THE CHALLENGE OF CREDIT SUPPLY

American Problems and Solutions 1650-1950

Michael Anthony Kirsch

VERNON PRESS

SERIES IN ECONOMIC HISTORY

www.vernonpress.com

In the Americas:

Vernon Press

1000 N West Street,

Suite 1200, Wilmington,

Delaware 19801

United States

In the rest of the world

Vernon Press

C/Sancti Espiritu 17,

Malaga, 29006

Spain

Library of Congress Control Number: 2016935298

ISBN: 978-1-62273-076-6

For the American people

Table of Contents

Introduction

This book investigates the central economic challenge of credit supply in American history and the different methods by which it was met from 1650 to 1950. It looks at the major developments in banking and credit policy in each era and the economic problem that each sought to address, their mechanics, impact, and shortcomings. It asks which financial institutions were essential to support economic growth and which financial powers were needed to achieve this goal. By studying the relationship of each major development to the next the reader gains an understanding of three hundred years of financial evolution.

It is important to study the financial policies and institutions that were historically successful and unsuccessful, and how and why. Failure to understand the financial system has too often led to legislation with negative results or inhibited and blocked legislation that would have facilitated economic development. The differences between successful and unsuccessful financial policies in American history cannot be explained without attention to historic detail. Financial legislation that had a beneficial impact in one period was sometimes ineffective during a subsequent period. Other legislation, a change in the mode of its implementation, or institutional mismanagement had an impact on economic and financial outcomes. Ideas both wise and ill-advised had powerful impacts. It has been a challenge for each generation to clarify which specific elements of past policies and institutions were sound and should be employed and which should be discontinued.

This book is written to guide readers through this financial labyrinth, and to make these subjects comprehensible. It uses the language of primary sources in each period so that the reader is brought into the often fascinating original discussion. Parts begin with a brief overview, chapters are kept to a manageable length to aid readability and comprehension, and the division of parts and chapters aims to lead the reader through the content.

Part I discusses the financing challenges facing the American colonies from the 1650s to the 1760s. It describes the problems leaders sought to address, the plan of Blackwell's bank of 1687, and why it was short lived. Absent a working bank, it reviews the rise in the use of bills of credit by the individual colonial governments as a general currency and as a basis for loans. The qualities that made bills of credit successful or unsuccessful in serving their purposes are examined.

Part II presents the developments in credit policy from the Declaration of Independence through to the conclusion of the Washington Administration and their relation to the events and processes that transformed the newly independent states of America into a firm union. The issues that weakened the credit of the Continental Congress are reviewed along with the remedy designed in the form of a Bank of North America. The important role of the Bank in serving the Congress and the economy through the Treaty of Paris, its key credit characteristics, and the difficulties it faced from the effect of insufficient Congressional revenues are thoroughly reviewed. An inspection is also made of the ineffective and burdensome tax system in place during and after the war. It is demonstrated that the design and drive for expanded federal power to raise taxes in order to fund the national debt was intricately related to the creation of a successful financial system. The legislative steps taken in the 1790s to establish a bank-based funding system are reviewed in detail. This system drastically reduced previous tax burdens, created an adequate supply of capital to support expanded credit, a currency plentiful enough to facilitate the growth of commerce and trade, and generated revenues needed to maintain a union despite some limitations.

Part III reviews the period from the expiration of the first Bank of the United States in 1811 to the demise of the second Bank and its aftermath. It describes the currency and credit crises which occurred during the War of 1812 as state banks tried with limited success to fill the place of the first Bank. It follows the design of policies for restoring public credit and a plan for financial order developed by the Madison Administration involving a second Bank of the United States. It shows that after an unfortunate beginning the second Bank was extremely successful in achieving its intended purposes. The specific mechanisms and management practices that made it effective in supporting the growth of industry, infrastructure, and commerce are detailed. It is seen that this public-private entity was useful in averting a number of economic disasters and banking crises. The actions taken by the government from 1833-1841 to sever relations with the Bank, and later the state banks, are reviewed to ensure that lessons for successful and unsuccessful credit policy are extracted from this difficult period. The short and long range negative effects of utilizing state banks as depositories of federal revenues are reviewed as are the consequences of creating an enlarged demand for gold and silver that was contrary to established business and banking practices.

Part IV is devoted to generating an in-depth understanding of the dramatic financial policy developments which took place during the Civil War. The context for these wartime actions picks up from the creation of the Independent Treasury System and the rise of state banking in the 1840s. The relation between the 1861-1863 planning for a federally controlled currency and banking system and the 1862-1865 wartime use of government bills of credit as a general currency is dissected in order to clarify the complications growing out of these measures in later years.

Part V is a step by step treatment of banking and currency developments under the National Banking System from 1865-1913. The complicated factors that made these banking arrangements only partially successful are examined closely. The failure to replace legal tender notes with national bank currency, the repeated recommendations by the Comptrollers of the Currency and others for improving the system, and the consequences of not implementing these suggestions are examined. The continual discord between an artificially restricted National Banking System, the Independent Treasury, and inelastic government currencies is discussed to show how each element contributed to the numerous credit contractions, financial crises, and depressions between 1868-1908. In this way the problems of the National Banking System are made clear and the elements that were missing for a more functional system are brought into focus.

Part VI encompasses the period of 1913-1950. It discusses the founding of the Federal Reserve System and its key characteristics. The focus is in particular on the limitation in the Fed's discount and loan provisions which significantly worsened the Depression and slowed recovery. Many types of assets held by banks simply were not accepted by the Fed for discounts, which sharply reduced the ability of banks to lend and remain solvent. This increased the crisis in the years after the stock market crash. Small and medium sized businesses and industries were not able to obtain bank credit. The many different ways that this problem was addressed during 1934-1950 are reviewed in detail. These included a number of proposed and actual amendments to the lending and discount powers of the Federal Reserve and the banking system.

This book prepares the reader to understand this financial history and to use it to comprehend today's issues relating to money and capital markets, credit institutions, and the Federal Reserve System.

Part I
Early American Banking and Credit

Overview

The first fully developed plan for a bank in the American colonies was put forward in 1686, with the Winthrop family prominent in its design. It was conceived as a solution to an insufficient means of payment and a lack of gold and silver to serve as currency, a recurring problem in future centuries. By mortgaging land, property, and goods, colonists were to receive bank bills of credit accepted as money with which they could pay their workers and make purchases. Though this plan was the outcome of thirty years of discussion and careful experiment, with full security pledged for its stock, the plan was abandoned in 1688 due to royal interference.

In 1690, a military engagement with Canada led the colony of Massachusetts to issue colonial bills of credit for military expenses, which then circulated as a means of payment. Other colonies began using similar bills for the same purpose. Designs and uses for banks and bills of credit to finance specific projects and industries were debated into the first decades of the 18th century. Banks based on specie (gold and silver coin) reserves were not possible in the colonies due to their inability to retain adequate amounts of specie.

Beginning in the 1720s, a widespread shortage of specie led to the use of colony-issued bills of credit both as a general currency and for directed loans. Of all the colonies, the paper currency of Pennsylvania was the most successful. In addition to its issue by the legislature for general expenses it was made available to all colonists as direct loans in return for pledged land. Along with landed security, the value of the bills was upheld by sufficient taxation and the quality of legal tender.

Bills of credit proved to be an effective currency when colonies practiced appropriate regulation in taxation and limited their quantities to real need. From the 1720s to the 1760s, the use of colonial bills of credit as a legal tender supported growth and enabled the domestic economy to save its silver for the purchase of foreign goods. This constant outflow of precious metals, primarily to Europe, perpetuated the need for credit creation along with the development of domestic industries. The use of legal tender paper currency came under attack by the English crown and parliament in the 1740s and 1750s, leading to an Act banning its use in 1764.

Chapter 1
The 1687 Bank of Credit and the First Colonial Bills of Credit

The central economic problem holding back the development of the Massachusetts Bay Colony was an insufficient medium of exchange. Unlike in Central and South America, the North American eastern seaboard colonies lacked gold and silver mines. England meanwhile kept its sterling at home leaving its colonies reliant on Spanish silver and Portuguese gold. The amount of gold and silver in circulation was not adequate to make needed transactions as most of it was used by colonial merchants to import goods from Europe. During scarcities of coin, costs were high, land value declined, debts increased, businesses failed, and immigration slowed.[1]

Massachusetts attempted to keep Spanish dollars and the coins of its own mint within the colony by setting their value above British legal tender standards. Increasing their local values encouraged spending of coins in the colonies and discouraged their use for buying British imports. In 1642, the Massachusetts General Court valued the Spanish silver dollar at 11% above its worth in Britain (five shillings instead of four and a half). Similarly, when Massachusetts began minting silver coin in 1652 it made a shilling with 22% less silver than a British shilling, making it worth 22% more if spent in the colony. In 1672, Massachusetts set the value of the Spanish dollar at six shillings, 33% above parity with Britain. Though a partial remedy, these attempts were largely unsuccessful and were repeatedly opposed by the crown.[2]

In the 1660s-1680s, various attempts were made to create an alternative payment method to metallic currency in the form of bank and fund credit. These led to the design for a "Bank of Credit" facility, supported by the third generation of the Winthrop family and other leaders of Boston and chartered in 1687. The Bank was to establish the country's wealth on its own foundation and to create a medium of exchange based on the products of its own lands rather than one based on foreign imports of gold and silver.[3]

The origins of the plan for a Bank of Credit lay in the early designs of John Winthrop Jr. (1606-1676) during his third and longest term as the Governor of Connecticut (1659-1676).[4] In 1661 Winthrop developed a proposal to remedy the deficiency in the circulating medium available for trade. In 1663, Winthrop submitted a plan to the Royal Society of England, titled "Some Proposals Concerning the Way of Trade and Banks without Money."[5] It was to involve pledges of land but in contrast to other proposals for land banks it would not require the land be taken out of use. Winthrop wrote, "money would flow in abundantly." Winthrop described the benefits of his non-specie bank as follows:

> [It] would greatly advance commerce and other public concernment for the benefit of poor and rich in Great Britain and the good of these plantations. . . . It may be quickly brought into a practical way, to the great advance of trade, and settlement of such a bank, as may answer all those ends that are attained in other parts of the world by banks of ready money.

An inspiration for Winthrop's plan was William Potter's 1650 book, *"The Key of Wealth: Or, a New Way of Improving Trade,"* which Winthrop had received from his associate Samuel Hartlib.[6] Its theme was how to increase the trade and productive capacity of a nation lacking gold and silver, or as Potter wrote, to show "how all things which may be got for gold throughout this earth, are obtainable in all respects as happily and effectually," by other means.[7] Potter discouraged the hoarding of money (specie) and said that by keeping estates in goods, ships, and lands, whose value exceeded "the value of all the moneys," wealth would be formed without increasing the quantity of money by accelerating the circulation of commodities. He argued that trade and commodities would be increased proportional to "the revolution" of money or its equivalent, describing an early form of a multiplier effect.[8]

For places that lacked mines for silver and gold and found it difficult to increase the quantity and flow "of money or credit," Potter said the only feasible way to multiply trade was "*by increasing amongst tradesman some firm and known credit or security . . . fit to transfer from hand to hand.*" The "multiplication thereof throughout the land" he wrote, would lead to the same effect in furthering trade "as the increase of so much money amongst them would do."[9] To this purpose he wrote:

> Admit therefore that several tradesmen of known and sufficient credit do cause a certain number of bills to be printed, and putting a value upon them . . . do lend the said bills each to other, upon no less security than if the same were so much ready money, or gold out of the . . . mine, and bend themselves jointly to make good the same according to the terms following.[10]

In this direction, Potter outlined several proposals for a company of tradesman that would furnish credit similar to banks of money but to be drawn on their personal credit, land, houses, and other capital. The bills would serve as a medium for adjusting accounts and conducting business. They were to be further secured by a form of stockholders who would make good on them if the company could not redeem the bills in specie on schedule. These conditions would make the bills, "no whit inferior" to the Chamber of London or the Bank of Amsterdam, he said.[11]

John Woodbridge, John Winthrop Jr.'s associate by marriage, had numerous discussions on the topic with William Potter in 1649 while in London. In 1667, Woodbridge submitted a formal proposal to the colonial leadership of New England to remedy the effects of the lack of a medium of exchange, consisting of a fund to pass credit without the use of money. Similar to Winthrop and Potter, Woodbridge thought it was not imperative to increase the amount of gold and silver. He spoke of "how little value coin, as the measure of trade, need be, in itself," and that "cash . . . is but a ready conveniency" since "intrinsic value is not essential to a thing merely good for exchange." New England attempted Woodbridge's plan on a limited basis in 1671, and it was tried again by a group of merchants in 1681 who approved of its benefits. This small-scale success led Woodbridge to elaborate the details of the experiment and outline a system that could be used more generally. In 1682, he wrote "A Proposal for Erecting a Fund of Land. . . . in the Nature of a Money Bank." In describing his fund, Woodbridge said that "credit passed in fund by book, and bills" would "fully supply the defect [lack] of money." The association was to give credit to individuals on the security of mortgages on land and other property, and this credit would be passed by bills of exchange (similar to checks), book entries, and bank notes.[12] Payments with deposits in the bank or the bills it issued would have "a *fund*, or deposit in *land*" as their basis. They would be free of the common problems involved in the use of gold and silver as a medium of exchange, i.e hoarding, theft, idle money, etc. The acceptors of fund credit would secure the necessary transfer of its amount at the office of the fund. Letters of credit would be transferred and accounts would be adjusted.

At the end of the 1680s the continuing gravity of the economic situation demanded a more developed plan for a payment structure based on credit. This came in the form of a design spearheaded by John Blackwell and Waitstill Winthrop, the son of John Winthrop Jr. In the draft of the plan, Blackwell wrote that a "great scarcity of money [specie] here, for carrying on the ordinary commerce amongst traders," threatened the colony. In July 1686, drawing on the earlier plans and attempts, Blackwell submitted a draft plan to charter a bank of credit to the president, council, and standing committee of Boston. "Bank-bills of credit," were to be "signed by several persons of good repute joined together in a partnership" and credit would be given for the mortgages of lands and deposits of staple goods and merchandise. The bills would circulate among those satisfied with the security of the bank's credit.

Through the bank, those with property in mines and shops, etc., but without gold and silver, would transform their property into a distributable credit, increasing the potential and usefulness of their wealth. Weavers of cloth and linen, builders of ships, manufactures of ropes, and sails, would pledge their workhouses for bills of credit with which to increase their supply of needed commodities, such as wool, yarn, dyes, hemp, iron, flax, timber, etc. Merchants in turn would pledge their land and receive bills to buy additional wares and other commodities from the manufacturer and husbandman, or pay their debts. Shopkeepers would pledge their shop and receive bills to buy goods from merchants. A mine owner would mortgage his mine for bills to obtain additional capital to employ laborers.[13]

Over time, wrote Blackwell, the bills were to become "esteemed as current moneys in all receipts and payments . . . by the treasurer and receivers thereof as any other occasion for money." The bank would not redeem in gold, but the notes would become as valuable as gold, and sold for it. He continued:

> Bills, in a kind of circulation . . . would through their experimented usefulness, become diffused by mutual consent, pass from one hand to another . . . as ready moneys, in all their ordinary dealings of buying and selling . . . and so have (at least) equal advantages with the current moneys of the

> country attending them, to all who become satisfied to be of this society or agreement, and that shall deal with them.

Increased employment from businesses financed by the bank would increase consumption of home manufactures and imported goods. The Bank would improve fisheries, navigation, shipping, the value of land, interest rates, and public taxation.[14] In addition to creating an adequate means of payment, Blackwell's plan would create the potential for merchants to transition from an equity based capital structure to include debt, putting the idle capacity of the colony into motion.

The bank plan was reviewed favorably by the council that September.[15] John Blackwell and Wait Winthrop were designated its directors. Other key leaders of the standing committee of Boston such as Adam Winthrop, Elisha Cooke, and William Stoughton were endorsers.[16] The council approved the plan, granting the directors the liberty to begin "issuing bills" on security of real and personal estate, and imperishable merchandise." In their statement they cited a "great decay of trade" and the difficulties created for "manufactures and commerce" by the scarcity of coin. The council believed that the "bank bills of credit" would be exchanged with greater security and ease for large payments than "monies coined."[17]

The Bank of Credit was formally chartered in April of 1687 with a partnership established, securities pledged, shares divided, and an administration arranged and appointed. However, before the plan was circulated to the public in pamphlet form, a supplement was added on behalf of Royal Governor Edmund Andros conflating the plan with his opposition to New England coinage. When Andros had arrived to fulfill his appointment as Governor of the Dominion of New England in December of 1686, his orders were to regulate the Spanish dollar as appropriate for trade. According to the notes of council secretary Edward Randolph, Andros was opposed to proposals for raising the rate of New England coin above its intrinsic value put forward in the spring of 1687.[18] In accord with this opposition, the supplement to the Bank plan was titled "An account of some of the many prejudices that will inevitably ensue, as well to his majesty and to his subjects by enhancing the value of Spanish coin &c. above his majesties." It advocated a return to English sterling as the measure of value for coinage instead of the Massachusetts shilling, proposed letting trade balances set the quantity of money, and posed the Bank as relief for expected shortages of sterling. Having grown used to six shillings to the dollar instead of four and a half according to English valuation, this proposal was unacceptable to the colonists and the Bank plan was abandoned by July 1688.[19] This was an early example of sound legislation becoming victim to amendments making its implementation untenable.

Government Bills of Credit and Bank Plans 1690-1720s

Without the private Bank of Credit to emit bills as money, a major military expedition to Canada in 1690 required recourse to a different method of financing. To pay soldiers and buy supplies, the colonial government emitted its own bills of credit. While the credit of the Bank bills was to be issued on the property and credit of the stockholders and depositors, the credit of the colonial bills of credit was based on public taxes. After achieving their original purpose in funding the military expedition, these bills circulated as payment among the colonists until being absorbed in payment of taxes.

In 1690, after some protested the use of these government bills, Cotton Mather (1663-1728), the signer of the bills for the colonial office, and John Blackwell, the author of the "Discourse on the Bank of Credit" published wide ranging articles illustrating the function of the bills and arguing for their necessity.[20] Mather, in his, "Some Considerations of the Bills of Credit, Now Passing in New England," spoke of the "desperate circumstances of the country," and urged the population to comprehend the necessity of accepting the bills as payment, to both honor the soldiers and obtain needed supplies:

> We are surrounded with adversaries: if we cannot find a store of *men* to expose themselves for us at this time, no man in his wits, can think the country can stand: these *men* must have money to reward and support them in their services, or they can do no more. But *silver* we say we have not; credit we may have and it will do as well, if by this *credit* we permit our friends to command the same useful things as if they had ready silver in their hands.

Mather elaborated how the bills functioned, explaining that the credit of the bills was based on the country itself, not on the administrators of the loan office issuing the bills. The security of the paper money was the credit of inhabitants of the country. As he described it:

> If the country's debts must be paid, whatever change of government shall come, then the country must make good the credit, or more taxes must be still raised, till the public debts be answered. I say... all the inhabitants of the land, taken as one body are the principals, who reap the benefits, and must bear the burdens, and are the security in their public bonds.

Mather argued that when receiving payment, a discount in accounts was just as good as money since it allowed debts to be settled. Bills of exchange (credit instruments of individuals) were used similarly. He therefore asked why the country's credit should not pass for a means to pay the country's debts and in which taxes could then be paid. Blackwell agreed that they were functionally equal to silver for obtaining commodities.[21] With echoes of Boston's Bank of Credit, Mather pushed the question beyond an emergency measure, and went so far as to question the utility of using any specie as a circulating currency.[22]

After the use of these government issued bills in Massachusetts for military purposes they were employed in other colonies to similar effect.[23] South Carolina printed their first currency emissions to finance military operations in 1703 and 1707, New Hampshire, Connecticut, New York, and New Jersey in 1709, and Rhode Island and North Carolina in 1710, and 1712, respectively. Though they were to be funded (the quality of having resources or actions pledged for the maintenance of value) by taxation at distant periods, many of the military emissions involving enormous sums were not regulated by sufficient taxation and depreciated in value, those of South Carolina and Massachusetts in particular.[24] Serious depreciation by 1712 in Massachusetts bills from insufficient tax receipts led to the use of mortgages as security for its bills in 1714.

Economic Bills of Credit

While some of the military related emissions had a secondary economic effect by their subsequent circulation as a means of payment, they did not meet the full demand. Consequently, numerous plans for banks of credit continued to be put forward to remedy the shortage of money substitutes.

In 1716, one author saw the long-term solution to currency shortfalls in government emissions of large sums of bills for decreasing the cost of transportation and creating new fields of industry. He proposed a board of trade to determine government loans for the "construction of public works and encouragement of industries," such as "lending large sums upon good security, without interest for some term of years" to pay for cutting a canal for more speedy passage of vessels. Or, he wrote, "the country could give or lend a sum of credit" to pay for the building of an iron finery and slitting mill to produce sufficient quantities of nails, pots, and kettles. By lending a few hundred to set up an iron refinery the government would save the country thousands a year in import costs. It read:

> And here being both iron ore, and a plenty of wood to work it, and this country having great occasion for all sorts of iron work; it may be advisable to advance considerably in bills, either by the way of loan or gift, to such as will undertake to set up a finery . . . which would work the iron better, and in greater quantities . . .[25]

In 1720, more bank proposals were written, citing the exorbitant interest which the province was paying to borrow money from the province agent in London and the dire consequences of a lack of exchange. One called for a public bank with twenty year, six percent loans, the interest to be paid in domestic manufactures, such as hemp, flax, and oil. This interest would become a fund and sold for bullion with which to redeem the bills of credit lent. Another outlined a private bank to operate in cooperation with the government, loaning bills of credit on "improved lands or any sufficient security," likewise emitted for the construction of public works and industries. The profit of the bank was to be invested in specie for the province treasury until the sum on deposit in the bank equaled the value of notes emitted.[26]

A chief factor in the problem of an adequate coin based medium of exchange was the trade status of the colonies. Without their own manufactures and ability to regulate trade they were unable to restrain the export of coin for the purchase of imports. The negative balance of trade carried away the coin as fast as it was replaced. In the late 1710s and early 1720s, the problem became severe and led to conditions necessitating barter in many colonies.

Chapter 2
Expanded Uses of Bills of Credit in the 1720s-1760s

Since the bank proposals between 1686-1720 were never effectuated, issues of bills of credit by individual North American colonies became the chosen means to supply a general medium of exchange. Their value was secured by land, the anticipation of future taxes, and by the legal tender quality they were given.

In 1723, the government of Pennsylvania faced petitions requesting the use of paper currency in order to address "a great decay of trade and credit" and "want of a currency of cash."[1] The legislature authorized an issue of bills of credit to serve as a general currency. The emissions gave "new life to business" and "promoted greatly the settlement of new lands."[2] The majority of the bills emitted were held by a colonial office and were lent in "small sums to beginners on easy interest." They were based on mortgages of double value of the sums emitted, the land held by the loan office in case of default by the debtors. The remaining bills were used by the assembly for its expenditures and withdrawn by payments of taxes as before. The loans were for eight years, and the interest and principal were paid back in installments. The bills were made a legal tender. The interest payments on the bills were applied to the expenses of the government, and when the principals were paid the bills were retired. Later that year, a second sum was authorized since the initial amount was, according to the legislature, "found by experience to fall far short of a sufficient medium in trade."

In 1729, the legislature issued a new amount. The loans were extended to sixteen years, reducing the annual installment amount of interest and principal. England was in opposition to the new issue, so Benjamin Franklin wrote a piece that year defending the action of the legislature and its paper currency. He described how the value of the currency was ensured through buying back of mortgages, punctual payments of interest by its holders, and payments of public debts by the legislature.[3] Seeds of discontent between the American Colonies and England were being sowed in the need for and resistance to a functioning credit market. In 1730, the first loans expiring were reissued, and in 1739 an improved Act was passed which incorporated the lessons learned from previous years, solidifying its strong regulation features.[4]

Rhode Island began economic related emissions of bills in 1721 in order to supply merchants with a medium of exchange, "always proportioned to the increase of their commerce." They became a key feature in putting their navigation industry ahead of the other colonies.[5] Massachusetts and other colonies also engaged in the use of bills of credit as an economic means of exchange in the 1720s and 1730s.

Thomas Pownall, the Governor of the Province of Massachusetts Bay from 1757-1760, wrote that the credit capability supplied by the paper currency of the colonies was key to their development as it made it possible to grow economically even while maintaining a negative balance of trade. It was true that "an increasing country of settlers must always have the balance of trade against them . . . because they are increasing and improving, [and] continually wanting further supplies which their present circumstances will neither furnish nor pay for."[6] But contrary to theory, he said, in "a commercial country of settlers" a negative trade balance, a consequent loss of specie, and a necessity to borrow the materials for trade and business did not guarantee a declining state. After applying their loans to improvements, they were able to "not only pay those debts, but create also a surplus to be still carried forward to further and further improvements," Pownall remarked. He continued, describing how loans of paper money made this possible:

> In a country under such circumstances, money lent upon interest to settlers, creates money. Paper money thus lent upon interest will create gold and silver in principal, while the interest becomes a revenue that pays the charges of government.

In 1767, Franklin wrote similarly that though the use of paper currency had allowed the debts of the colonies to Britain to increase with the increase of population and trade, "the improvement and increase of estates in the colonies has been in a greater proportion than their debt." By serving as a basis for loans and an adequate means of payment, paper currencies, enabled a great increase of settlements, population, buildings, improvements, agriculture, shipping, and commerce. From 1723-1767, while using paper currency, Pennsylvania's exports increased tenfold. The colony was able to obtain large quantities of gold and silver from its trade with other colonies for its imports of manufactures from England. Similar results were seen in New York and New Jersey. For New England as a whole, from 1696 until 1760 when paper money was regularly used, the number of farms, churches, buildings, and exports increased nearly five times.[7]

Parameters for Successful Bills

Overall, from the 1720s to the 1760s, bills of credit issued by individual colonies worked well as a medium of trade without reliance on specie, but were only successful to the degree they followed certain parameters: were made legal tender, were properly secured by adequate taxation or land security of at least double the value, were emitted of a quantity in proportion to proper needs of trade, and punctually regulated for payment of interest and principal. Pennsylvania's currency was more successful than other colonies due to the punctuality of payments of interest and principal by the mortgage debtors and the legislature. This was because the loans were not in excess of the need for a medium of exchange and because of its methods of redemption.[8] While Massachusetts and Rhode Island issued paper currency against mortgages, they did not demand annual installments of the principal of the loans, only the interest, with payment of the principal at the expiration of the loan. This, along with inadequate taxation for their large emissions, led to large fluctuations in the value of their paper currencies.

Where the sums were moderate and did not exceed amounts required for trade, their value was upheld and retained a fixed value when compared with silver. Due to the regulated nature of the Pennsylvania currency, it did not cause spikes in the prices of needed commodities when compared with the price of silver, a claim of Franklin proven by the records of commodity prices for the period.[9] This was also true for New York and New Jersey bills.

In addition, in order to maintain the value of bills of credit, it was imperative that they were made a general legal tender, acceptable for all debts. Without the quality of legal tender they would not continue to circulate as currency. This took place because promissory notes payable in the future depreciated in proportion to their maturity. As a case in point, in 1723 Pennsylvania and Maryland both issued a similar amount of pounds in bills of credit on loan, on landed security, for a similar amount of time. Pennsylvania made theirs a legal tender for discharge of all debts while Maryland did not. Pennsylvania's bills maintained their circulation and purchasing power, whereas Maryland's bills lost value and then disappeared from circulation and were hoarded until maturity, no longer serving their intended purpose as a currency.[10]

Opposition and Defense of Colonial Currency

The English crown and parliament made multiple attempts to contract and restrict the use of bills of credit in the colonies. In 1739, the Royal Governor of Massachusetts, Jonathan Belcher, was instructed to take action and contract the currency of the colony. In response to Belcher's actions, the Massachusetts Assembly appointed a committee to design a sufficient medium of trade that would not depreciate. A land bank similar to Blackwell's Bank of 1687 was designed by John Colman, a Boston merchant, and established in 1740. The following year, Governor Belcher interposed against the bank and obtained an Act of parliament in England ordering it closed. However, Massachusetts and other colonies continued to issue different forms of bills of credit.[11]

In 1751, parliament passed "An act to regulate and restrain paper bills of credit in his majesty's colonies or plantations of Rhode Island, Connecticut, Massachusetts, and New Hampshire, and to prevent the same being legal tenders in paper money." However, it allowed bills of credit to be created for administrative needs or emergencies, a difficult distinction to define, leaving open many opportunities to continue emitting bills. But since legal tender was necessary for keeping up the value of paper currency, the New England colonies attempted to mitigate parliament's ruling by adding interest to their non legal tender bills to keep up their value. This attempt was unsuccessful. To earn the interest on the bills required timely computations that hindered business transactions, and the interest led them to become hoarded as investments rather than to continue to circulate as promissory notes, defeating their main purpose.[12]

In 1764, more serious action was taken by Britain to restrict their use. During January and early February 1764, the Board of Trade held discussions about extending the Act of 1751 to the rest of the colonies. Franklin addressed the parliament in London in response, suggesting that colonial legislatures should be empowered to lend bills as required for specific purposes, on collateral security, with deficiencies guarded against by taxes. Many British merchants trading in America were opposed to the Board of Trade's proposal. Colonial agents asked for time to consult their constituents. The Board declined these requests, and on February 9, 1764, submitted its objections to legal tender issues in the colonies to the King, recommending action to restrain "the emission of paper bills of credit in America, as a legal tender." The result was the April 19, 1764, Currency Act of parliament, designed "to prevent paper bills of credit, hereafter to be issued in any of his majesty's colonies or plantations in America, from being declared to be a legal tender in payments of money."

From 1764-1766, Franklin and Pownall proposed a remedy in the form of a general paper currency for all of the American colonies, modeled on the success of the Pennsylvania loan office system.[13] Franklin and agents to the colonies also worked to repeal the Currency Act. Many British and American merchants opposed to the Currency Act were unconvinced by the Board's arguments to restrain the use of paper bills of credit as a legal tender and requested Franklin give a point by point reply. Franklin wrote two such pieces on the subject in 1767.[14] Franklin reviewed their successes and failures and gave a detailed rebuttal of the Board's arguments relating to the depreciation of paper currency, the export of gold and silver, and intrinsic value.

To the Board's statement that paper money carried away specie from the colonies, Franklin remarked that their negative trade balances had already done so before its use. To the statement that a medium of trade should have an intrinsic value he pointed out that the Bank of England's notes did not have intrinsic value but rested on the credit of those that issued them, just as paper bills in the colonies rested on the credit of the respective governments. If England had lacked trade laws to prevent merchants from exporting specie it would also have faced shortages.

To its statement that in the middle colonies [New Jersey, New York, and Pennsylvania] the paper money was constantly depreciated, he said the increased demand for silver to pay for imports made it 10% more valuable than paper, but that it continued uniformly at this rate for forty years, regardless of new emissions.[15] There had been no alterations due to paper money "in the price of the necessaries of life when compared with silver: they have been for the greatest part of the time no higher than before it was emitted, varying only by plenty and scarcity according to the seasons, or by a less or greater foreign demand."[16] Franklin stated that this uniformity remained throughout the period, even when the currency increased in large amounts, demonstrating that its volume did not determine its value in silver and gold. It was sometimes claimed that increases in the prices of foreign bills of exchange signified a depreciation of the bills of credit. While the cost of buying bills of exchange did vary between the colonies and Britain, this price differed just as much if they were bought with silver, as they were if purchased with bills of credit. In other words, the latter had not depreciated, there was rather an increase in the cost to buy a bill of exchange due to a scarcity of foreign bills of exchange. This took place under large negative trade balances (see footnote for definition of bills of exchange).[17] However, depreciation of the bills did take place when large sums were emitted for military operations without adequate taxation to retire them, as their amount caused excess imports of British manufactures, an increased demand for silver, and temporary depreciations of the currency relative to silver. In sum Franklin argued that the paper money of the Middle Colonies had not been structurally debased but that cyclical declines could occur, particularly in instances of war.

After meeting the objections, Franklin recommended removing the legal tender restraints on paper currencies as it would allow the colonies to pay their debts to England in silver. On the other hand, he said, a consequence of restricting legal tender bills would be to impede trade in Britain from the lack of trade with the colonies. In 1773, the effects of a long series of action taken against the colonies along with their own plans toward greater sovereignty, economic and otherwise, culminated in the American Revolution.[18]

Part II
The Bank of North America, the Bank of the United States, and the Development of the Funding System

Overview

With the advent of the American War of Independence, the bills of credit of the individual colonies were augmented by those issued by the Continental Congress. The severe depreciation of the Congress' bills by 1779 resulted from inadequate taxation and use of Congress' power. A solution to the effects of this depreciation was devised in the form of a bank chartered by Congress that would restore credit to the currency and support the economy and government in loans.

This design became expressed in the Bank of North America, the first successful bank in the American colonies and states. In the final stage of the American Revolution from January of 1782 to the signing of the Treaty of Paris in September of 1783, the Bank became a crucial element to American success by reviving economic confidence and supporting the government. Based on the unity of public and private credit, the Bank's currency had more credibility than the depreciated continental currency.

The missing ingredient to the long-term success of the Bank of North America was Congress' power to utilize the resources of the independent states. Without taxation powers in Congress the Bank's size was limited and its capital became almost wholly expended in loans to the government. Notwithstanding, its currency approximated one that was reflective of economic demand and demonstrated the benefits of an institution of public and private credit dedicated to making loans and discounts. Hamilton's congressional messages in December of 1782 and April of 1783 expressed in kernel form the potential of the congressional funding system of the 1790s, as well as the close knit relation of the funded debt with banking capital.

The inability of the Congress to obtain a taxing power from the states in 1781-1783 led to a dependence on a burdensome system of state collected direct taxes for paying war-time debts and expenses. A post-war depression took hold in 1784 amplifying growing currency and credit shortages. The increasing weight of direct taxation under conditions of depression led to farmer's revolts, movements and legislation for debt and tax relief, depreciating currencies and property values, and a further weakening of the Congress. Economic demand for a uniform and efficient tax system, a sufficient and stable means of exchange, and adequate credit and capital became central to the struggle for a new constitution that would replace the Articles of Confederation.

With the ratification of the Constitution, the first Administration and Congress of the United States of America was poised to make use of its hard won economic powers. With the power of taxation, the debts were adequately funded then transformed into a medium of commerce, creating a basis for banking.

In accord with plans outlined by Treasury Secretary Alexander Hamilton, Congress passed a number of Acts in 1790 that created new taxes and allocated sufficient funds to turn the domestic, foreign, and state debts into a funded debt. The debt rose in value and became a basis for economic transactions. Congress incorporated a Bank of the United States the following year, whose capital was largely based on the newly funded public debt.

The Bank's qualities and actions served as a means for Congress to effectively carry out the power to collect taxes, to pay its debts, and to regulate trade among other powers. The financial system for the nation became increasingly stable and the public debt served as a valuable resource for obtaining bank credit from the Bank of United States and other state banks. The Bank's note currency was uniform and accepted as money. It was a large saving from the previous reliance on specie currency and state bills of credit of uncertain value. Credit became available for merchants, laborers, farmers, and small-scale manufacturers.

As new borrowings were required during the Washington Administration, Treasury Secretary Hamilton made it his policy to ensure their integration into the overall funding system. He proposed that each new borrowing be accompanied with new taxes, especially those designed to stimulate domestic enterprise, in order to guarantee final extinguishment of the debts and uphold the value of the public debt. Unfortunately, due to the monetary demands of foreign and internal military conflicts from 1792-1795, combined with a growing resistance in Congress to lay adequate taxation for these purposes, a large portion of the Bank's capital was absorbed and tied up in direct loans to the government.

In January of 1795, Hamilton issued an extensive final report on the present and future state of the public credit. It incorporated all previous Congressional legislation pertinent to providing for the public debt into a unified plan to guarantee adequate revenues for growing expenditures. The use of Hamilton's funding methods during the Thomas Jefferson Administration declined as taxation was brought to a minimum and the public debt diminished as a resource for reserve assets. The Bank of the United States continued to perform most of its lending and fiscal functions until its charter ran out in 1811.

Chapter 3
Designing a Currency with Credit

Beginning in 1775, the Continental Congress of the United Colonies created a "continental currency" to pay for the revolutionary war. A total of $226 million worth of continental currency (bills of credit) was printed by the end of 1779.[1] Though imperative at the time, the bills were not issued in the same manner that had made many of the colonial currencies of previous years successful. Despite having implicit power to tax from the Declaration of Independence, the Continental Congress did not collect taxes or issue regular securities to absorb them.[2] In its first issues, the Congress assumed that the state legislatures would absorb the paper through taxation in sufficient amounts to uphold its value. However, they did not levy taxes in 1775 or 1776 and the currency began to depreciate in 1777. In November of that year the Congress officially requested that the states collect taxes but they did not comply. By 1778-1779 the depreciation of the currency was severe. Further contributing factors in the depreciation were a growing lack of confidence in the union of the states and the high prices of goods caused by the war.[3]

Alexander Hamilton served as an aid de camp to General George Washington and managed the communications for army supplies. In this capacity, he saw from an administrative level the consequences of a weak Continental Congress. On a number of occasions between 1779 and 1781 Hamilton outlined his thoughts on the problems and solutions to the crisis. "The fundamental defect," Hamilton believed, was "a want of power in Congress." Congress had "descended from the authority which the spirit of the act" of 1776 had vested within it. Growing "diffident toward its own authority," it had bent to please the states. Having "scarcely left themselves a shadow of power," they therefore lacked sufficient means to answer the needs of the public.[4] The lack of power to put resources behind the currency was the main cause of currency depreciation, Hamilton wrote, not an intrinsic problem related to its quantity.

Hamilton had begun planning innovative financial arrangements to deal with this state of affairs in 1779. To restore and secure the government's ability to borrow for the success of the war he proposed a more permanent solution than annual loans, which were becoming increasingly difficult to obtain. Since private interests could make more of a profit by investing in trade than lending to Congress, he proposed turning future loans to Congress into a permanent fund. The fund would be directed so as to be beneficial to the investors in commerce, making it in their interest to uphold the value of the currency. "The plan I would propose," he wrote in the winter of 1779, "is that of an American Bank . . . under the denomination of 'The Bank of the United States.'" This plan, he said, would lead to a "restoration of paper credit, and establish a permanent fund for the future exigencies of Government." The Bank would benefit the government in loans for the war. Also, he wrote, it would "promote commerce, by furnishing a more extensive medium, which we greatly want in our circumstances. I mean a more extensive valuable medium. We have an enormous nominal one at this time. But it is only in name." Half of the Bank's capital was to come from a foreign loan and its notes were to replace the depreciating continentals as the main currency of the states.[5] As had been attempted under Blackwell, and as Pownall had explained the success of Pennsylvania's loan office system, Hamilton envisioned a currency that would be primarily lent into circulation for trade and commerce, with a built-in incentive for making good on the bills.

Meanwhile, the crisis deepened. That winter the Congress became increasingly conciliatory to the states. They urged the states to collect taxes and hoped the continental currency would increase in value if its quantity was increased no further. When depreciation continued, with the bills dropping to one-fortieth of their original value by the spring of 1780, the Congress made a drastic attempt to prevent further depreciation. On March 18, 1780, the Congress asked the states to collect $180 million of continental currency by April 1781 and deliver it to them for retirement. But the Congress redeemed the bills at a rate of only one-fortieth their face value. A total of $120 million was paid in by the states in this way over the year, for which the states were credited $3 million in specie.[6] The 40 to 1 measure failed to achieve its effect, and the remaining currency continued to depreciate. It dropped to one-hundredth its face value by the end of the year. It was a failure for which Congress was often chastised in later years, including by Hamilton. The credit of the Congress was severely damaged as it had essentially repudiated over $200 million of paper currency.[7] Congress also issued a smaller amount of bills bearing interest. This time the states were given most of the bills to distribute to creditors themselves and were asked to provide funds for payment of the interest. Congress was also forced to ask the states to collect more taxes to finance expenditures. The actions by Congress that winter signified a weakening of Congress' authority. Accordingly, in the Articles of Confederation ratified in March of 1781 the Congress was legally prohibited from levying taxes and was limited to making requests to the states.[8]

By the spring of 1781, the remaining continental bills became of little use in serving as a currency and were gradually removed from circulation. In their stead only the currencies of individual states and scarce specie circulated. There was a growing lack of currency with which to pay taxes. Congress's obligations mounted and the high prices of goods driven by the war's demands required the issue of more debt to buy them.

In response to the growing crisis, Congress asked the states on February 3, 1781 "to pass laws laying an impost (import duty) of 5%" on "all goods, wares, and merchandise of foreign growth and manufactures" imported into the states, and to vest Congress "with the full power to collect and appropriate" the amounts needed to pay the principal and interest on the debts of the U.S. This impost request was effectively an amendment to the Articles of Confederation ratified the following month. To strengthen its position, Congress replaced the finance committee with a single Superintendent of Finance on February 20, 1781. Robert Morris, a member of the Continental Congress from 1775-1779, was appointed to fulfill the post. Morris' plan was for the interest on Congress' debts to be its own responsibility and the expenses of the war to be apportioned among the states. A state of national accounts showing the balance of credits and debits between Congress, the states, and the public became one of Morris' chief tasks.[9]

Morris set to work on a plan for a National Bank three days after being appointed.[10] He saw bank currency lent into circulation as the best replacement for the discredited government paper. "There is no reason why paper should not pass equivalently with silver," Morris wrote, "if it be issued on proper funds, and with proper precautions, so that the demand for it be great."[11] On April 30, 1781, while Morris was composing a design, Hamilton wrote him a letter with his thoughts on the crisis and the solution. Addressing the depreciation of the currency, he said it was the result of a lack of confidence in the union and of active power in Congress. It was not a shortage of resources of the country, he said, as the country possessed ample commodities and labor. Building on his plan from the year before, Hamilton outlined his own example charter for a national trading and banking corporation that would enable Congress to obtain a permanent source of credit from individuals. He proposed that by uniting the wealth of private merchants and traders with the public, a sizable "mass of credit" could be established that would "supply the defect of moneyed capital." The plan would "offer adventurers immediate advantages analogous to those they receive by employing their money in trade, and eventually greater advantages . . . " It would "give them the greatest security the nature of the case will admit for what they lend." In addition, it would "secure the independence of their country" and spur the country's commerce and strength.[12] A dependable medium of non-depreciating bank notes would increase the quantity of the currency, trade and commerce, and the payment of taxes. One of the main factors of the depreciation of the earlier emissions of paper currency had been for lack of a close integration with economic demand, a factor which the Bank's currency would cure, as it would be issued through loans and discounts. The Bank would turn the pledges of commerce and industry into an accepted form of payment between individuals. The currency would obtain greater credibility as it became increasingly reflective of economic activity. "The tendency of the national bank," he wrote accordingly, "is to increase public and private credit . . . Industry is increased, commodities are multiplied, agriculture and manufactures flourish, and herein consists the true wealth and prosperity of the state." He called for new taxes to be deposited in the Bank, increasing the fund on which it would operate. The states would pledge to pay into a fund devoted to the interest payments on the required loans that the Bank would make to Congress for the war. He detailed a feasible manner for the existing and new debts of the states to be paid over a thirty-year period. This national debt, Hamilton wrote, would serve as a powerful cement of the Union, keeping up a necessity for taxation.

On May 17, Morris put forward a plan of his own with a much simpler design than Hamilton's and a smaller initial capital. Gouverneur Morris, serving as the assistant financier to Robert Morris from 1781-1784, wrote out its final language.[13] Congress approved the plan on May 26, as "the Bank of North America," to be chartered when subscriptions were filled. Morris remarked to Hamilton that day that receiving his letter had strengthened the confidence he had in his own judgment, as many points coincided with his own. He foresaw the establishment of "a paper credit that cannot depreciate." He said that although the Bank's authorized capital stock was much less than what Hamilton had proposed, and less than it should be, it was wiser to start small. After securing an amount of $400,000 it could then "be increased almost to any amount."[14] Similarly, Morris wrote to Franklin in July that the plan was to eventually increase its capital by an order of magnitude. Three days after Congress passed a resolution approving the Bank, Morris addressed the nation with an open letter. "To ask the end which it is proposed to answer by this institution of a bank is merely to call the public attention to the situation of our affairs," he wrote. He went on to describe the depreciation of the currency and the financial and contractual distress it had caused. Public credit had suffered and the needs of the U.S. demanded an ability to anticipate revenues. The continental currency had been a form of anticipated revenues, but a method now exhausted. Confidence in the government was lacking for it to obtain these anticipations as individual loans. However, an incorporated Bank would supply this necessity and make loans to the government in advance of taxes collected. "The use, then, of a bank is, to aid the government by their moneys and credit, for which they will have every proper reward and security," Morris explained.[15]

On July 13, 1781, Morris wrote to Benjamin Franklin explaining his new position as Superintendent of Finance and included a copy of the plan for the Bank of North America. "No Country is truly independent until with her own credit and resources she is able to defend herself and correct her enemies," he wrote. Morris described the problems of collecting revenue from the states and the over reliance on bills of credit. He referred to his work on the Bank of North America the previous month, telling Franklin that he was drawing from the "experience and example of other ages and nations." He hoped it would become a "principal pillar of American credit," making it possible to put private capital to use for the country and "bind" the moneyed class "more strongly to the general cause." Franklin responded later on November 5, 1781, writing in agreement with Morris's plans, adding that "all good patriots" should support him in his efforts. In connection with "our Bank," wrote Franklin, "I clearly see . . . the advantages that you show would arise from the operation."

That July Hamilton began publishing a series of short papers, under the title, *The Continentalist.* They argued the case for needed powers of Congress and supported Congress' February call for revenues from import duties, to which only half of the states had agreed. Hamilton developed a theme about avoiding the fate of other weak unions in history, such as the city states of ancient Greece and the Swiss Cantons. Congress' ideas, he wrote, were not those "enlarged and suited to the government of an independent nation." He said it had conceded, "the powers implied in its original trust," since by the Declaration of Independence it was stated that the Congress had "full power . . . to do all . . . acts and things which independent states may of right do." These included needed economic actions, which, Hamilton stressed, meant going beyond covering expenses for the war. He wrote:

> The separate exertions of the States will never suffice. Nothing but a well-proportioned exertion of the resources of the whole, under the direction of a common council, with power sufficient to give efficacy to their resolutions, can preserve us from being a conquered people now or can make us a happy people hereafter.

On August 30, 1781, in his fourth installment, Hamilton went into more specific detail on the need for funds to pay the debts and provide for the Bank of North America which Congress had established. The Congress, he wrote, "can neither have dignity, vigor, nor credit" by remaining entirely dependent on the occasional grants of the states. Credit was necessary for carrying on the war, as taxes year to year could not suffice. Hamilton referred to the newly approved but not yet chartered Bank and the needed components added to Congress' powers if it was to serve the purposes he had in mind. He said that "the restoration of public credit" could be expected from Morris's administration provided the federal government could raise sufficient taxes. The Bank would give the government "that durable and extensive credit of which it stands in need," if, he wrote, Congress had "it in their power to support him with unexceptionable funds." He said if the "practice of funding the debts" had been begun in 1777 then the depreciation of the continental currency and the loss of credit that accompanied it could have been avoided. The Bank was now the means, he wrote, "to prevent a continuation and multiplication" of the ill effects of depreciation.

Chapter 4
The Bank of North America Takes Action

The victory of Yorktown in October 1781 was the last major battle of the Revolutionary War. However, the war did not end with this victory as even then it was the hope of Great Britain that the finances of the states would prove fatal to its ultimate victory and independence.

After the capture of Yorktown, the army returned through Philadelphia hailed as heroes but without pay. Little had taken place to change the course of financial discord in the states. Long and short-term debts were mounting. The continental currency no longer circulated and was being withdrawn through tax payments. Morris prohibited loan officers in October from issuing more certificates bearing interest. "The confidence of the people is so entirely lost that for the present no bills of credit whatever can be made use of as money," Morris wrote to Franklin on November 27, 1781. He described the "deplorable situation of credit for want of funds to secure, or means to redeem the debts for which the public faith is pledged." The impost request of February to pay the debts still had not been approved. Its initiation required agreement from all the states before the tax could be collected in any one state. Rhode Island, Massachusetts, and Maryland had yet to assent. In accord with the Articles of Confederation, Congress began annually requesting the states fulfill quotas of the sums needed for Congress to pay its war time expenses. The compliance rate was roughly 50% in 1781 and 1782.[1]

In this situation, with public credit dwindling, without adequate revenues, and scarce currency, the credit supplied by the Bank of North America was of the utmost necessity. Subscriptions to the Bank had been slow and smaller than expected, as people had little money and even less confidence in the Union. By November, only $70,000 had been subscribed by men of trade, both at home and abroad. In December, the private subscription increased to $85,000, and a loan from France of $470,000 arrived. With the funds from France, the United States government subscribed to the stock of the Bank for $250,000, enabling it to receive a charter from Congress. On January 7, 1782, Morris wrote to Franklin to celebrate the chartering of the Bank, "the commerce of this country will lie under great obligations to an institution long wanted among us."

The Bank of North America and the economic changes it brought about were essential to sustaining the nation's credit in the period between the victory at Yorktown and the official ending of the war, nearly two years later. A dramatic change took place in the solidity and prospects of the union from the loans and bank currency it provided. In direct loans, it benefited the government greatly, making four monthly loans to the Congress for a total of $400,000 in the first six months of its operation. The Bank provided discounts to individuals and aided in the anticipation of receipts of public money, including contractors for war rations. The bank aided the state of Pennsylvania in the payment of its taxes to Congress in the amount of $80,000. This allowed the state to defend its frontiers, as it had been forced to relieve officers from the failure of internal revenue. The anticipation of state tax payments was crucial for Congress since the states had only paid $30,000 in taxes by June. With a capital of $300,000 the Bank advanced $480,000 for the public service in the first six months of its operation.[2] Robert Livingston, then Secretary of Foreign Affairs, wrote to John Jay on February 2, 1782, and to John Adams on March 5. "Public credit has again reared its head. Our bank paper is in equal estimation with specie." He described a renewed confidence of the public in distributing paper as currency, and that "Paper ceases to be a medium, except the bank paper."[3]

The Bank signaled the potential unity and increasing power of Congress. The economy was able to renew semi-regular transactions of trade and commerce. James Wilson, a signer of the Declaration of Independence and member of Congress, had been appointed a director of the Bank by Congress in 1781.[4] In 1785 he wrote that the success of the Bank in the spring of 1782 came as a blow to the Tories, the British, and their agents among the states, all who had desired financial failure. Throughout 1782, he wrote, the Bank "was viewed as the source and as the support of credit, both private and public: as such, it was hated and dreaded by the enemies of the United States: as such, it was loved and fostered by their friends."[5] Wilson explained that the British knew three years into the war they would not defeat the United States militarily. Instead, their success depended "on the failure of our finances." He continued:

> By this thread our fate was suspended. We watched it with anxiety: we saw it stretched and weakened every hour: the

> deathful instrument was ready to fall upon our heads: on our heads it must have fallen, had not public credit, in the moment when it was about to break asunder, been entwined and supported by the credit of the bank.

At the close of 1784, Robert Morris summed up the Bank's essential service through to the end of the war. By July, 1783, the government had been able to borrow over $820,000 in anticipated revenue on the basis of the renewed credit and confidence brought about by the Bank. "It may then be not only asserted, but demonstrated," Morris wrote, "that without the establishment of the national bank the business of the department of finance could not have been performed." Without the Bank, continued depreciation and a state of insolvency would have made the Treaty of Paris more difficult to obtain.[6]

The Economic Potential of the National Bank

The Bank facilitated a good deal of commerce and demonstrated the potential of payments made with bank credit. Before the Bank, farmers often returned from their locations of sale empty handed, as buyers and merchants could not obtain sufficient amounts of currency, even though they possessed sufficient property. Cash was hoarded, since full payment was often required up front. Merchants preferred to deal with one another and with farmers in specie since accepting payment in a personal promissory note or bill of exchange often required holding onto the note for a long duration before receiving final payment. Merchants would only loan their money to each other for short periods when they had idle money to spare. The shortages caused importers and brokers to charge farmers high rates of 15-20% for loans. Even so, farmers were able to become highly productive with the supplies obtained, making it worthwhile to borrow. The Bank was able to facilitate the same process at a much lower interest rate of 7-8%, for much longer periods, and with greater regularity.[7]

With a Bank that could turn promissory notes for economic transactions into a trusted form of payment in bank credit, merchants and traders now had an alternative currency with which to exchange with farmers. Merchants could bring promissory notes and bills of exchange to the Bank and it would purchase them at a slight discount, giving bank notes (promissory notes of the bank) or a deposit in return. In other words, the Bank exchanged its own credit for the personal credit of merchants. Merchants and tradesmen could then use the deposit credit and banknotes as a means to pay for their subsequent purchases. Tradesmen able to obtain these facilities of the Bank could therefore turn the credit of their future production and trade into a means of exchanging labor and capital. The amount of credit the Bank could issue for the purchase of private credit assets was not limited to its specie capital but it was prudent to keep the proportion relatively small since bank notes would occasionally be presented to the Bank for redemption in specie. Nearly a century after Blackwell's plan was attempted, a national institution had been achieved that could create a stable form of currency, supply needed credit, and provide liquidity.

This role of the Bank in trade was not as extensive as Morris had hoped since much of the Bank's funds remained expended in loans to the government. Despite this fact, it represented the possibility of a sufficient payment system for the economy. And though highly imperfect, a correlation between the currency and the economy was achieved by the Bank's issue of its own credit in response to economic demand. The Bank also represented the potential to facilitate the collection and distribution of revenue and to equalize exchange rates.

However, due to insufficient contributions from the state requisitions and the non-compliance of the states to the impost, the Bank was unable to retain a lasting national scope or increase its capital stock to the level intended. Hamilton described Morris' predicament to a French officer, Louis-Marie vicomte de Noailles in the spring of 1782. He told Noailles that the Bank had the support of the commercial interests and had aided the government. The missing factor allowing it to expand its operations and reach its potential was "moderate funds, permanently pledged for the security of lenders." Hamilton held out optimism to Noailles that the Congress's request for a duty on imports would take effect.[8] But by 1784, the institution formed to organize the resources of commerce into a source of credit for the currency and needs of the government was fated to wane into national insignificance.

Chapter 5
The 1782-1783 Origins of the Bank-Based Funding System

The requisitions of Congress to the states became increasingly burdensome as the war came to a close and as debts accumulated. The taxation methods available to the states were direct taxes on lands and polls (uniform taxes irrespective of property) and indirect taxes on trade. There was not enough manufacturing in the states in the 1780s to make excise taxes on consumption a serious factor. Duties were a supplement to direct taxation for states on the coast but inland states had to rely exclusively on land and poll taxes.[1]

Direct taxes became more difficult as the output of the economy suffered a steep decline throughout the war. Families lost the labor of soldiers and many went into debt. After the decline of the credit of the continental currency, taxes were increasingly ordered to be paid in scarce specie or in kind. The Bank of North America's currency was crucial in 1782 and 1783 but not alone sufficient to fill the void. Declining money and credit supply led to a drop in prices. During the 1780s land lost two-thirds of its value and the price of livestock fell by half.[2]

Lifting the weight of direct taxation was a leading argument for the impost request of 1781. Taxes on trade were collected from merchants in places where specie was most plentiful. Duties translated into price increases on goods consumed and were thus borne in proportion to consumption and wealth. A federal import duty would therefore be a way to obtain a large sum without putting a burden on the majority of taxpayers who were farmers with property but little money.[3] In April and July of 1782, Hamilton addressed the lack of a federal impost from this standpoint in two more Continentalist papers. With prescience, he depicted the conflicts that would later arise in 1784-1787 from the inability of Congress to impose duties and regulate trade. States would end up not imposing their own duties for fear that neighbor states without duties would be at a commercial advantage. Potential revenue from duties would be lost. Revenue would then have to come from increased taxes on property, resulting in decreased land value and increased prices for necessities required by the laboring poor. Hamilton also included a proposal for how to decrease the burden of direct taxation in the long term. The establishment of "permanent funds," rather than unpredictable and "temporary" appropriations and taxes, was the best way to ease the burden on the people. "With this basis of procuring credit," he wrote, "the amount of present taxes might be greatly diminished." In other words, a government able to pay its bills in the long-term would create the confidence and stability needed to make credit a source for covering current expenses. This would allow the government to increase economic activity and draw on its future revenues. As Hamilton put it:

> Large sums of money might be borrowed abroad at a low interest, and introduced into the country, to defray the current expenses and pay the public debts; which would not only lessen the demand for immediate supplies, but would throw more money into circulation, and furnish the people with greater means of paying the taxes.

In July 1782 Congress appointed a committee to consider how best to support the credit of the United States. On July 29, Morris issued a statement arguing that financial security depended on permanent revenues raised internally, not on foreign loans. His design was for a comprehensive system of poll, land, and excise taxes to fulfill the state requisitions. These taxes were rejected in favor of maintaining unique levy and collection policies state by state.[4] By the summer, Maryland, Georgia, and Rhode Island still had not complied with Morris' repeated requests to approve the 5% import duty.[5]

Hamilton traveled to the New York legislature on July 14 in his capacity as tax collector for Morris. He communicated several matters that Morris had specified and his own proposals about the defects of the tax system. The legislature passed a bill to collect money for Congress but he obtained the impression that as the amount of taxes imposed was already so high further taxes would be fruitless. Resolutions he helped to draft were introduced proposing a convention of the states to expand the powers of Congress. On the 24th, the legislature then appointed Hamilton to begin serving in the Continental Congress that November.[6]

At the end of September, Morris described the continuing financial problems of the country in a letter to Franklin. He said the modes of laying and collecting taxes remained unnecessarily harsh and the amounts that the states were collecting themselves remained inadequate. On September 3, in addition to the impost, he asked the states for an immediate $1.2 million necessary to pay the year's interest on the domestic debt. Referring to the same, Morris wrote: "The smallness of the sum which has been paid will doubtless astonish you." Morris blamed legislators for seeking popularity and hoped "the consequences of not being taxed" would lead to a change in response. On the basis of his personal credit Morris kept creditors at bay and collected just enough from the state requisitions to pay operating expenses and interest on the foreign debt during his time as Superintendent of Finance.[7] He continued to hold out hope that the future approval of a federal duty power would prevent default on the principal of the debts. That fall Maryland belatedly complied with the impost request, leaving only Rhode Island to put it into operation. Morris employed Thomas Paine to write essays defending the impost from Rhode Island's continued objections.[8]

The Address to Rhode Island

Despite the attempts to bring Rhode Island on board with the approval of a federal import duty, the state officially rejected it in November. Congress deputized a three-man committee in response to deliver an appeal to reverse its decision.[9] Congress members Hamilton, James Madison, and Thomas Fitzsimmons were appointed to write the message.[10]

Contrary to Rhode Island's claims about the effects of import duties, the committee argued that duties were ultimately a consumption tax and did not fall heavier on merchants and commercial interests than any other class. Instead, they fell in proportion to the amount of goods consumed. They explained that this merchant-consumer example held for the amount of the tax borne by commercial states on the coast as compared with non-importing states in the interior. Each type of state would only pay their just share of duties in proportion to their consumption of dutied goods. They pointed out that the duration of the requested impost was coextensive with the existence of the debt, the duties to be raised were those specifically for the debt, and the interest rate was fixed. Therefore, the impost was not "repugnant to the liberty of the U.S," as Rhode Island had maintained, nor did it represent indefinite power.[11] While most creditors wanted the principal in practice, it was outside the power of the Congress to pay both principal and interest. The "next expedient," they wrote, "is to fund the debt," to uphold its full value by providing for the interest.

This would allow it to be negotiable and traded for money. Hamilton's plan for a funded national debt, which he would implement as Treasury Secretary, was foreshadowed and explicitly enunciated here for the first time:

> Besides the advantage to individuals from this arrangement, the active stock of the nation would be increased by the whole amount of the domestic debt, and of course the abilities of the community to contribute to the public wants; the national credit would revive, and stand hereafter on a secure basis.[12]

By funding the national debt, it would be transformed into a tremendous resource for industry and commerce. Hamilton explained later that this defined the fuller purpose of the February 1781 impost. It was not merely for an amount with which to satisfy creditors.

The written address to Rhode Island was a victory of reasoning but a political failure. By the end of December Virginia had repealed its earlier ratification of the impost amendment and Maryland signaled it would do the same. The committee's journey was suspended.[13] Adding in Pennsylvania's threat that November to not pay its due proportion of taxes for the year, it appeared that financial disunion was on the horizon, even as the war was coming to a conclusion.

In December of 1782 European newspapers reported the fact that not all of the colonies had agreed to the 5% duty on imported goods requested in February 1781. Franklin wrote to Morris on December 23, chastising the states: "Our people certainly ought to do more for themselves. It is absurd pretending to be lovers of liberty while they grudge paying for the defense of it." He said that the world had now become acquainted with "the non payment of taxes by the people, and with the non payment of interest to the creditors of the public." This knowledge had badly hurt our credit abroad and the ability to obtain foreign loans. In the future, the foundation of credit should be within the nation, he wrote, and before loans were made, funds should be "established beforehand, for the regular payment at least of the interest."[14] This latter point by Franklin would become one of Hamilton's main principles of operation when serving as Secretary of the Treasury of the United States.

The Funding Attempt of 1783

On January 11, 1783, with the war's end uncertain, the system of taxes having failed, and debts mounting, Morris wrote distressfully to Franklin of the near impossibility of managing the finances with little revenue. His frustrations included working under a Congress whose power was limited to "framing recommendations," dealing with creditors whose constant complaints made it more difficult to respond, and facing an army on the verge of disbanding for lack of pay.

On January 24, in coordination with Hamilton and James Wilson, Morris took bolder action. He sent a letter to Congress threatening to resign if "permanent provision for the public debts" was not achieved by May. Instead of progress on the provision for the debts, circumstances had increased the debt and decreased the collection from the states. "I must, therefore, quit a situation which becomes utterly insupportable," he wrote. His letter provoked great reaction from Congress and General Washington.[15] Morris told Washington that Congress was more afraid of offending the states than adopting the necessary measures. Washington wrote to Morris that he could have received no worse news and said the effect of his resignation would be grim. Hamilton explained to Washington on April 11, 1783, that Morris's only alternative was the course of making further engagements that could not be paid, which would "have sacrificed his credit and his character; and public credit already in a ruinous condition would have lost its last support."[16]

The next day Congress took up the subject of providing for the whole debt, with Wilson and Hamilton initiating the debate. Madison, Oliver Ellsworth, and Thomas Fitzsimmons among others were involved. From then until the end of February, Congress discussed the subject of providing permanent revenues for the whole debt, domestic and foreign included, and the ongoing war's demands. They argued that funds extending generally and uniformly throughout the United States and collected under the authority of Congress would be preferable to those collected by the states. They approved a proposition that stated, "the establishment of permanent and adequate funds on taxes and duties . . . are indispensably necessary towards doing complete justice to the public creditors, for restoring public credit, and for providing for the future exigencies of the war." The proposition was generally accepted by the delegates but the method for establishing these funds was vigorously debated.[17] The debate garnered immediate reaction from Virginia and Rhode Island, the main states which had blocked the federal impost. These states blamed the mounting debts upon Congress' own mismanagement. Others wanted Congress to attend to debts due to them before others. Rather than force the issue, many in Congress sought compromise and moved for acquiescence. A small committee of five, consisting of delegates Carroll, Gorham, Fitzsimmons, Hamilton, and Ramsay argued in response that it was Congress' duty to persevere with its original 1781 impost request, for "revenues equal to the purpose of funding all the debts of the United States."[18]

The final result of Congress's winter debates for permanent funds was issued on April 18, 1783. The 1781 impost had been a request to the states for a general power to raise a 5% duty on goods to an amount equal to paying off the debts. The 1783 Act in contrast asked for the power to levy duties equal to roughly 50% of the amount needed to pay the interest on the debts, leaving the states authority to choose and collect their own taxes (mostly direct taxes) to make up the other 50%. The 1781 impost requested a power to collect taxes for a period coextensive with the time of the debt, 30 years or more. In the 1783 Act the duties were set for a period of 25 years.[19] Morris objected to its final form and thought it gave the states too much power over the selection of taxes. As in 1782 he was in favor of a uniform system of land, excise, and impost taxes.[20]

Hamilton was one of only three delegates who voted against passage of the Act.[21] Included in his objections he stated that by not making the duration of the collection equal to the maturity of the debt, the debt would not assume sufficient credibility as a resource of commerce or capital for banks. He wrote:

> For want of an adequate security, the evidences of the public debt will not be transferrable for anything like their value—that this not admitting an incorporation of the creditors in the nature of banks will deprive the public of the benefit of an increased circulation, and of course will disable the people from paying the taxes for want of a sufficient medium.

In other words, the Act did not make the debt a resource for the economy. This objection was reflective of his role in the address to Rhode Island the December previous and foreshadowed his policies in later years. Hamilton saw the need to coordinate the nation's finances as a system in order to obtain an integrated economic effect. He recognized early the importance to the banking system of reserve assets in government securities, "evidences of public debt."

Despite Hamilton's opposition to the overall plan he was nevertheless appointed to a committee along with James Madison and Oliver Ellsworth to prepare the Act's accompanying address to the states. The committee argued the benefits of duties as a form of taxation.[22] In addition, the committee discussed three points that were strikingly similar to the arguments and steps taken later by Congress in 1790, when passing legislation for establishing public credit. First, the committee wrote that the total collection requested would provide for all of the debt in a single act, which was necessary to establish national credit. The domestic creditors, soldiers included, had become involuntary creditors, since the duration for which their initial loans were made had passed. These creditors were "entitled to clear principles of justice and good faith to demand the principal, instead of accepting the annual interest." But since it was impossible to pay the principal, they deserved at least a secure payment of the interest. This would allow them "to transfer their stock at its full value," as a full-value mechanism for trade purposes. Secondly, by secure funding, "the capital of the domestic debt,"—which was at a high interest of six percent—could be "cancelled by other loans obtained at a more moderate interest." Thirdly, they addressed in detail that all of the creditors should be treated equally, whether they were of France, individuals in Holland, patriotic soldiers, domestic lenders of their property for public service, or those who had purchased certificates of debt from the original lenders. "To discriminate the merits of these several descriptions of creditors would be a task equally unnecessary and invidious. . . The voice of policy, no less than justice, pleads in favor of all," they wrote.

But only half of the states acted on the measure in 1783. None responded with full authorization, and only two states, Delaware and Massachusetts, gave full compliance with the funds required of the federal impost portion. None of the states made provision for the supplemental funds to be chosen by themselves with their own taxes.[23] Instead of compliance, Congress was attacked by the state legislatures for claiming power and neglecting other responsibilities.[24]

The collective action of Congress and the states had led to a weakening of federal power. But it had also led a number of political figures to privately discuss plans for strengthening the union. In February 1783, Henry Knox wrote to Gouverneur Morris asking him, "why do not your great men call the people together and tell them . . . to have a convention of the States to form a better Constitution[?]" In April of 1783, Jonathan Jackson, a former Congressional delegate, wrote to Benjamin Lincoln, the secretary of War, of a plan "to throw the States into one large family and the separate sovereignties into one united." In April of 1783, Hamilton told Congress that he was developing a plan for a general convention whose goal "would be to strengthen the federal constitution."[25] On June 30, 1783, still as a member of Congress, Hamilton wrote a series of resolutions that detailed each error of the Articles of Confederation. The Articles lacked general powers equal to "the purpose of effectually drawing forth the resources of the respective members for the common welfare and defence," he wrote. In addition to describing the lack of a judiciary and the numerous, ill consequences of "confounding legislative and executive powers in a single body," he included a list of their central economic errors. Congress had been given the power to tax in its right to ascertain sums to be raised and to appropriate them. But this power was mute, he wrote, since the Articles withheld, "the control of the laying and collecting of the taxes equal to the required sums." He attacked the Articles for authorizing Congress to borrow but without also giving them the power of establishing funds to secure repayment, which led them to "emit an unfunded paper as the sign of value." This created a lack of credit to circulate the bills emitted, a depreciation, and a breach of contracts.[26] He also objected to the inability to regulate foreign coin and trade. Hamilton's resolutions ended by stating that Congress "recommended to the several States to appoint a Convention . . . with full powers to revise the Confederation, and to adopt and propose such alterations as to them shall appear necessary." These resolutions were not introduced.

Chapter 6
The Economic Path to the U.S. Constitution

After the Peace of September 1783 the economic situation in the U.S. became drastically worse. The consequences of not giving Congress the power to collect adequate revenues or regulate trade accumulated. A deep depression set in during 1784, forcing many of the currency and taxation issues of previous years to a head.

Two immediate effects of the Peace were trade volatility and currency contraction. "When hostilities ceased," wrote James Wilson in 1785, "the floodgates of commerce were opened. An inundation of foreign manufactures overflowed the United States." Purchases were made beyond the ability to pay. This resulted in a negative trade balance and specie fled the country to pay for the imports. Circulation was diminished, including that of the Bank of North America. Many domestic importers did not make good on their purchases from European merchants, injuring credit and increasing the interest rate for loans. Retailers paid domestic importers with specie. "Every operation, foreign and domestic," Wilson continued, "had an injurious effect on our credit, our circulation, and our commerce."[1] In Pennsylvania, merchants who had expected assistance from the Bank pledged credit beyond their means. Those who had drawn too many bills of exchange consequently failed in great numbers. The Bank could not possibly back them up, since without state support for its debts Congress still required the bulk of the Bank's funds.[2] Limited credit capacities had led the public sector to crowd out the private sector. Trade was sent into a further crisis as the British closed their ports in the West Indies to the U.S. and put trade restrictions on fish, rum, meat, and other products. Economic downturn after the war caused prices to fall and revenues to decrease. Credit contracted, money was removed from circulation, and specie for borrowing was largely unavailable. The growing depression through 1784 and 1785 led to an almost total loss of access to private credit for most classes.[3]

The demise of the Bank of North America was another relatively immediate impact of the post-war environment. The Bank had never become the commercial oriented institution of the size required, nor was it able to fully support and integrate itself into domestic commerce. Along with its erosion from the negative balance of trade and financial condition of the Congress, opposition from speculators and Tories in the Pennsylvania legislature and other politically related ills rendered it an ineffective national entity by 1784. Instead of expanding its operations to make up for the growing scarcity of specie, its currency declined in tandem.[4]

As the post-war depression worsened in 1784, the response of the states to the 1783 funding plan of Congress moved through the state legislatures with even less uniformity than the year before. Connecticut and South Carolina partially acceded to the terms, bringing the total to eight states.[5] "The people of this country still continue as remiss as ever in the payment of taxes," wrote Morris to Franklin on September 30, 1784. In his view each state was desirous of shifting the burden onto the shoulders of the other.[6] The amounts delivered to Morris from the state requisitions became insufficient to finance the debt and he was forced to begin postponing payments in 1784. Congress took a new approach to financing its debts, paying interest on loan office and settlement certificates with certificates of interest. But without confidence in Congress to eventually pay interest in specie, or in a currency tradeable at par with specie, the market value of federal certificates fell between 10-40%.[7] Like in the winter of 1780 a transfer of financial authority from Congress to the states increasingly took effect. Many states did not want to bestow on Congress a power of taxation or wait for other states to comply with the request of April 1783. They began to pay off the creditors of Congress themselves, issuing their own bills of credit to redeem the federal notes held by creditors for their share of Congress' debts. In other words, the states became creditors of the Congress. This dampened the arguments of those like Morris and Hamilton who saw federal powers to finance the debt as strong bonds of union.[8]

On November 1, 1784, Morris finally resigned his post and issued a lengthy volume on the accounts. The report concluded with a recommendation that while paying debts was expensive, it was "infinitely more expensive to withhold the payment." The latter action eliminates the source from which to obtain money when the government is in need. "That source, abundant, nay, almost inexhaustible," he stressed "is public credit." If the debts were provided for they would become "a real medium of commerce," he wrote, since the "possessors of certificates would then become the possessors of money." This was the meaning of a funded debt, and echoed Hamilton's sentiments in 1782 and 1783. Morris urged the states to create a federal government with powers to command the resources of its members: "If there be not one government which can draw forth and direct the combined efforts of our united America, our independence is but a name, our freedom a shadow, and our dignity a dream . . ."[9]

Morris was correct about these goals, but the economic reality of the depression had become a bigger obstacle than the willingness of state legislators to adopt his recommendations. Heavy direct taxes became unbearable for those who were poor or of moderate income and who lacked a personal source of credit. Farmers had livestock, tools, their buildings, and land, but not gold and silver.[10] Large war debts increased the need for debt payments, increasing in turn the amounts that states were attempting to collect, on top of what Congress had requested. Taxes paid to the federal government accounted for only half of the money the state governments were raising in direct taxes. In Connecticut, taxation "embraced every object and was carried as far as it could be done without absolutely oppressing individuals." In Massachusetts "taxation was carried still farther even to a degree," as a large government debt in the state led to severe direct taxes. It is estimated that the average per capita tax burden in Pennsylvania, Rhode Island, Massachusetts, and South Carolina in the early 1780s increased severalfold above the prewar amount. The scarcity of currency magnified these burdens on taxpayers. One author estimates the increase in taxes was as high as five to ten times that previous. Another author has compared the conditions of the decade following the war with the Great Depression of the 1930s.[11]

Therefore, despite the attempts of the legislatures to implement the requisitions of Congress they were simply not bearable by the public. The result was political and financial turmoil. Many taxpayers refused to pay their creditors. Others interfered with court proceedings and the forced auctions of farmers' property. Relief legislation was demanded by farmers and passed by many legislators. This legislation included issues of government bills of credit to allow debtors to pay creditors in state paper currency instead of specie. These bills of credit were also issued to allow taxes to be paid. Some states rejected relief measures and insisted upon strict enforcement of tax collections in specie. These states faced serious opposition, most famously in the case of the 1786-1787 uprising in western Massachusetts known as Shay's rebellion. Uncertainty and instability decreased investment.[12] In Federalist Paper No. 12, Hamilton succinctly characterized how direct taxation became impossible under these conditions: "Real scarcity of money, incident to a languid and mutilated state of trade, has hitherto defeated every experiment for extensive collections, and has at length taught the different Legislatures the folly of attempting them."

Currency and property values fluctuated between and within states as relief efforts increased. In 1786 the value of New York's paper currency was at par with its face value in specie, Pennsylvania and New Jersey's was 10-15% below par, while North Carolina, Rhode Island, and Georgia's was far below.[13] As the states and Congress grew increasingly bereft of revenues, so the value of the government securities they had issued during and after the war increased in fluctuation. Speculators in bonds profited greatly from these fluctuations, leading to a growing animosity against domestic bondholders. Taxpayers protested. Many felt their heavy taxes were being borne for the benefit of speculators. Some writers argued that government securities bought by speculators should not be paid at the market value or should be brought down artificially. Others argued that legislatures should not direct certain types of tax collections to pay bondholders. These protests and debates made the impost request of April 1783 unpopular and made it more difficult for states to fulfill the requisitions of Congress.[14]

In competition for commerce and scarce revenues, states began imposing rival duties. In a February 1787 address on the impost to the New York legislature, Hamilton described how each state competed for imports and kept duties to such a low amount as to be unprofitable. Pennsylvania had only a 2.5% duty and Connecticut and New Jersey were duty free. The latter states considered the impost of New York as a tax upon them. New York was forced to keep its duty small and unprofitable in competition with Pennsylvania. Smuggling was widespread. Internal trade conflicts and debt problems between the states worsened through 1784-1786.[15] The weakness of the union became further evident.[16]

These economic conditions led to a steep decline in the collections of the required amounts to pay the debts of the United States for the war. Morris had been able to bring in over 50% of the amounts requested to the states during 1781-1784, a little over $2 million. But in 1785, a requisition bill for $3 million ($1.7 million of which was to be paid in specie) brought in only 20% of the amount. By 1785 Congress began defaulting on interest payments to the French. In 1786 only 2% of the requisition for the year was paid. An attempt was made that August to vote a new requisition of $3.7 million to pay the interest and principal on the foreign loans. The results were equally poor. By January of 1787 the states would cease all payments to Congress.[17]

The decline in direct taxation by the states made the inability of the Congress to tax ever more troublesome. On February 15, 1786, a congressional committee appealed to the states regarding their belated and varied compliance with the April 1783 request to invest Congress with a power to levy duties to pay the debts and restore credit. They wrote that the moment of decision was upon the "people of these United States" whether they would "support their rank as a nation, by maintaining the public faith at home and abroad" or, for want of revenues would put the "existence of the Union" in jeopardy. The committee called for seven of the states to modify their resolutions and the remaining states to adopt the system.[18] But when New York finally passed a resolution in response on May 4, 1786, rather than completing the acceptance of an impost, it rendered the other twelve state resolutions useless. Unlike the other states, it refused to grant any power of Congress to collect the impost. It only granted money. Since none of the state resolutions of 1783-1786 were considered law until they all complied, the exercise of over three years was rendered futile.[19] Congress held out hope that the mistake could be overturned. In August it requested that New York hold a special session to reverse its stance that the grant of the legislative power to collect taxes to Congress was unconstitutional. On February 15, 1787, the New York legislature belatedly took up the issue. Having been elected the previous April to serve in the 1787 session of the legislature, Hamilton gave an exposition on the subject of legislative power: that which was properly due to the federal government and that to the states, with respect to the power of taxation. His speech contained the substance of many of his arguments later seen in the Federalist papers, especially No.'s 30-36. It argued that the powers of legislative authority had been granted, and that the degree or nature of powers was a matter of expediency and prudence, not of principle. He added that duties levied by a common direction would be much more profitable than rival duties from each state.[20] His resolution was defeated by a silent vote of the opposition. By September 1787, Congress would be insolvent, with no money to pay the first principal payments that were due to foreign creditors.[21]

On February 21, 1787, Congress took up the matter of a commissioner's report from a trade convention in Annapolis held the September previous and its accompanying resolution that a convention should be had in May of 1787, "to render the constitution of the Federal Government adequate to the exigencies of the Union."[22] Amid debate, similar resolutions were introduced by New York and Massachusetts delegates from their legislatures echoing the call for a convention to establish an adequate government that could preserve the union.[23] The debate resulted in the approval of the Constitutional Convention taking place between May and September of 1787 that produced the U.S. Constitution.

The U.S. Constitution arising from the convention of 1787 created a government that could address and solve the economic and financial problems of the 1780s. Congress was empowered to create a tax system that could provide sufficient revenues without unduly burdening the public. More efficient, indirect consumption taxes using federally levied and collected imposts and excises could replace direct state taxation. It prohibited state governments from issuing further bills of credit or enacting legislation that would impair the obligation of contracts. While states had used these powers to respond to the currency, debt, and tax revolts of the 1780s, the responsibility to prevent and deal with currency and debt crises was now placed in the hands of the Congress. The Congress acted on this responsibility in the creation of a bank-based funding system. As explained in detail in the following chapter, this involved an integrated system of federal taxes, new borrowings, a unified national debt, among other measures. Restoring public credit increased and stabilized the value of U.S. securities making them a tradeable security equal to money, expanding the supply of credit. The subsequent creation of a newly designed banking corporation of national scope then solidified a stable and growing economy. These financial measures were among the driving motivations for the Constitution.[24]

Chapter 7
The Bank of the United States and the Funded Debt

By 1789, the scarcity of money had led to a decrease in the value of property by 20-50%. The foreign debt was $12 million at the time. Domestic debt, made up of numerous types of debt of creditors and veterans, totaled $42 million. In addition, each state had its own separate debts, in total another $22 million. There was no way to pay the principal and interest of the entire debt outstanding through annual taxes alone. The first step taken by Alexander Hamilton as Treasury Secretary closely followed the proposals developed in 1781-1783 by himself and others.

On January 9, 1790, Hamilton delivered a report to Congress describing the nature of the debt incurred during the war not as a burden to be shrugged off, but "the price of liberty." He affirmed that the rights of all creditors would be held equally and that the debt would be paid in full. He outlined a single plan for reorganizing the debt, providing for the interest, and reducing the principal outstanding.[1] His plan was debated for sometime, finally passing as three Acts of Congress in August of 1790. With the passage of these Acts, the public debt was converted into a medium of commerce and exchange. The ensuing prosperity transformed the relations between debtors and creditors. The union of the states would become cemented based on increasing land value, industrial growth, and expanding agriculture that uniform and creditworthy debt bestowed upon the new nation.

In the August 4 Act of Congress, "An act making provision for the debt of the United States," the foreign, national, and state debts, were remoulded into a shape favorable to the nation, and dealt with in a way that unified the resources of the country available through taxation. The Act authorized new loans to be taken out for the full amount of the domestic and state debts, assuming and transforming the latter into national debts. The subscriptions to the loans were paid in the various types of domestic and state certificates of debt issued during the war. In exchange, the creditors received new U.S. debt certificates with an interest payment guaranteed by a permanent appropriation from Congress. The new loans were part of a unified plan to fund the entire national debt.[2]

In accord with Hamilton's "fundamental maxim," the August 4 Act which created these debts included a means for extinguishing them. The "proceeds of the duties on imports and tonnage" and all revenues of other taxes were allocated accordingly: $600,000 was set aside "for the support of the Government of the United States, and their Common defence." After reserving this, a sum was pledged for the foreign debt until final redemption of the whole, for the payment of the interest on the outstanding foreign debt, and the interest on a new foreign loan of 12 million (also authorized in the August 4 Act to discharge arrears of interest and installments of the principal of the foreign debt). The residue, after the foregoing, was then pledged and appropriated for the payment of the interest on the newly issued U.S. certificates of domestic public debt, of varying interest but averaging 4%. Finally, the remainder was applied to the interest on the new state debt certificates. The interest on the new certificates was paid out quarterly in order to increase the available money in circulation for commerce.

The source of these funds was chiefly duties on imports and other internal excise taxes. The first major Act of Congress on July 4, 1789 "An Act for laying a Duty on Goods, Wares, and Merchandises imported into the United States" had been an application of its new power "to lay and collect taxes, imposts and excises, for the payment of debts and for the encouragement of domestic manufactures." Also on August 4, an extensive Act was passed for a more effective collection of duties.[3] More importantly, on August 10, in an "Act making further provision for the payment of the debt of the United States," Congress enacted Hamilton's April 23 recommendations for providing for the debt and greatly increased the number and amount of duties on imports and internal excise taxes, all to be appropriated according to the manner of the August 4 Act.

In his 1790 report, Hamilton wrote that it should become "a fundamental maxim in the system of public credit of the United States, that the creation of debt should always be accompanied with the means of extinguishment." In this context, he recommended the authorization of a new foreign loan up to $12 million to assure regular payment of the principal on foreign debts, and if necessary the principal of domestic debts, the interest of foreign debts, and purchasing of public debt while it remained below value. For the "sinking or discharging of the debts" the Act of August 4 appropriated the proceeds of the sales of the lands in the Western territory. A further Act on August 12, "An Act making provision for the reduction of the public debt," legislated that the surplus revenues of the duties on imports and tonnage (after the allocations of those mentioned above for interest payments) would go toward purchasing the public debt at its market price while it remained below its true value. These purchases were made in order to increase its value and protect it from speculators who would take advantage of its low and fluctuating value. To ensure this latter ability to protect the price of the debt from speculation, the Act authorized a further loan by the President up to $2 million to be applied to purchases of the public debt.[4]

The set of Acts taken as a whole created a funded national debt. Instead of a drain on the nation's resources and currency, contributing to scarcity, the new U.S. debt certificates became a medium of commerce, an asset, and a vast pool of capital for trade. A new capital was created equal to the whole amount of the domestic debt. By funding, the debt rose in value from $15 million to $45 million by the end of 1790. Congress effectively created a capital resource of $30 million for the economy which could be readily traded for specie or as a security for which lenders would readily issue credit. The equivalent of $30 million in liquid assets were added the economy. The result was a reviving of commerce and trade.[5] In 1791, Hamilton summarized the effect of the 1790 Acts of Congress:

> In a sound and settled state of the public funds, a man possessed of a sum in them, can embrace any scheme of business, which offers, with as much confidence as if he were possessed of an equal sum in coin. This operation of public funds as capital, is too obvious to be denied...
>
> Though a funded debt is not in the first instance, an absolute increase of Capital, or an augmentation of real wealth; yet by serving as a new power in the operation of industry, it has within certain bounds a tendency to increase the real wealth of a Community, in like manner as money borrowed by a thrifty farmer, to be laid out in the improvement of his farm may, in the end, add to his Stock of real riches.[6]

As the value of the public debt rose, so did the available credit in the economy. Likewise, as the strength of the nation's economy increased so did the value of the public debt. By facilitating commercial exchange as a source of credit and money, funded debt became a productive source of wealth and enhanced the value of all other property. The increase in money and credit supply improved trading volumes and allowed merchants to trade for smaller profits.[7] In addition to upholding the public credit for further loans, the funding of the foreign debt made foreign investment a renewable resource for domestic agriculture, commerce, and manufactures, where the domestic profits far exceeded the interest paid out to foreign lenders. U.S. bonds became an alternative substitute to land for investing profits and a security invested for domestic purposes.[8]

The First Bank of the United States

The factor that ensured the success of the new financial system was the Bank of the United States. Unlike the Bank of North America, the Bank of the United States was able to fulfill the role which Hamilton and Morris had written about for properly funded U.S. debt when working for the Continental Congress. While the Continental Congress did not possess a power of taxation to turn its debt into a valuable security, the U.S. Congress did have this power and had utilized it for this purpose. On December 13, 1790, Hamilton urged Congress to authorize private parties to incorporate their claims of public credit into a Bank under joint proprietorship with the government.[9] On February 25, 1791, the Bank of the United States was incorporated, uniting the benefits of banking with the resources of public debt.

While not circulating as money itself, the capital Congress had created with the funded debt was utilized to form the majority of the Bank's capital. Those who had subscribed to the loan for the domestic and state debts, and received new 6% certificates, used them to become subscribers to the capital stock. A total of $8 million dollars of shares were subscribed in one part specie, three parts certificates of public debt. To unite the interest of the bank with the public and increase the lending capability for the economy, the United States subscribed for $2 million of stock, one-fifth its total capital.[10] The act of subscribing to the Bank's capital with public debt securities, which converted the debt into bank stock, accelerated the rise of the value of the public debt. In addition, the potential utility of the public debt was transformed and its value was augmented by its new service to the economy and the government.

In his letter to President Washington on the constitutionality of the Bank, Hamilton demonstrated that the Bank was not only a trading company that possessed capital, but served as the expression and means of the powers of Congress, increasing the facility of some of them and making others possible. By creating an effective medium of taxation in bank notes and deposit credit, the Bank facilitated Congress' powers "to collect taxes, duties, imposts and excises, to pay the debts and provide for the common defense and general welfare of the United States." The increase in the size and speed of circulation of the currency made payments more feasible as they could be made on credit. In addition to the large capital stock, the coin of depositors, promissory notes of merchants, and public debt securities were put to use and magnified in loans and discounts by the Bank. It became possible to make payments on credit by checks on the Bank and its branches, or more locally in bank notes.

The Constitution proscribes that "all duties, imposts and excises shall be uniform throughout the United States." The Bank made it possible for the taxes laid to be collected in a uniform fashion by replacing the various paper circulating at fluctuating values between states with a single currency of uniform value. This uniformity aided Congress in carrying out its power to regulate commerce between the states. This power was also assisted by the convenient medium of exchange and by the loans the Bank provided, which encouraged the nation's merchants, navigation, and manufactures. It aided the government in the collection of duties and regulation of trade by lending to individuals, companies, and importing merchants in lieu of their possession of money.

The Bank was further integrated with the collection of taxes by serving as a depository for government revenues, which increased the available credit to the economy. Without the Bank, the revenues of duties pledged for the contracted payments of interest on debts would have remained idle in preparation for payment. Instead, the government deposits were available for loans and discounts during the period between the collection and appropriation of the government funds. This function also assisted Congress in its power to "dispose of and make all needful rules and regulations respecting . . . property belonging to the United States."

The Bank's currency facilitated Congress' power of paying the debts by making it possible for the government to pay the interest on the domestic and state debts in the legal tender of bank notes rather than gold. This assisted the Treasury and increased the available currency in circulation. The Bank was the designated instrument to carry out the power of borrowing money and it lent to the government in anticipation of its revenues. During the Revolutionary War, under conditions of bad credit, the loss of specie and lack of circulating medium, the private credit of the Bank of North America had been necessary and essential for the government to borrow. The Bank of the United States was a similar auxiliary for low interest loans for the government.

The currency in circulation became largely that tied to the promise of the funded debt, in the capital of the bank, as deposits, and as a security for discount. The notes of the Bank were made a legal tender and "receivable in all payments to the United States," and could be redeemed for specie if desired, "payable on demand, in gold and silver coin." In the 1790s, other state banks rose into place to facilitate the growth of internal regions. With the memory of depreciated state currencies from 1783-1790 receding into the background, people became accustomed to the bank notes, and merchants to obtaining discounts for their notes and drawing on deposits. The banking system made it possible for numerous people to keep accounts with others and to make purchases between themselves through the medium of credit. Hamilton summarized the economic facilitation supplied by this expansion of credit in his final 1795 report:

> Credit . . . is among the principal engines of useful enterprise and internal improvement. As a substitute for capital, it is little less useful than gold or silver, in agriculture, in commerce, in the manufacturing and mechanic arts. The proof of this needs no labored deduction. It is matter of daily experience in the most familiar pursuits. One man wishes to take up and cultivate a piece of land; he purchases upon credit, and, in time, pays the purchase money out of the produce of the soil improved by his labor. Another sets up in trade; in the credit founded upon a fair character, he seeks, and often finds, the means of becoming, at length, a wealthy merchant. A third commences business as manufacturer or mechanic, with skill, but without money. It is by credit that he is enabled to procure the tools, the materials, and even the subsistence of which he stands in need, until his industry has supplied him with capital; and, even then, he derives, from an established and increased credit, the means of extending his undertakings.[11]

The Bank increased the efficiency of domestic bills of exchange and individual promissory notes, moderating the interest rate and friction of private brokers. These factors were of great significance, as Hamilton put it, to the "whole system of internal exertion." By facilitating a currency on credit, the raw materials of farmers were able to be bought by the credit supplied to merchants. The Bank aided in keeping the currency uniform and sound by regulating the issues of state banks through its ability to demand prompt payment for their circulating notes and other obligations. In addition, the Bank contributed to a positive balance of trade by promoting domestic industry in its loans and general circulation, thereby decreasing the need for sending specie abroad in purchase of goods.[12]

In comparison with a hypothetical specie currency, the use of a bank-note currency saved the country a large portion of capital for investment in commerce and agriculture that would have otherwise been traded for specie to form a currency for exchanging goods. Since banks held on reserve roughly one dollar of specie for every three or four bank notes in circulation, it was a saving of two-thirds to three-fourths the capital cost of providing a means of exchange as it would have been if capital was traded directly in specie. In 1790, the circulating currency was $20 million, and $3 million of the circulation was gold and silver. This saving through the use of bank notes therefore amounted to roughly $10-12 million.[13]

The design of the Bank of the United States included numerous changes from the charter of the Bank of North America with respect to guarding interests of the public and the government. In his report outlining the Bank of the United States Hamilton said that the Bank of North America had made the "the interest and accommodation of the public" more subservient to the interest of the stockholders than proper. Hamilton wrote that though banks depended on stockholders and private profit, public utility was the greater object of public banks, and should not be made subservient to the former. According to his suggestions, the size of the capital stock of the Bank was determined by the needs of the economy not the discretion of the shareholders for a desired dividend.[14] In addition, foreigners owned stock, but they could not become directors, regardless of their shares, which protected the Bank from foreign direction. The Bank could only make or receive large loans to and from state and national governments with the authorization of Congress. The interest rate was reduced to 6%. The Bank could sell the public debt portion of its stock but it was not "at liberty to purchase any public debt whatsoever."

The many benefits made possible through the bank based funding system were paired with a dramatic reduction in the tax burden experienced by the general public and the states. Assumption and federal taxes had freed the states of the biggest part of their state budgets. In Massachusetts and North Carolina, where this effect has been precisely measured, direct taxation fell by 75 to 90 percent between 1785 and 1795. It is estimated that direct taxes were cut throughout the states by as much as 85% on average in the same period. Though the amounts collected by federal impost duties rose at the same rate as state taxes decreased, the indirectness of the former was experienced throughout the country as the lifting of a tremendous weight. "Men wonder at the lightness of their burthens and yet at the capacity of the Government to pay the interest of its debt," wrote Hamilton in 1795. In his December 8, 1795, address to the union, President Washington spoke of the same: "Every part of the union displays indications of rapid and various improvement . . . with burthens so slight as scarcely to be noticed." The efficiency of the new tax system was extraordinarily impressive. The taxes collected by the Treasury Department in 1792 were greater than all of the state requisitions from October 1781 to March 1787 combined. The record of prosperity was seen in other ways. Trade and commerce rapidly expanded. Between 1790 and 1795, the value of American exports doubled from $20 million to $40 million. The total tonnage of U.S. ships entering U.S. ports with cargo increased 63% within that time, while that of British ships fell by 87%. By 1795, 90% of American trade was transported by American ships.[15]

Treasury Department Policies of 1791-1795

The reorganization of the public debt and the establishment of the Bank of the United States were only the first steps in securing a sound banking and financial system. In his subsequent reports, Treasury Secretary Hamilton continued to follow through on his maxim that new and old debts must be inseparable from new income. Therefore, further borrowings included new taxes proposed for final extinguishment, especially those which would spur the development of the nation's own resources and manufactures.

In December 1791, Secretary Hamilton proposed that Congress promote manufactures using its powers to lay and collect taxes, duties, imposts and excises. He also proposed Congress appropriate money to a special fund for infrastructure projects and premiums for encouraging "new inventions and discoveries."[16] On March 5, 1792, Congress passed an Act for raising an army necessary to protect the frontiers. Days later, Hamilton submitted a financing proposal to the House to incorporate the new expenses of the Act into the previously established system of federal revenues, while maintaining and upholding the public credit.[17] Hamilton wrote that the interest of national credit and prosperity required building upon the previous system of taxes for funding the debt and to "avoid, as much as possible, the incurring of any new debt."

In this 1792 report, Hamilton outlined a series of annual funds, consisting of new taxes, dividends from the government's stock in the Bank of the United States, and freed up funds that had previously been part of the 1790 funding of debts. On the credit of annuities from these funds, the government would borrow about five times the amount of each fund to be reimbursed within five years. Each year, a new fund would be constituted, made up of different taxes from the longer list he had proposed. The basis for the first was a tax on horses. The fund would begin accruing interest a year later, with a new sum borrowed on the credit of this annuity, likewise reimbursable within five years. Rather than simply borrow more money for the expenses of the frontiers, or divert the use of dividends from the stock in the Bank as an appropriation, like some had suggested, he outlined a more integrated plan of additional import duties.[18] In May 1792, Congress passed most of the tariffs he proposed and his other recommendations.

In January 1795, Hamilton issued his final report on the public credit. In it, he listed numerous ways to follow through on the payments on the public debt as intended in 1790. This included new borrowings sufficient to provide for the increasing cost of external conflicts. Hamilton listed a series of propositions which were "necessary to be adopted," he wrote, "to complete our system of public credit." Damaging to the potential thriving of the new financial system was the growing and pressing demands of western and foreign conflicts. Building up for the Quasi-War with France, financing the Northwest Indian War, and paying a volunteer army to suppress the Whiskey Rebellion were exceptional expenses and had an unfortunate impact on the funding system. There was also a strong inclination in the government to shift burdens from the present to the future.[19] Both of these circumstances led to the necessity of large amounts of borrowing from the Bank of the United States, tying up a large portion of its capital in the first four or five years, and decreasing the Bank's ability to serve as a vehicle for the expansion of the economy. By March 1792 the Bank had lent the government over $2.5 million and by January 31, 1795, total loans amounted to $4.7 million.[20]

To maintain the funded debt and uphold the value of government securities and the stability of the financial system, Hamilton proposed a special and sufficient fund to reimburse and redeem the debt. The fund would come from temporary duties made permanent, redirected surpluses of import duties, dividends on the government's stock in the Bank, exonerated revenues from interest and principal payments, and other surpluses not appropriated.[21] The funding system was designed to be flexible and managed with adjustments as necessary. Therefore, instead of a specific annual appropriation, Hamilton proposed appropriating from imports only so much each year as necessary. In this way, any amount in a year could be paid in emergencies, but not an amount such that it would tie up more revenue than necessary in the sinking fund. This flexibility was necessary to uphold and maintain the usefulness of the public debt as a resource for a growing amount of currency and credit. Hamilton thought that diverting more than was necessary to pay the interest and meet installments was a waste, since other applications could contribute to more national income and facility to make good on the debt.

Congress passed Hamilton's January 1795 recommendations to complete the system of credit on March 3, 1795, in "An Act making further provision for the support of Public Credit, and for the redemption of the Public Debt." However, under Hamilton's successor Oliver Wolcott, the amount finally owed to the Bank at the close of the year 1795 was $6.2 million. The government had borrowed over 60% of its capital. The continued resistance of the Congress to raise a sufficient amount of revenues to make regular payments on this debt led to the sale of a large portion of the government's stock in the Bank in 1796 to pay back some of its loans from the Bank.[22] The sale of stock disturbed Hamilton's proposed sinking fund for funding the debt, eliminating the dividend as a source for the government to draw upon, and reduced a source of interest between the Bank and the public.[23]

Funded Bills of Credit

After resigning as Treasury Secretary, Hamilton proposed another method of funding for the Treasury Department, as seen in his correspondences with Treasury Secretary Oliver Wolcott Jr. After the experience of 1782-

1788, the Constitution of the United States wisely prohibited the state governments from issuing their own bills of credit. But the federal government was not so prohibited. In 1783, Hamilton had specified that it was the emission of *unfunded bills of credit* by a government without power which he had opposed. Once the Treasury Department's revenue system, banking system, and the credit of the government had been firmly established, Hamilton saw a potential usefulness for a measured use of bills of credit under necessity, limited to the anticipation of revenues. As Treasury Secretary Wolcott faced growing expenditures from foreign conflicts in April of 1795, Hamilton wrote to him that upon facing similar expenses, he had contemplated "the expedient of issuing warrants upon the treasurer, payable at future periods, from two to twelve months, in the nature of exchequer bills."[24] This was an alternative to loans from the Bank and a means of using the credit of the United States directly when under pressure to make up for shortfalls. These credits would be negotiable, and though costing more than a loan from the Bank, could be useful in times of need. In June of 1796, the government was called upon to build frigates but no money was available. Hamilton proposed that Wolcott should place in the hands of his building agents, "Treasury bills from one hundred to one thousand dollars, payable in a year with interest."[25]

Hamilton was most explicit about using funded bills of credit in a letter to Wolcott in August of 1798. He wrote of the difficulties in collecting taxes without a proper circulation. Individual capitals for loans was sometimes limited, he said, and "The banks can only go a certain length and must not be forced." He continued:

> Yet Government will stand in need of large anticipations. For these and other reasons, which I have thought well of—I have come to a conclusion that our Treasury ought to raise up a circulation of its own. I mean by the issuing of Treasury notes payable some on demand, others at different periods from very short to pretty considerable—at first having but little time to run. This appears to me an expedient equally necessary to keep the circulation full and to facilitate the anticipations which Government will certainly need.[26]

Part III
The Second Bank of the U.S. as an Instrument for Economic Growth

Overview

The second Bank of the United States was formed by the James Madison Administration under strong recognition and experience of the dangers of state based currency control. In 1811, the charter of the Bank of the United States was allowed to expire, leaving the circulation of the nation's currency to state banks. Disorder ensued from unregulated state banking and excessive issues contributed to wartime inflation, higher interest rates and rates of exchange, and bank closures. Without the Bank the government faced numerous difficulties in raising and distributing taxes, borrowing money, and making payments.

In 1814-1815, Alexander Dallas designed a new Bank of the United States with President James Madison as part of a system of measures to restore public credit and financial order, repeating many of the steps of Treasury Secretary Hamilton. Only after beginning under misguided direction and an economic environment of financial crisis and depression was the Bank able to accomplish its stated purposes.

From 1823 to 1832, the Bank was economically successful by many standards and consolidated numerous financial policies, both by its own actions and in cooperation with the Treasury Department. The Bank kept exchange and interest rates low, created a currency of constant value, and was indirectly and directly involved in the nation's largest strides in manufacturing and infrastructure building up to that time. By its regulation of state bank emissions through forcing specie payments, decreasing or increasing its loans and discounts, and by the use of its assets, the Bank prevented various economic catastrophes and severe banking crises.

Its success depended upon the methods of its president and directors in determining the purposes for which its credit was used and using discretion in the manner in which it was lent or restrained. Under proper direction it proved to be a central tool to the economic success of the second term of the James Monroe Administration, the John Quincy Adams Administration, and the first term of the Andrew Jackson Administration.

Contrary to statements made in the subsequent period, it provided credit for infrastructure, industry, and agriculture without endangering the banking system or causing inflation. This accomplishment was not repeated under a different political and economic context in 1833-1836, or under a similar institution estranged from the U.S. government between 1836-1841.

The actions of the U.S. government taken during the period of 1833-1841 to break relations with the Bank and the state banks lacked proper justification and were largely responsible for the financial instability experienced in those years. An examination of this Administration discord with the Bank and its economic impacts brings the lessons to be drawn from its successes into focus. From 1829-1832, the Jackson Administration made numerous allegations against the Bank concerning its performance, management, and safety. Congressional investigations made in response found insufficient evidence to vindicate most of its claims. The Administration maintained a course to veto the re-charter of the Bank in 1832, about which former President James Madison had provided prospective constitutional analysis the previous year. After the veto of the Bank, the Administration called attention to an apparent danger of maintaining the Bank as a federal depository of public revenues and proceeded to plan the removal of the Bank's public deposits. In response, Congress investigated the safety of the public deposits, and returned a majority vote in favor of maintaining them in the Bank. The Administration's removal of the public deposits from the Bank in 1833 involved a number of legal violations and led to negative economic consequences. The loss of credit previously made available via loans funded with public deposits led to a short-term financial crisis. Longer-term impacts resulted from utilizing selected state banks for public deposits, including the use of these deposits to create loans for land speculation in 1835 and 1836.

The Specie Circular and mismanagement of the Distribution Act by the Jackson Treasury Department in the fall of 1836 and winter of 1837 had dramatic impacts on the financial system and became a significant factor in the financial crises of 1837. In 1837, the Martin Van Buren Administration held state banking to be as undesirable as the Bank of the United States, and proposed that the Treasury Department no longer accept payments on credit through banks, but only utilize specie, leading to the Independent Treasury Acts of the 1840s.

Chapter 8
Currency Disorder and the Finances of Madison's Second Term

In 1810, the question of whether or not to renew the charter of the first Bank of the United States was a major debate in Congress. Regardless of party views, the propriety of disordering the finances of the nation before a war with England was questionable.

The lack of an adequate replacement for its long-standing function in facilitating duty payments to merchants and supporting commerce was a cause of apprehension. Lost revenue for the government and increased competition for gold and silver was a very real danger. Of greater concern was the potential rupture in established punctuality and credit lines, which could overturn commercial confidence with unforeseen and widespread economic effects. Much of the Bank's record in the previous years stood in conflict with the arguments against renewing the charter, most of which were based on claims that the Bank was a foreign directed institution, threatening to create an aristocracy of wealth, and harmful to the interests of agriculture. Foreign stockholders were not allowed by law to take part in the Bank's direction. Its capital, including the foreign owned portion, was mostly lent to merchants who purchased the output of agriculture. The interest gained by stockholders in the loans, a cause of party complaint, was in proportion to the surplus earned by citizens above their own income from the loan.[1]

In the end, the renewal of the first Bank's charter failed by one vote in January 1811. The costs to general economic activity and to the government of not renewing the charter of the Bank without an alternative in place were extensive. The economy experienced rapid and uneven inflation, high interest, non-uniformity of state currencies, high rates of exchange, and banking failures. The government's revenues decreased while borrowing rates increased. The government experienced difficulty collecting and distributing taxes, and making timely payments.

From 1811-1814, the number of banks nearly doubled from 118 to 202, while their total authorized capital increased by only 50%.[2] Without the check of the Bank upon them, state banks were able to inflate their issues.

The state banks increased the size of their circulation by over 50% in the next few years, while its value decreased by over 30%.[3] On top of the depreciation of the currency from excessive issues, the bank notes of the various states depreciated in comparison with one another from 5-20% in port cities, and 20-25% in interior cities. Without the Bank, businessmen trading between states had to turn to brokers for the exchange of bank notes. The esteem of state bank notes decreased in proportion to distance from the bank, requiring losses for those transiting notes from one region to another, especially for those using western notes for eastern purchases. In addition to distance, the knowledge of a state bank's condition and the length of the period before the state notes could be cashed influenced discount rates. Observed instances of substantial depreciation increased these rates. The discount increased further when the capital was small, making it less worthwhile to transmit for redemption. This made it even more burdensome for those starting new ventures. Within five years of the Bank's expiration the cost of a bill of exchange to pay debts in large eastern cities for western businessman increased by 15% because of the depreciation of western bank notes. These losses were charged to the final consumers, primarily farmers. Brokerage costs amounted to a 15-20% tax on business transactions (see footnote for definition of bills of exchange).[4]

In addition to these general effects from the lack of federal currency regulation, there were more harmful ones for much of the economy. Financial disorder created a demand for specie and funds, placing the poorer classes at the mercy of those with great wealth, as a section of the latter preyed upon desperate debtors needing to avoid default. These included money-lenders, brokers, and new banks. Some of these lenders were previously investors in the capital of the Bank and now sought profits with idle capital. In addition, there was a great amount of fraud, swindling, and breach of contracts.[5] Speculators primarily benefited from large fluctuations in the issues of bank paper, while other classes did not. Misuse of bank privilege led to the creation of banks with very little security for their bills, often leaving participating farmers to take the loss.[6]

During the period of the first Bank, the value of the currency was largely maintained in proportion to the currency needs of business. Because of this, the currency was kept "at par" meaning that in the rare event a note was presented for payment in specie, it could be redeemed, with banks keeping roughly one dollar of coin for three or four banknote dollars.[7] This made transfers of money to distant places cheaper, as no discounts were suffered. By mid-1814 however, due to the excessive issues, the demands of war with Britain, price speculation, hoarding, and financial insecurity, banks were drained of their specie reserves. Though some attempted to reduce loans to maintain the payment of specie available in relationship to their notes outstanding, by the summer many banks were forced to suspend redemption in order to keep circulation of their notes proportional to demand. Many banks failed. The resulting attempt to contract outstanding notes led to a recession and with it widespread bank failures.[8]

For the government the effect was an increase in the cost to borrow money, obtain sufficient revenue, collect and distribute taxes, and make payments on time. The varying value of state currencies and their depreciation imposed premiums upon the Treasury for the transfer of government revenue from one point to another. Transferring revenues through state banks rather than a national bank increased this cost. In 1814, $9 million of Treasury funds were in 100 different state banks that had suspended. Bank credits in western banks were rendered useless to the government by the specie suspension, and transferring public funds from one place to make payments at another became impracticable. This inability to transfer funds caused the Treasury Department to fail in meeting its engagements, damaging public credit.[9]

Public credit became severely depressed. Under the distressed condition of the currency, the larger populace was not disposed to lend to the government. Without an institution to facilitate government loans, the government was forced to borrow and issue treasury notes at a loss. By 1814 the public credit had reached a point that resulted in $42 million of government bonds being sold for $35 million. For a $9 million loan to the government to be secured at par in 1815, the rate of interest had to be raised to 7%. Treasury notes, issued as payment in anticipation of revenues, fared worse than bonds and were accepted by creditors at a larger discount. The varying value of state currencies resulted in a drop in overall revenue. By the end of 1814 state bank notes which were received for duty payments varied from par in Massachusetts to a discount of 20% from par in Maryland.[10] At that point the collection of taxes was not enough to pay the interest on the national debt.[11] By the end of the war, the market for importers seeking to pay reduced duties became an incentive for states to depreciate their currencies, as during 1784-1787.

In addition to the burdens the financial system placed upon the government, it also raised constitutional issues. Congress had relinquished its control to the state banks and the state legislatures, which under the constitution were not designed to supply the national currency. It became difficult for Congress to carry out its taxation power according to the letter of the law, which states that all taxes collected "shall be uniform throughout the United States," and that "no preference shall be given by any regulation of commerce, or revenue, to the ports of one state over those of another." Due to the depreciations, the taxes could not be uniform to collect the same amount in value from each state. The crisis demonstrated the importance of the exclusive control over the currency given to the Federal government by the Constitution, as seen in its prohibition of the states from coining money and emitting bills of credit. Congress could not control and regulate the currency without an instrument for this purpose in place.[12]

Dallas, Madison, and the Bank

In the middle of the financial crisis, President James Madison brought Alexander Dallas into the Treasury Department as Secretary on October 7, 1814. Dallas proved to possess the character traits necessary to meet the task, and provided a sober analysis for Congress. With the coffers of the Treasury drained, the pressing demands of the war and creditors, and bankruptcy of the banks, he was aware of the monumental task that lay before him. His stated goal was to restore public credit and rescue the nation's finances. The course he took was contradictory to party beliefs and adopted methods.

In his first report of October 17, 1814, to the Committee of Ways and Means, he was plain in stating the facts of the situation as well as the required remedy.[13] The leading cause of distress was "the inadequacy of our system of taxation to form a foundation for public credit," he wrote, and the absence of the means to "anticipate, collect, and distribute the public revenue," referring to a national institution for credit. Just as Alexander Hamilton had described the situation in his letters during the revolutionary war, Dallas wrote that the resources of the people were then large, but the means to incorporate them for the use of the government were small. This state of affairs had begun as a policy under the Administration of Thomas Jefferson which had championed extensive reductions to most taxes except on foreign commerce. The policy had been popular with the people, who felt its short-term benefits. Many internal expenses had been dropped including those in preparation for war.

For a solution, Dallas stated that though treasury notes could provide limited relief, "the establishment of a national institution operating upon credit combined with capital" was "the only efficient remedy for the disordered condition of our circulating medium."[14] In addition to fixing the state of the currency this institution would be a safe depository and auxiliary to the public credit for borrowing needed amounts beyond taxes. Dallas put forth six propositions to fund the public debt, establish a new system of internal revenue, provide a method to borrow, and bring order to the currency. These repeated many of the steps taken by Treasury Secretary Hamilton:

- Provision for punctual payment of interest upon all forms of public debt, both those existing prior to and those created for the ongoing war;
- Creation of a gradual sinking fund for new war debt;
- Raising of revenues equal to debt payments and normal expenses by the doubling of existing taxes, and adding new duties and domestic taxes;
- A national bank;
- New loans or issues of treasury notes to be accepted in payment necessary for the annual expenses of the war.

Having outlined this plan, he addressed party prejudices which had become commonplace. On taxes, which he saw as fundamental to revive public credit, he stated that he already anticipated that the plan would "doubtless, generate many and very various objections." To the prejudice against the national Bank, which his own party had voted against reestablishing just three years before, he addressed the question of constitutionality with a long statement, one utilized by President Madison in his addresses on the subject the following year. In it Dallas remarked:

> In making a proposition for the establishment of a national bank it would be presumptuous to conjecture that the sentiments which actuated the opposition have passed away; and yet it would be denying to experience a great practical advantage, were we to suppose that a difference of times and circumstances, would not produce a corresponding difference in the opinions of the wisest, as well as of the purest men. . . .

> When . . . we have marked the existence of a national bank for a period of twenty years, with all the sanctions of the legislative, executive, and judicial authorities; when we have seen the dissolution of one institution, and heard a loud and continued call for the establishment of another; when, under these circumstances, neither Congress, nor the several states, have resorted to the power of amendment, —can it be deemed a violation of the right of private opinion, to consider the constitutionality of a national bank, as a question forever settled and at rest?
>
> But, after all, I should not merit the confidence, which it will be my ambition to acquire, if I were to suppress the declaration of an opinion, that, in these times, the establishment of a national bank will not only be useful in promoting the general welfare, but that it is necessary and proper for carrying into execution some of the most important powers constitutionally vested in the government.[15]

The October version of Dallas's bank plan, introduced into the House on November 13, 1814, was for a large capital of $50 million, based almost entirely on public debt, 40% subscribed by the government. In response, John Calhoun proposed a capital of 10% specie and no government subscription. Dallas wrote back to the committee that capitalization with treasury notes would have an injurious effect on the credit of the government and on needed loans the next year, and that the $40 million proposed as its capital would not circulate without depreciation. Various other plans were then proposed. In summary, the Congress rejected Madison's original war measure and both Houses passed a bank plan though with a much reduced amount of capital, a portion being treasury notes, and with no right to suspend specie redemptions. On January 30, 1815, Madison vetoed this bill because of its small capital and the proportion of it capital in treasury notes. Without sufficient capital, Madison wrote, its capitalization would not increase the value of the public debt.[16]

Though a Bank bill was not passed that year, the system of revenue proposed by Dallas was enacted. The subsequent use of treasury notes to make up for shortfalls of revenue became less and less necessary.[17] One of Madison's greatest concerns was the lack of Federal control of the currency, and its domination by state banks. If the state banking system could not be brought under control he was not against excluding state bank paper altogether.[18]

On December 6, 1815, Dallas wrote to Congress that the toleration of unredeemable currencies of state banks made necessary under the pressure of war had ceased, and that a "recurrence to the national authority was indispensable for the restoration of a national currency."[19] He reviewed the options of applying national authority over the currency, and discussed why currencies based on specie, state banks, or treasury notes were inexpedient, not possible, or not necessary. The best application of the power of congress over the currency, he concluded, was to re-establish a national bank that would lead and aid the state banks with its resources and by its example. As he wrote:

> Authorized to issue notes, which will be received in all payments to the United States, the circulation of its issues will be co-extensive with the Union, and there will exist a constant demand, bearing a just proportion to the annual amount of the duties and taxes to be collected, independent of the general circulation for commercial and social purposes. A National Bank will, therefore, possess the means and the opportunity of supplying a circulating medium of equal use and value in every State, and in every district of every State. . . . The National Bank will be the ready instrument to enhance the value of the public securities, and to restore the currency of the national coin.[20]

The services to be performed by the Bank's capital, Dallas wrote, on December 24, 1815, were the accommodation of government, commerce, agriculture, manufactures, and the arts, and to restore and maintain the national currency. "In short," he wrote, adding color to the sketch, "they will be required, under every change of circumstances, in a season of war as well as in the season of peace, for the circulation of the national wealth; which augments with a rapidity beyond the reach of ordinary calculation." Beyond these economic features, Dallas captured its national character:

> The national bank ought not to be regarded simply as a commercial bank. It will not operate upon the funds of the stockholders alone, but much more upon the funds of the

> nation. Its conduct, good or bad, will not affect the corporate credit and resources alone, but much more the credit and resources of the government. In fine, it is not an institution created for the purposes of commerce and profit alone, but much more for the purposes of national policy, as an auxiliary in the exercise of some of the highest powers of the government.[21]

Two months later, on February 26, 1816, a design of the Madison Administration for a second Bank of the United States, nearly identical in form to the first Bank, was introduced in Congress. It passed the House without important amendment on March 14, 1816, by a vote of 81 to 71, and the Senate on April 3. Madison signed the bill on April 10, 1816. Its capital was to be $35 million. The U.S. subscribed to one-fifth of the total with 5% bonds. The second Bank of the United States served as the nation's depository and was required to transfer the funds of the government without charge and to negotiate public loans. In Madison's annual message to Congress on December 3, 1816, he spoke of the imperative of a currency of "equal value, credit, and use wherever it may circulate," and Congress' responsibility to ensure one of that kind. He applauded the measures taken for "creating and regulating a currency of that description," citing the Bank as an essential part of the plan.

Chapter 9
The Bank and the Economic Depression of 1818-1822

The second Bank of the United States officially went into operation on January 7, 1817. The economic and financial state of the country required a Secretary of Treasury and President of the Bank closely collaborating to handle the delicate balance of securing national interest and reigning in the plethora of over extended state banks.[1] It would appear that Dallas was the appropriate person for the task, having demonstrated his capabilities from 1814-1816. Unfortunately, he was unable to serve in that capacity. Two administrations of the Bank ensued during which many of the original intentions were unfulfilled due to an economic crisis and poor leadership.

A central issue was that the Bank's capitalization was precarious. It had been intended that shares were purchased with one-fourth part specie and three fourths holdings of public debt. But after the first installment, the Bank was unable to obtain sufficient specie in its capitalization from would-be stockholders and allowed them instead to leverage their public debt holdings to receive bank notes, with which they could pay the specie portion of their shares. The Bank then borrowed from Europe for the rest of its specie capital. Within the first four months of its operation, it was hit with an unexpected demand, when the government paid off 50% of the government bonds which made up its capital. For their sale, the Bank received depreciated state bank paper, and lost the interest from the government bonds, forcing it to lend the amount it received to make up the lost revenue in whatever investments it could find.[2]

Another, greater challenge to its early beginnings was dealing with the effects of an economic crisis, as a recession took root by the end of 1817 and became widespread in 1819, continuing for a number of years. The crisis of 1817-1819 was driven by several economic problems:

During the war of 1812, many branches of domestic manufacturers became established; however, the 1816-1817 tariff and duty laws were insufficient to protect domestic cotton, wool, and other manufacturers from the flood of cheap goods entering American ports after the war and a large portion of them were forced to close. Unemployed mill and shop owners and laborers entered the agricultural field for employment and investment, creating a glut of agricultural produce by 1818-1819, combined with agricultural loans which could not be repaid.[3]

Making matters worse was the decline of agricultural prices and demand in Europe after the Napoleonic wars. From 1800-1815, the U.S. had been able to maintain an even balance of trade wholly from its agricultural exports due to increased demand from Europe. Now, demand for U.S. agriculture declined and agricultural products fell to one-half the prices attainable in 1808 and 1810, and one third the value they possessed during the inflation years of the state banks.[4] In addition, a surplus of shippers of agricultural products entering the market led to numerous bankruptcies in commerce and trade.

Consequently, agricultural exports fell far short of paying for manufacturing imports from Europe and a negative trade balance beginning in 1817 proceeded to deplete the banking system of its specie reserves. The economic hardships of manufactures, agriculture, and commerce further strained the financial system and banks renewed loans in hopes of eventually collecting from suffering debtors. Land speculation also arose in the West. These circumstances made it difficult for the Bank to force curtailments of state bank notes and a resumption of specie payments.

The new Bank of the U.S. did not cause these problems, but the actions of its first administration under William Jones did not improve the situation either. When the Bank tried to keep state banks in check by presenting their notes for redemption, forcing the banks to call in debts and reduce loans, it received harsh protest. Jones reacted to this criticism and was not strict enough with over leveraged banks and speculators. He loaned more than was prudent in the western states, inviting many unwarranted applications for loans. Even so, the second Bank continued to receive protests from the modest pressure it did apply. After going bankrupt, many state banks blamed the Bank for having allowed them to excessively extend their businesses.

The Bank's own condition suffered for two other reasons. Where state bank notes were less credible, as was the case in the western states, the Bank's own notes were often sought to pay debts. Since most debts were to merchants in eastern cities, this normal pattern of sending national bank notes east led to a continuing demand for coin at the Bank's eastern offices. However, involvement by the Bank's western offices in land speculation led to exceptional demand for the coin of its offices in the East.

Less important to the overall economic impact was the internal corruption by Jones and other directors in fueling a speculation of the Bank's stock for their own profit. Directors encouraged trading in stock and issued loans on pledges of stock to its full market value. Shares were bought and sold without any money transacted by simply applying for a loan on the security of shares that were not yet paid for. As prices rose, shares were sold and money was made, including by Jones, who apparently saw nothing wrong with the practice. The value of the Bank's stock rose from $100 to $156 a share by August 1818, before corrective measures were introduced.[5]

Despite all of these problems, the Bank performed desired functions for the Treasury, receiving state bank notes on deposit for the Treasury and transferring funds in a stable currency. The government was able to borrow on better terms due to its influence in the public debt.

The Crash and a New Director

In July 1818, a new group of directors of the Bank took over its direction and began curtailing loans. This put pressure on merchants, speculators, and state banks. Bankruptcies were common. A more general drop in real estate and commodity prices took place. Many banks began to close. In November 1818, the House investigated the Bank under Jones, publishing their findings in January 1819 of its discount of stock notes, speculation, sales of securities, and undue accommodation to state banks. Afterward, it became popular, though incorrect, to blame the ongoing banking crisis entirely on the Bank.[6]

On March 6, 1819, the board of the Bank elected Langdon Cheves as its new President. Nicholas Biddle, who had declined to serve as a director under the Jones' administration, was appointed by President James Monroe to its board of directors. By the time Cheves took the helm, the Bank was overextended and drained of much of its coin from the causes mentioned. In April of 1819, some worried the Bank had lost so much of its coin that it was only months away from no longer honoring its notes.

As stated, the necessity of honoring its notes in coin at all offices was an important reason for its condition. Duty payments at its eastern offices made them the eventual destination of most bank notes. Cheves therefore ceased carrying out this part of the Bank's charter and its offices only honored their own notes.[7] In addition to this measure, Cheves issued a directive to its western offices to no longer issue any notes and it had a large portion of their coin and federal deposits sent east to shore up its eastern offices. State banks were no longer shown any leniency and the Bank's holdings of state bank notes were returned to them for redemption. The emissions of state banks were curtailed, bringing an end to any remaining speculation.[8] As a result state banks went bankrupt in greater numbers and many farmers and manufacturers lost their savings. In the spring of 1819, bank bubbles broke and the prices of exports declined by 50% or more. Merchants, businesses, and agricultural operations went bankrupt and closed in large numbers.[9]

Cheves returned the Bank to a sound condition but took his corrective measures farther than necessary. Productive borrowers engaged in prudent business and land purchases suffered the same consequences as those involved in speculation. The Bank restricted its own loans and purchases of bills of exchange, reducing business activity even further. State banks in turn reduced loans and discounts, few bills of exchange were purchased, and trade in all forms of credit was slow. With credit lines broken, markets for goods were reduced to items that could be sold at once.[10]

What characterized the stringency of Cheves' administration was his continuing suspension of the Bank's role in maintaining a national currency. He did not see the possibility of resuming redemption of notes at all offices, and used state bank notes for the Bank's circulation to supplement its own in loans and discounts. As made clear in the next chapter, by using state bank notes instead of its own the Bank lost two of its best methods of currency control, keeping the rate of exchange down and the amount of state bank currency within reason. With a capital larger than its notes, and by not issuing its own currency in sufficient amounts, the second Bank lacked a balance against the state banks with which it could press them for coin. Nor could it influence the rate of exchange. These shortcomings played an important role in depression conditions continued through 1822. In summary, Cheves restored order to the currency and reigned in the state banks, but he did not use the Bank's resources to engage in commerce to the degree required, and was over protective of its own security.

Chapter 10
The Bank and the Economic Growth of the 1820s and 1830s

In January of 1823, Nicholas Biddle became the new Bank President and initiated a series of measures that assisted in reviving the economy.[1] Though he had commended Cheves for saving the currency from unsound banks and their depreciated bank notes, he viewed the previous two years of continued depression as a result of needlessly restrictive policies. He thought it was time to make better use of the Bank's resources for the benefit of the country.[2] Rather than the more generic view of loans and discounts held previously, he thought it was possible to use them for specific purposes so as to ensure the ability to later redeem them.

Biddle viewed two interconnected steps as immediately necessary; bringing the notes back to par in their various regions and giving the bank a more commercial role.[3] By bringing notes back to par they would be able to carry out their regional requirements, and less currency would be needed overall. The Bank was given a more commercial role by linking its use of discounts together with the patterns of national trade. He issued a directive to western offices to resume issuing their notes instead of continuing to use state bank notes. But they were required to issue them mainly for those seeking to pay debts in eastern cities, i.e. for discounts of bills of exchange drawn on eastern commerce hubs. Those offices sent the bills of exchange to eastern offices where they paid off other bills upon maturity. When the western bank notes so issued made their way east for duty payments, the eastern offices then possessed sufficient coin for redemption. Biddle had solved the riddle that had led Cheves to conclude that it was impossible to issue notes receivable at all offices. Though originally issued a thousand miles away, there were ample funds in the eastern banks resulting from the economic activity for which the interior notes were issued.[4]

A third step was instituted towards regulating the rate of exchange. Buying bills of exchange from merchants in locations where goods were being produced and selling the bills where they were being traded at the ports resulted in a reduction in extreme price variations. Another factor in keeping the exchange rate low and stable was the Bank's transfer of government revenues on behalf of the Treasury Department for government expenses.[5] Objections to this stability came only from the private money lenders and those engaged in speculation who profited largely from low rates of exchange where bills were bought in the interior and high rates where they were sold in the coastal cities.[6] The Bank eliminated brokerage charges in trade transactions by its discounts of bills of exchange, which increased profits available to farmers and merchants.

With these steps taken, the Bank could more easily regulate the state banks. Since its notes and deposits made up a significant amount of the currency, it could use its regulatory abilities to bring state banks back into order and reduce their issues. While people generally used the Bank's notes for commerce between states due to their constant value, they used state bank notes in their own state to pay taxes. As depository for federal taxes, the Bank would collect a greater amount of notes of the local state banks in each of its offices than the local state banks would collect of the Bank. The Bank could therefore deliver state notes at their counters for redemption in coin, forcing them to contract their circulation when it sought to apply pressure. With a currency at par, and a stable rate of exchange, the cost of business decreased. In less than a year, the four year long economic depression began to abate. Along with employing capital in bills of exchange the loan policy was shifted from real estate to short-term business loans for goods in the process of production.[7] By 1825, the currency of the nation was once again stable.

The Bank also became integral to the general economic progress of internal improvements and industry, as Dallas had proscribed in 1815. By 1832 more than half of its resources were used to advance agriculture, infrastructure, manufacturing, and other construction projects.[8] By 1823-1824, with the Erie Canal coming to completion, other states began measuring their untapped resources and initiated plans for development.

The majority of the canal, turnpike, and railroad companies were financed through the sale of state and municipal bonds purchased by the Bank and state banks. The banks also made loans to promoters of projects on the security of stocks and bonds. Between 1823-1832, the Bank itself served as the underwriter for numerous canal, turnpike, and railroad companies, purchasing and reselling their bonds, and directly lending over $20 million on their securities, often directly to the companies themselves.[9] The Bank's involvement encompassed about half of the capital of the major canals in the 1820s and early 1830s. Under the well balanced and regulated financial system of that time, the output of industry and agriculture that was made possible by new infrastructure garnered a sufficiently high rate of return to pay back the principal and interest of loans. The states viewed their own application of revenues as investments, and calculated the rise of public wealth and annual revenue to be gained from the extension of trade, new industries, and increased value of land and agricultural output.[10]

In federal financing of infrastructure, the government utilized its growing annuity from its ownership of one fifth of the Bank's stock. In 1825 and 1826, Congress gave the Treasury the power to subscribe for $2 million shares of the Chesapeake and Delaware Canal Co., and the Chesapeake and Ohio, by paying for the shares with potential dividends due to the United States from its Bank stock. In other words, the Treasury Secretary purchased stock of the canal companies, with which they would pay their workers, on the credit of expected profit made by the Bank from the economic growth it facilitated.[11] The John Quincy Adams Administration also supported furthering the Cumberland Road to the Ohio River, the Portland to Louisville Canal, and a connection between the Great Lakes to the Ohio River.

The operations of the Bank enabled tradesman, manufactures, and farmers to obtain their needs from merchants on the credit of expected returns. Farmers increased the value of their land ten times the original borrowing cost, and manufacturers doubled their wages.[12] The route by which they received the Bank's credit was not always direct. Small workshops, home industries, and farmers purchased from country stores on credit and the latter obtained their goods from country merchants on credit. Country merchants received loans from city merchants who in turn received loans from the Bank.[13] Through the credit facilities of the Bank, families cultivating new lands in the west could apply their surplus produce to obtain further supplies by trading with merchants at country stores, who in turn transmitted the produce to the more developed seacoast for consumption and export. This created a process of growth with increasing wealth on both sides, though the interior remained debtors. The debtors were able to pay what they owed by their future sale of crops and improvements to the land. Though they remained in debt, they grew richer in property value each year, and became increasingly able to pay their loans.[14]

Through the Bank's prominent role in the domestic and foreign exchange market through its discounts, the Bank balanced accounts with little expense for the various parties involved. It allowed payment for commodities and other debts to be made when credits came due from the cycles of trade. By extending loans to agriculture, seasons of bad crops that could have led to bankruptcy for many were much less detrimental. Instead of selling crops at a great loss, they were saved for a better market.[15]

Under proper management of this kind banks were a representation of the farms, factories, and infrastructure to which they had lent their funds.[16] These increasingly diverse investments of surplus capital were unique in the world at the time, as was the increasing ability to borrow surplus capital on interest. In many places in Europe, although manufacturers, smiths, masons, and canal engineers possessed ample capital in the form of labor and workers, they had to keep their designs shelved since there was no developed means for borrowing money to serve as a currency between the commodities to be exchanged. The primary reliance on gold and silver specie in Europe limited the ability to expand credit and thus the money supply in this manner.[17]

In addition to these sound loan and exchange policies of the Bank, another element was involved in the ability to create a large amount of credit without inflation. Central to the success of the non-inflationary bank currency was the practice of keeping capital invested. Otherwise, a large amount of deposits relative to a given amount of bank capital would lead to a less sound and secure banking system. Accumulated deposits and stores of cash, i.e. capital seeking investment, were prone to uses in speculation.[18] Unemployed capital made the currency less stable as it tended toward speculation in commodities rather than investment in new production. Large deposits also created a larger demand for specie on reserve for redemption. Under the confidence and stabilized payment system provided by the Bank from 1823-1832, capital was kept invested, and excess currency in the form of deposits did not create inflation driven by speculation. By keeping capital employed, the amount of currency was kept in proportion with the real demand for production. While the amount of loans and bank credits continually rose, they rose in rough correlation with productive demand. With the proportion of currency to the amount of trade kept small there was greater stability in its value. Its increases and decreases followed the ebbs and flows of economic activity.[19] In this period, deposits were usually invested into capital goods, and most deposits were not idle cash but bank credits for bills of exchange representing goods in circulation. This supported the safety of the banking system. Therefore, the prevention of inflation and a stable currency was chiefly the result of keeping capital engaged in valid investment more than the amount of coin kept on reserve.

The well-structured and profitable system of 1823-1832 required a large amount of direct management from the Bank in coordination with the Treasury Department. Various regulations were taken to protect the domestic economy from the influence of speculative tendencies on specie reserves. Because of its role as depository, when it restrained its own loans for importers in periods of speculation it often chose to regulate the activities of state banks. On other occasions it could expand credit from its own books to relieve panic.

Most transactions were based on payments with bank credit. Though coin was sometimes utilized as a standard of payment to settle domestic balances and accounts it was chiefly used to settle trade deficits with foreign nations or individual payments by merchants for imports. Under conditions of confidence and an even balance of trade there was sufficient coin for ordinary demand. During an overabundance of outgoing foreign payments in gold, the internal currency underwent shocks, as lending by banks decreased with the exported coin. Under these conditions, the Bank tried to prevent the necessity for payments in coin to maintain stability in the domestic system of bank payments. In these instances the Bank regulated the state banks in an indirect manner by decreasing its own loans.

Successful Crisis Management

When the nation's banks emitted too much bank credit, the prices of domestic goods rose, creating a market for cheaper foreign goods. In these circumstances foreigners selling the goods did not purchase an equal amount of domestic goods and a trade deficit in favor of foreigners was created. Gold and silver reserves were drained, and often led to an increased failure of banks.[20] To prevent these events, the Bank took measures to inhibit merchants from borrowing the coin to purchase foreign goods by curtailing its own loans. With less bank notes and credits in circulation than before, debtors were forced to sell their goods at cheaper prices to obtain the scarce notes; foreigners lost their competitive edge, imports declined, and the remaining domestic coin, formerly used to purchase imports, sought domestic goods. The trade balance shifted, and coin remained in the U.S. until the next cycle of excess bank paper.[21] On other occasions, to prevent merchants trading in the far east from withdrawing specie from banks for trade, the Bank sold bills of exchange drawn on London, as payment instead. Bills of exchange drawn on London were a means to effect the cancellation of a debt owed in London and were just as valuable as specie to merchants trading in the far east who regularly traded with England.

The other key consideration which entered into the Bank's method of regulation was to provide time for the adjustment of debts. Under stress among the banks and trading community, the drain of specie was not an indication of a lack of capital but of an inability to turn their capital, once invested, back into money for payments. In effect, long-term investments and debts could not be collected or turned into cash immediately. Therefore, extended time was necessary for borrowers to realize returns from production then underway.

As a specific example of its crucial policy, the Bank prevented the U.S. economy from being drawn into the 1825 London bank panic.[22] Offices of the Bank were ordered to tighten lending in order to remain in a position to stop the coming panic among the state banks due to the panic in London. As the crisis worsened, state banks shut down activity, as expected. Calls for specie at all banks and between states would have led to a systemic banking crisis if the Bank had not increased loans and initiated an extension of due dates at the proper locations within the system.[23] This was achieved at a moment when over one hundred banks closed in London, and many other companies went bankrupt throughout Latin America. The Bank was able to remain sound because of its measures taken to create economic stability.

In another case, its regulation and credit capability prevented a domestic banking crisis in the winter of 1827. Due to a decline of agricultural production that year American farmers had not supplied the usual market for bills of exchange which merchants could use to pay for their imports. Under normal conditions these bills of exchange offset the demand for specie. This decline of American exports combined with a spike of imports caused a large export of specie. The Bank stopped lending to those paying for imports with specie and put its assets on the market in order to increase its balance of state bank notes with which to pressure the banks for redemption. Speculation continued, but the Bank continued to utilize its role as depository of taxes to use its collection of state bank notes to press the state banks for payment, eventually forcing them to reduce loans to importers.[24] In 1828, the Secretary of Treasury wrote that due to its ability to operate on both a state and national level a national bank was the only means by which Congress could efficiently control the currency.[25]

During periods of large payments by the Treasury department of the public debts the Bank proactively sought to prevent too large an amount of funds from accumulating into an idle mass, as well as too great a withdrawal of available credit after they were paid out. This was achieved by coordinating actions with would-be recipients of public debt payments. The Bank would advise the U.S. government's creditors to borrow the amounts coming due from the Bank in stages. The creditors therefore were not made sudden holders of large amounts of funds to invest in the market, which would have resulted in large swings. In this way, on the scheduled day of payment, most had already been paid, and the effects were minimal. The Bank was able to continue its support of normal activity and simultaneously serve as the government's fiscal policy tool.[26]

Chapter 11
Confirming the Success of the Bank

In Jackson's 1829 December speech to Congress, he expressed critical views of the Bank of the United States, stating that it had not created a stable currency. Though its expiration was seven years away, he broached the subject of renewing the charter and established an opposing stance. In response, the House and Senate conducted reviews of the state of the currency. Their reports concluded that after the previous disorder of the currency from 1811-1819, the Bank had established a currency of uniform value in all places, convertible into gold and silver on demand. They reviewed how the Bank's lending and depository function was used to regulate the effects of economic stresses by calling in or extending loans and debts; its prevention of speculation by checking state bank notes; its creation of a stable exchange rate; its transfer of funds at no loss to the treasury; and its provision for a lower interest than any private broker or state bank.[1]

While the Administration maintained a subtle opposition to the Bank throughout 1830, it did not become one of its political causes until 1831,[2] beginning with a speech in February by Thomas Benton, the voice of the Administration in the Senate.[3] Benton used phrases reminiscent of the 1785 attacks on the Bank of North America, and of speeches in 1810-1811 against the renewal of the first Bank's charter. He said it was a dangerous monopoly that threatened an aristocracy. Though it had been the desired fiscal tool of Congress and the Executive for thirty-five out of forty years since 1791, Benton said the Bank was hostile to the government and that some of its basic functions were mischievous. He accused it of charging high costs to the government as the public depository of funds and of excessively indebting people for its own profit. According to his argument, its power to regulate the currency and prevent over issuance of state banks represented a dangerous power to break the banks and gain control of the market.

Those viewing the Bank as an institution loaning capital at fair rates, and its stock as an opportunity to invest savings, questioned the distinction Benton gave to state bank stock and the national bank's stock, as he said the latter was aristocratic. His statement that the Bank was a monopoly was also questionable. Its offices competed with the circulation of nearly 400 other state banks; its loans, circulation, and deposits, were one fifth the whole amount held and issued by the banking system. The private portion of its capital was $28 million, on which it made a profit of 6%, while the capital of state banks was $124 million, on which they made a 7% profit.[4] Benton's address was widely printed in the news, along with Administration statements that the Bank was taking political sides in its loan policy.[5]

In January 1832, the Bank sent a resolution to both Houses of Congress applying for a renewal of its charter, though its expiration was years away. Preliminary votes showed majority support for charter renewal. Benton provided the leader of the House committee with a case against the Bank.[6] A seven person House committee investigation took place in March 1832 which was sent to the full House at the end of April, with two minority reports issued soon after.[7] The main point of the majority report was that the Bank was discriminating in its loans to newspapers to sway the election vote.[8] The official books indicated that newspapers in favor of the Administration obtained most of the loans. The two most questionable cases of loans, used as the source of the claim of bribery, were not found to stand in the cross examination of witnesses.[9] The opposition charges of excessive interest, public losses, and embezzlement similarly turned out not to be the case after further review.[10]

Consequently, the minority reports won the favor of the full House and a bill passed both Houses of Congress to renew the charter of the Bank on June 11, 1832, 28 to 20 in the Senate, and 109 to 76 in the House.[11] Two years later the leader of the minority report offered a public apology for his role in writing it and for many of its accusations of corruption against the Bank and its directors. He stated the he had wrongly wounded the feelings of men associated with the Bank.[12] Nevertheless, after the June vote of Congress, Administration aligned newspapers circulated the report and its accusations against the Bank. Irrespective of the findings of Congress, the charges made in the newspapers were popular and supported the upcoming July veto of President Jackson.

The statement explaining the July veto repeated earlier remarks of monopoly and oppression,[13] but its central point was captured in its phrase, that "The Congress, the Executive, and the Court must each for itself be guided by its own opinion of the Constitution." The veto said that the Supreme Court's 1819 decision of *McCulloch vs Maryland* upholding the Bank's constitutionality had no legal bearing on the other branches of government. The veto prompted political gatherings in opposition, some stating that to interpret laws and the constitution without deference to judicial rulings was a threat to the republic.[14]

Former President James Madison had addressed the potential of Jackson's veto the summer before in a letter to James Ingersoll, viewing it as incorrect from a constitutional and legal standpoint. He explained why Jackson's opposition to the Bank was not comparable to his original objection in 1791. Speaking to the topic of judicial precedents, Madison thought that a judge should not "vary the rule of law according to his individual interpretation of it," listing reasons why rulings deliberately sanctioned and confirmed repeatedly should be binding and authoritative in settling legal questions. Madison believed that to act according to one's individual opinions and reject past judicial rulings and precedents threatened the stability of the constitution and laws.[15] In his own situation as President in 1811, when Congress was voting on renewing the charter of the first Bank, he saw the choice between:

> . . . that which has the uniform sanction of successive legislative bodies through a period of years, and under the varied ascendency of parties; or that which depends upon the opinions of every new legislature, heated as it may be by the spirit of party, eager in the pursuit of some favorite object, or led astray by the eloquence and address of popular statesmen, themselves, perhaps, under the influence of the same misleading causes.

From this standpoint Madison explained his own reasoning, why, despite strong party views, he intended to approve a renewal of its charter in 1811: the original Act of 1791 had been discussed and settled through all the branches of government, the Bank had received "twenty years of annual legislative recognitions," "a positive ramification of it into a new State," and "the entire acquiescence of all the local authorities, as well as of the nation at large." He explained that the majority of his party who ended up voting against it did not deny the constitutionality of the power to establish the Bank, but disapproved of the plan, and had united with a small minority that denied the power. To have vetoed, therefore, he wrote, would have been "a defiance of all the obligations derived from a course of precedents amounting to the requisite evidence of the national judgment and intention."

Henry Cabot Lodge wrote later that there was an important distinction "between a new bill and one for continuing an existing law." In his veto, wrote Lodge, Jackson assumed "the right and the power to declare an existing law, passed by Congress, approved by Madison, and held to be constituted by an express decision of the Supreme Court, to be invalid because he thought to say so."[16]

The Effects and Legality of Charter Nullification

In December 1832, the President questioned the Bank's condition and its continuing role as a federal depository, citing its delay in paying government bonds earlier that year. The president of the Bank had informed the Secretary of Treasury in the spring of threats of cholera from Europe, and a needed extension for business and trade at the time the government bonds would otherwise normally be paid, recommending a delay in payment to prevent financial crisis. When cholera hit, it caused panic in business and among the banks, and New York City was hit hard as over two hundred thousand people fled the city limits.[17] The Bank was able to unwind the crisis with its credit resources. Notwithstanding these events, Jackson described the payment delay as a serious problem and told Congress that the Administration was privately determining the safety of the public deposits. Jackson said that the subject merited a serious investigation:

> An inquiry into the transactions of the institution, embracing the branches as well as the principal bank, seems called for by the credit which is given throughout the country to many serious charges impeaching its character, and which if true may justly excite the apprehension that it is no longer a safe depository of the money of the people.[18]

The Administration's private investigation by a political friend concluded contrary to the President's statements, but a Congressional investigation was still urged, which began in January of 1833.[19] After reviewing the matter, the majority report stated that the delay in bond payments did not present an issue of concern and that the Bank was sound and could fulfill all of its engagements. The minority report dissented, suggesting that a western office with unpaid debts and the case of payment delay implied insolvency. It recommended unilateral action by the Executive with regards to the Bank, stating that Congress's opinion did not change the urgency of the matter.[20] The House approved the majority report in March, and affirmed the safety of the government deposits by a majority of 109 to 46. From the standpoint of the press, the investigation and vote of Congress in favor of the Bank was fairly inconsequential, and the Bank was depicted as a monster opposed to the President.

Jackson directed Treasury Secretary Louis McLane to proceed with an order to remove the deposits at the end of March. McLane wrote to Jackson in May that he thought removal was unjustified without an alternative and opposed unilateral action without Congress's assent. He pointed to the probable disadvantages of using state banks as depositories, a prediction that would ultimately prove to be accurate. It was "not to be expected," he wrote,

> that with the temptations to extend their business which the possession of the deposits would create, with the chance of mismanagement to which such institutions are always liable, and with the hazard of loss to which they are ordinarily exposed, and their inability to withstand any extraordinary pressure, a loss should not occur in some one or all the selected banks.[21]

McLane maintained that the Bank had fulfilled its purposes as a depository, which the state banks would not achieve but rather lead to disorders in currency and trade, including suspension of specie payments and loss of credit lines.[22] McLane was then replaced as Treasury Secretary by William Duane, who also disagreed with the proposed action, and told Jackson he thought the removal would affect the general public more than the Bank.[23] Duane was replaced by Roger Taney at the end of September.

The Treasury stated on September 26 that new federal revenues would be deposited in state banks, but if a deposit had already been made in the Bank it would "remain there until it shall be gradually withdrawn by the usual operations of the Government."[24] Shortly after, however, the Secretary wrote orders to transfer deposits from the Bank. Both of these actions involved breaches of law.

In regard to the first action, while it was his discretion to stop the flow of new revenues into the Bank, according to the 1816 Act of Congress establishing the Bank, they should then have been deposited in the Treasury.[25] Instead, he made contracts with state banks which he was barred from doing since Congress had not passed a law for the purpose.[26] In regard to the second action, section sixteen of the Bank's charter stated that government revenues were to be deposited in the Bank unless the Secretary ordered otherwise, in which case he had to immediately lay before Congress the reasons. The Secretary's discretion involved money prior to deposit, and afterward it was to remain until transferred for payments of government expenditures. For the Secretary to transfer them beforehand was to break the chartered agreement with the Bank. Of greater constitutional relevance in removing the deposits, the Executive exercised Judicial power. By removing the deposits it was prematurely ending the government's contract with the Bank, rather than waiting until its expiration in 1836. If the corporation had violated its charter the appropriate course was referral to the judiciary, as it had a right to receive notice of its alleged offenses and a trial. Instead, by removal, the Secretary became prosecutor, judge, and jury.[27] In regard to the first and second action, the Treasury's deposit of new money or transfer of existing money from the Bank into the state banks was an exercise of Legislative power, as the Treasury Department's role is to collect funds and ensure that they are appropriated and deposited, while the Congress determines how they are appropriated and deposited. In the Secretary's statement justifying his actions, he incorrectly stated that it was his duty to determine new locations for the revenues.[28] Determining new locations put federal revenues in the hands of the Executive, giving it the power of the purse. Congress had placed the deposits in the Bank by the charter of 1816, and it was their duty to legislate the alternative.

Cancelling the deposit aspect of the Bank's charter three years prior to its scheduled expiration had many negative economic consequences, both in the short-term, from 1833-1834, as well as those contributing to the financial crisis of 1836-1837.

The disruption of the credit lines provided by the government deposits in the offices of the Bank around the country caused a credit contraction which lasted from the fall of 1833 until the summer of 1834. Removing government revenues that had been previously lent out by the Bank meant borrowers had to pay their debts or find a state bank to take them. While the Bank tried to reduce the exposure of itself and its creditors in anticipation, there was no quick replacement for the system that had been established. The substitute depositories were not reliable, had charters differing between twenty states, were in many cases of small capital and circulation, and were in competition with other local banks.[29] They reduced their loans in order to carry out government expenditures and transfers of funds. The disruption of removing the $7-9 million of deposits from the Bank began having a serious impact on economic activity. According to the Bank, it would have been able to extend credit through the difficult period of adjustment as it had previously, but due to actions by the Secretary in removing money already deposited, and runs on some of its offices, it was forced to reduce exposure for its own security.[30] Financial crisis set in by December 1833, as credit contraction led to shortage of money. Crops were sold at ruinous prices, and many farmers suffered.[31] Though the Senate reprimanded the President, and numerous memorials of protest were sent to Congress expressing their disapproval of the deposit removal, the Executive actions were sustained by both houses of Congress.[32] After a period of credit difficulties, resulting in loss of property, investments, and savings, the financial crisis subsided and trade resumed by the summer of 1834, with the Bank performing its other functions as best it could despite lacking the public deposits.[33]

With respect to the removal of the deposits, of greater consequence than the temporary credit crisis of 1833-1834 was the undue expansion and speculation of 1834-1837, driven by the new state bank depositories.

The large balances of bank notes previously received as public deposits had provided the Bank with a key regulatory power upon the banking system, which it used to keep state banks in check. With this removed, excessive issues, if they occurred, were difficult to restrain. Incidentally, this took place from the large deposits now available to selected depositories as well as a lack of direction given regarding loans created by those deposits. Above the $8-9 million in public deposits initially received, surplus of revenue over expenditures was increasing in an unprecedented manner, as a consequence of having paid off the federal debt and from increased sales of public lands. By November 1836, public deposits in eighty-eight state banks grew to $49 million. The banks used the money to leverage large issues of their notes and to extend their loans. Land speculation developed rapidly beginning in 1835. Some banks were created simply to join in the land speculation, many of which later failed.[34] Revenues from the sale of lands grew from $5 million to $25 million from July 1833-July 1836. The average revenue from land between 1834-1836 was $15.5 million per year, over five times the average from 1829-1833.[35] Another factor in rapid land speculation during this period was the extinguishment of the public debt by January 1835 which had led many investors to seek the former as a replacement for the loss of their annuity in the latter.

From 1834 to 1837, almost two hundred new banks were organized in the U.S.[36] The aggregate of their circulating notes, exclusive of the Bank, rose from $61 million in 1830 to $149 million in 1837. In his December 1835 address, Jackson described the growth of land sales as evidence of increasing prosperity, commending the state banks. He congratulated them in their service as custodians of the public revenue and said they had created an improvement to the currency and exchanges. He compared them to the Bank of the United States, stating that they were "not susceptible of dangerous extension and combination," and had proved the merit of his actions against it:

> The experience of another year has confirmed the utter fallacy of the idea that the Bank of the United States was necessary as a fiscal agent of the Government . . . The considerations on which the Bank of the United States rested its claims to the public favor were imaginary and groundless, it can not be doubted that the experience of the future will be more decisive against them.[37]

Months later, it became apparent that speculation was on the rise, and the failure of banks was increasing, costing the Treasury in specie. The Treasury, having received their notes from the land offices, was left with discredited notes and suffered the loss. Bank credit, both sound, and unsound, had facilitated large tracts of land to be held by speculators.

Effects of the Specie Circular and Treasury Mismanagement

To reassert the power of the purse, Congress passed "The Deposit and Distribution Act of June 23.[38] The Act regulated the deposits of public money, including the distribution of a surplus of $37 million, in four installments according to population, beginning January 1837. The eighty eight banks used as depositories by the Treasury held $77 million deposits, while the remaining seven hundred state banks in the country held $51 million. The Act sought to effect a more equal distribution of funds, to bring down speculation, and make the surplus available in commercial cities as the offices of the Bank had, for exchanges and tax payments, rather than overly concentrated in fewer banks whose deposits to capital ratio was becoming increasingly large.

The Administration had its own more drastic approach to the public deposit concentration issue. On July 11, 1836, without advanced notice, it issued the Specie Circular, whose effect was to discredit many of their notes. Referencing monopolies of speculators purchasing lands, and banks with excessive issues, the circular informed deposit banks that the government would no longer accept anything but gold and silver for public land. Gold and silver had previously been used only for settling trade balances, security against occasional redemptions, and for the occasional settlement of balances between banks dealing in exchange. The new government demand for specie led to great difficulties. The bank notes and deposits of banks that had made loans for land sales became illiquid since they were no longer receivable by the government. Their owners, including the depository banks, were therefore encouraged to convert bank notes and deposits into gold and silver, which had the effect of a joint run upon them. Banks in the West and other locations of land sales stopped loans and liquidated assets for gold and silver in anticipation of the pressure.[39]

Making matters worse, the banking system then received pressure from the Treasury's interpretation of the June Deposit and Distribution Act. To distribute funds among the banks, the Treasury was supposed to transfer funds to banks nearby those from which funds would be transferred, not from one state to another. If the deposit to capital ratio of a bank in a major city was too large, the Treasury was to distribute some of its revenue to the closest banks within that city or state. The intention was to uphold the trade for that city, and not disturb commerce. For the distribution of the funds among the states, it was not necessary to transfer actual funds from major cities to other states as delivery of bank drafts to deposit banks in major cities achieved this objective. Giving bank drafts to the state governments which they could sell for profit or use to settle debts was equivalent or preferable to orders to withdraw actual money. Similar operations had been done before.[40] Instead of bank drafts, the Treasury sent directives for the withdrawal of actual funds totaling $9 million. In order to diminish deposits in some depository banks in major Eastern cities, the Treasury sent directives to western states rather than sending them to other banks in the same city or state as directed by Congress. At the same time western states were given directives for the following year's appropriation, thereby transferring money from where it was fully in use to states where it could not be appropriated for a year.[41] Therefore, as the specie circular was pressing western banks, these states received withdrawal orders on eastern depository banks, making it a liability for the eastern states as well. The crisis was elevated to another level as the deposits of eastern banks in creditor states, which had been in high demand for trade, were withdrawn and sent to western banks in debtor states to have currency for those seeking to buy land.

The consequent specie demand upon depository banks produced an unequalled crisis. In self-preservation, banks stopped making new loans and brought pressure on their debtors for payment. They used whatever means possible to draw gold from other banks. Eastern banks were unable to aid merchants in purchasing agricultural goods as their gold and silver was withdrawn. At the same time, western debtors to eastern merchants were unable to pay, as there were no buyers for their goods, and similarly, their own debtors could not pay. The bank payment methods between creditors and debtors were discredited, prices fell rapidly, and the course of trade was arrested. By November, interest rates rose nearly twenty five percent and the rate for bills of exchange to transmit funds from distant locations to the East increased five times.[42]

Additional causes of the crisis were due to deflationary pressures from the Bank of England. From 1833-1837 the Bank of England had become overleveraged based on a great deal of domestic stock and commodity speculation. As a result gold had become cheap to export to the U.S. In the spring of 1837, English banking firms ceased facilitating the need for gold in the U.S. and cut off their normal U.S. merchants purchasing cotton. Due to the domestic crisis, no American buyers could stand in as substitutes for the foreign demand, and bankruptcy spread among southwestern merchants, banks, and farmers.[43]

When the second $9 million installment of the Distribution Act was due in April, requiring transfer of specie from depository banks to other banks throughout the country, the depositories nearly failed. In May, the redemption pressures on banks became too much, and deposit banks suspended payments of specie in New York quickly followed by other locations. The state banks followed suit after the government stopped paying specie through its depository banks and state bank specie demand soared in attempt to find any source of specie.[44]

Because of the specie circular, the federal revenues paid into the state bank depositories in the form of bank notes were not accepted by government creditors. In addition, revenues from the public lands declined. By September 1837, the Treasury was running a deficit. President Martin

Van Buren called a special session of Congress and $10 million treasury notes were authorized to make up the shortfall. In Van Buren's September 4, 1837, address to Congress, he did not question the validity of continuing the Specie Circular. He said the renewed charter of the Bank in 1836 would not have prevented the crisis or the speculation, though it had proven its ability to do so in the past. Notwithstanding his former praise for large numbers of banks established after 1833, he said the state banks were to blame and had failed to properly carry out the distribution law.[45] He noted the crisis proved his long distrust of banks, and concluded that they were inherently dangerous, proposing legislation to cut "any connection between the Government and banks of issue."[46] In place of bank depositories he proposed the establishment of subtreasuries in the states that would receive and pay gold and silver, separating the public revenue from business and trade. Congress voted against Van Buren's subtreasury plan that year. A similar proposal had been dismissed by Congress without much thought when Benton had proposed it in February 1831.[47]

Through 1838, unemployment increased, businesses remained closed, and credit lines remained difficult to come by. Van Buren pressed the banks to resume specie redemption and said that debts should be paid regardless of the sacrifice. Banks committed to continue suspension until the government repealed the Specie Circular, as resumption would have been equivalent to pressing all of their depositors for cash.[48] In response to the continuing depression a resolution for rescinding the Specie Circular passed the Senate 34 to 9 on May 30, 1838, and passed the House on the same day, by a majority of 5 to 1.[49]

Afterward, banks resumed specie payments, but confidence in banks continued to decline. The federal government and Treasury did not take action to repair the facility of payments by cooperating with banks or other forms of intervention. In 1839 Van Buren maintained his stance with respect to banks and again proposed the subtreasury system. To address the growing amount of bad debts, he urged cuts rather than refinancing, including for debts previously taken for infrastructure. He said the crisis proved that credit provided by banks was illusory and lacking in real wealth.[50] The struggle worsened between debtors and creditors as banks remained defensive of their solvency into the 1840's. The economic depression did not lift until 1842.

Reviewing the Political Struggles of the Bank

Looking back, the Congressional investigations from 1830-1833 had cleared the Bank of the charges made by the Jackson Administration. If the Executive had desired further action, prosecution by the Attorney General was the proper course. The debate regarding whether the removal of the deposits was justified was legally a question of whether the Executive had the ability to nullify the charter. This not being the case, Administration acted on the basis of popular support. Though the action of removal was unlawful, the Administration later cited the prosperity of 1834-1836 as justification, which turned out to be a result of excessive credit and speculative activities. Rather than a gradual remedy and slow unwinding, the choice to make an unprecedented demand on the specie reserves of banks without warning demonstrated disregard to the consequences. That banks had lent to speculators or engaged in speculation did not require or warrant jeopardizing the general system of bank payments. Precedent had shown that speculation had been successfully reigned in before without such action, as in the many cases between 1823-1828. John J. Knox, comptroller of the currency between 1872-1884, described the measure thus:

> The removal of the deposits to the State banks and the issue of the specie circular were both acts of financial recklessness on the part of the President, and the circular had the effect of unduly precipitating the collapse of the wild speculation in which the handling of the public deposits by the State banks had resulted.[51]

The facts presented indicate that the chief causes of the 1837 panic were a combination of the specie circular and the mismanagement of the distribution law. Knox supports this general thesis writing:

> The specie circular, by creating a fictitious demand for coin at a time when the banks were using a very large amount of currency in order to pay their obligations to the Government so suddenly called for, was no doubt very largely the cause of this suspension and the subsequent panic.[52]

While the Jackson and Van Buren Administrations had previously cited state banks as a contrast with the Bank, they eventually voiced opposition to all state banks in 1836-1841 by making similar accusations. This contradiction has the effect of discrediting many of the claims of the Jackson Administration's earlier opposition to the Bank from 1829-1836. The contradiction also supports the hypothesis that the deeper motive of the Jackson and Van Buren Administrations was an opposition to federal government involvement in the economy. The sympathy of the currency philosophies of Benton with those of Jackson and Van Buren support this thesis, as does the Administration's opposition to federal sponsorship of infrastructure and its expressed statements regarding simple government.[53] From this standpoint, the Jackson Administration's 1829-1833 acts in politicizing the Bank issue appear as a means to its political philosophy.

A final consideration is added with regard to the measures against the Bank. Since the welfare of the country was the explicit concern of the Jackson Administration, a valid alternative should have been first insisted upon. The method of action in removing the deposits during a recess, regardless of the consequences, does not support taking its statements at face value. Alternative charters and other plans for Banks had been proposed, and were discussed, as mentioned in the minority reports of 1832.[54] Constructive action, as the Administration's own Secretary of Treasury McLane had said, would have been to form an alternative first. Later, during the crisis of 1837, another design for national regulation of banks, without the elements the Administration had publicly opposed, and very similar to the later National Banking Acts of 1863-64, was made available at the request of the Administration's Secretary of War.[55] In sum, the financial consequences of government policy between 1833-1841 further illustrate the merit of the intended functions of the Bank of the United States when in concord with the Congress and the Executive, as executed between 1823-1832, and as first established under the direction of Treasury Secretary Alexander Hamilton.

Part IV
The Return to Currency Management and the Promise of the National Banking System

Overview

The Independent Treasury System, first proposed by Martin Van Buren in 1837 and fully established in 1846, proved to be a burden on the financial system and reduced the specie supply of banks. The combination of the Independent Treasury and unregulated state banking led to an increase in private brokerage costs for financial transactions and greater instability during the 1840s and 1850s.

In 1861, along with the demands of the Civil War one month after its formation, the Abraham Lincoln Administration faced a Treasury with little revenue, a country in poor financial health, and a banking system that was unreliable. Having long been one of Lincoln's personal priorities, the Lincoln Administration planned to initiate a system of federally controlled banks as soon as feasibly possible.

However, the demands of war and the Administration's maintenance of the Independent Treasury policy resulted in an inability of the banks to meet the high borrowing demands of the government. With the suspension of the banks in the winter of 1861, the necessity to issue legal tender postponed the formation of federally controlled banks.

Legal tender notes provided the first occasion of a national currency since the second Bank of the United States in 1836, and provided a similar uniform means of payment, but one that came into far more widespread use. Lincoln saw the notes as an effective auxiliary means of exchange in the period before a national banking system could be established.

In 1863, the Treasury Department successfully funded all of its war demands with the largest sale of long-term U.S. bonds in American history up to that time, and at little discount. The great degree of economic activity, sufficient means of payment provided by the legal tender issues, and high prices of gold and commodities made the needed borrowing and taxation by the government a smaller burden on the public.

The National Banking Act of 1863 was intended to replace bank note currency with one created by the Treasury, secured by U.S. bonds and reserves of individual banks. Its aim was to provide a national currency accepted for payment at all banks, with greater security and less expense through uniformity. Despite its failure to adopt reserve methods that acknowledged the growing use of deposit credit rather than bank note transactions, and its lack of centralized credit controls, it was an improvement on the previous system.

By the end of 1864, the National Banking System had been effectively established and the Lincoln Administration planned to fade out legal tenders as the system grew to meet economic demand, with the former serving as a reserve for the latter.

Chapter 12
The Independent Treasury and State Banking

In 1840, Congress approved the subtreasury system previously described, which President Martin Van Buren had proposed between 1837-1839. This system was in response to his opposition of the Bank of the United States and the state banks. The public's opposition to Van Buren and the banks' opposition to the subtreasury system were each strong. The subtreasury system was short lived as a result and Congress repealed it in August 1841. However, President John Tyler's veto of a national Fiscal Bank the same year effectively continued Treasury payments in the same manner as the subtreasury until its official reenactment with the Independent Treasury Act of 1846.[1]

Under the Independent Treasury, the government did not use banks to handle its payments. The Treasury ceased relation with bank notes, deposit accounts, and bills of exchange, which had become the common mode of effecting payments. Instead, subtreasuries received and paid out specie. In surplus years, this meant that the amount paid by the banks on behalf of taxpayers into the subtreasury was a reduction in their loanable funds for that amount.

While the Treasury adopted this method of payments, the general public continued to rely on banks and left the gold and silver to the government. They continued to rely on bills of exchange, checks, and bank notes to conduct their own payments.[3] Regardless of its merits, it was not possible to retain enough specie or move it from place to place with sufficient speed. Apart from the Treasury's new demand for it, specie was otherwise used only in the payment of balances of foreign trade, in occasional domestic settlements, and in very small retail transactions. It accounted for one hundredth of the total value of property transferred in the payments and settlements of debts made by domestic industry and commerce. Its continued decline in use over the previous century was due to the increased demand for payments in trade, with more efficient methods taking its place. Specie became relegated to a more limited but useful role in serving in the payment of foreign trade deficits and as the legislated reserve security for bank circulation.

Therefore, by making specie required for the whole amount of revenue to the government, the Independent Treasury aggravated the burden of taxation in the increased demand for what was otherwise rarely used domestically. This created discord between the government and the rest of the creditors in the country.[2] As the depositories of the nation's specie, paying it when required for security and foreign exchange balances, the banks, not the public, experienced the burden of the Treasury's demand for it. The banks conducted payment transactions to and from the government for the public at large on the credit of their accounts, reducing the direct negative effects of the subtreasury system on businesses and individuals.

However, due to the high demand put upon the banks to both facilitate the government's demand for specie, and the demand of importers for specie, their reserves shrank, leading the state banks to decrease their loans and discounts. In the 1840s and 1850s, they were not able to meet the increasing demand for payments in commerce to support normal economic growth. Individuals and businesses had to turn to other means to pay their liabilities. A surplus of private brokers and other entities lending money and conducting transfers and exchanges of money was the result, often charging rates of interest of 15-20%.[4] The high demand for payments in the major cities brought a large class of capitalists to begin the profession of discounting notes and lending money. From 1847 to 1857, the number of private banks increased by twenty times, while the number of people employed in discounting private securities grew a hundredfold. Private money lending and involvement in domestic exchanges exceeded many times over the capital of banks.[5] The system became unnecessarily expensive. Interest rates increased to levels far exceeding those of the Bank, creating a burden upon industry and commerce, with interest charges totalling $50-100 million. Legitimate banking business began to find it difficult to make a profit and many banks were forced to adopt risky practices in order to earn their dividend. The rate of interest continued high until the crash of 1857, which was driven by the double demand on banks for specie. The high cost of the payment system between 1846-1857 was essentially a business transaction tax paid to private lenders for the valuable service they provided in lieu of the national government's involvement in the currency.[6]

Along with becoming more expensive, the banking system became non-uniform and increasingly risky. Most states did not require any stocks deposited for the security of bank notes and there was no security beyond the capitals of the banks, which were frequently non-existent. In instances where stock security was required there was no limitation as to the amount. The number of different currencies became increasingly diverse. By the opening of the Civil War, there was over 1600 different types of bank notes in circulation and these varied widely in value. Counterfeit currencies were also very common and banks were not compelled to receive the notes of other banks.[7]

Chapter 13
The Departure from the State Banking Era

The incoming Abraham Lincoln Administration faced a hazardous financial situation. The Treasury had no uniform method of control over the banks or the currency. Unemployment was high, thousands of businesses were idle, and hundreds of thousands were unable to sell goods. There was a general lack of an adequate medium of exchange, and the cost of money was high, with a 10-15% borrowing rate in the cities and much more in the country. Meanwhile, revenues from duties, which had become the country's main source of revenue, declined rapidly as the war began in April.[1]

In July 1861, the war placed a demand on the Treasury for $318 million in the coming year. Confronted with this expenditure, Lincoln's Treasury Secretary Salmon P. Chase saw few options for immediate relief. An issue of treasury notes for the full amount would disturb domestic trade, but borrowing from private money lenders at the exceedingly high rates offered would lead to crushing interest payments. Relief came in a third option from the largest state banks of the country, primarily in Boston, New York, and Philadelphia. Officers of these banks counseled Chase and negotiated a loan to the government of $50 million at 7.3%. By December 1861 additional loans of this type amounting to a total of $150 million were made. Chase wrote that these loans "were necessarily made at an interest which he regarded as high, though lenders strenuously insisted on higher." The loans revived the nation's credit. Individual capitalists who had been willing to lend at higher rates were vocal in censuring Chase for turning to the banks.[2]

The next action by Chase was questionable, as it reduced the potential of the state banks to serve as partners with the Treasury department. As reviewed in the previous chapter, the Independent Treasury System effectively ended dealings between the treasury and banks. All payments to and from the sub treasuries were made in specie. But given the fact that the government now required almost the entire capital of the largest state banks in loans, it stood to reason that the Independent Treasury system should have been modified so that the banks could be utilized for the government's fiscal operations. This would have allowed the loans to the Treasury to be kept in deposit accounts at these banks, and payments from the Treasury for war purchases and to creditors paid with drafts on the banks requiring no movement of gold. Indeed, when making these large advances to the government, the banks had requested to be made into depositories for the sums lent to the government. That was the customary mode of using bank loans. In addition, Congress had granted permission to suspend the Independent Treasury Act in certain respects. That September, a very detailed plan to avoid the transfer of the large amounts of specie to and from the subtreasuries was printed in the New York Times.[3]

Functionally, the one hundred associated banks in New York, Philadelphia, and Boston were very suitable to act as fiscal assistants to the Treasury. The notes of their banks held the highest credibility in the country and checks from them would have been received in payment as good as gold throughout the Union states. They possessed a capital of $120 million. While the necessary unity between each other and their preparedness to regularly coordinate such large loans and payments was questionable, they had demonstrated a willingness to be used for fiscal operations of the Treasury. These banks had greater skill and knowledge of the money market than Treasury officials and may have been able to coordinate and distribute new loans for the Treasury in coming years more efficiently than the Treasury alone. The latter became a problem in 1864, and the national banks did not become effective for this purpose until 1865.[4]

Instead of this arrangement, the Independent Treasury system was upheld and Chase withdrew the full amount of the loan in specie from the banks, the first fifty million in August, the second in October, and the third in November.[5] This method exhausted the resources of the banks and the specie reserve of the banks became dispersed. Had it been retained it could have been a useful reserve later on for the banks and the Treasury's future issues from 1862-1864. This action began a pattern of alienation between the banks and the Treasury.

Lincoln and the National Banking Plan of 1861

While serving as an Illinois state representative, Abraham Lincoln had opposed the Subtreasury system of President Martin Van Buren and defended the merits of the Bank of the United States. As a member of Congress, he was less explicit about the Bank but maintained support for national regulation of the currency.[6]

In his campaign for President, Lincoln made slavery the central issue and did not take a firm stand on any leading economic issue due to the need to unify his party.[7] It then remained to be seen how his previous record on financial regulation would translate into practice after assuming the presidency in 1861. This was answered in December 1861 when Secretary Chase issued a plan to reinstate federal banking regulation, bring uniformity to the currency, and regulate its quantity. With precedents dating back to 1815, the keystone of the plan was to require banks to deposit U.S. bonds with the Treasury who in return would provide U.S. notes to the banks to circulate.[8] As Chase described it, the new national banks would be required "to purchase United States stocks to hold as securities for their circulating notes."

In this way, if bank circulation could not be redeemed by the banks themselves it would be redeemed by the Treasury after the Treasury sold the bonds held as security. This was a major improvement from the state banking system, which had largely placed its security on individual reserves of gold and silver. This had proved unreliable in times of crisis. Though the government would not be not a joint owner of the capital of the national banks, as it had been in the Bank of the U.S., it would have a similar arrangement in that their capital and circulation would be largely based on the public debt. The other chief improvement promised by the national banks was the establishment of a uniform currency subject to no discount. Each national bank would accept the other's notes at par. This was unheard of during the previous twenty years, and would drastically reduce the cost doing business and effecting transactions. Existing state banks were to be transformed into national banks and new banks would be formed as well.[9]

In addition to Lincoln's previous record on the subject of banking, the importance of the plan can be seen in the fact that it was one of the only economic subjects on which he worked closely with Chase. In contrast to taxation, the tariff, and the legal tender, issues about which President Lincoln was mostly silent and left the work and debates to Congress and Chase, he did weigh in on the National Banking Acts.[10] This is evidenced in Lincoln's addresses to Congress, and also confirmed by one of his aides, John Hay, who wrote:

> [Lincoln] thought Chase's banking system rested on a sound basis of principle, that is, causing the Capital of the country to become interested in the sustaining of the national credit. That this was the principal financial measure of Mr. Chase in which he (L) had taken an especial interest. Mr. C. had frequently consulted him in regard to it. He had generally delegated to Mr C. exclusive control of those matters falling within the purview of his dept. This matter he had shared in, to some extent.[11]

The National Banking Plan Postponed

From July to December 1861 the Treasury relied upon $150 million it had borrowed from the banks, and an issue of $50 million in demand treasury notes (treasury notes redeemable in specie on demand). In Chase's December 1861 Treasury report, he laid out the Administration's plan for financing the war. The U.S. government was to rely on continued borrowing from state banks during a rapid transition into a proposed national banking system, along with a continued use of demand treasury notes. This plan was never pursued.[12]

At the end of December 1861 the Treasury funding was nearly exhausted from the demands of the war while the banks were in no position to provide anywhere near the funding needed. The government needed to raise $350 million during the first half of 1862. On December 30, 1861, the banks of New York suspended the payment of specie, a policy soon followed by the rest of the banks throughout the country. The Government then also suspended the specie exchangeability on its $50 million of demand notes. Chase viewed the bank suspension as a result of increasing demands of the war, military delays, bank strain, and diminished confidence in the government. This in turn made bonds unsaleable in the ensuing environment. These factors, he wrote, "made a suspension of specie payments inevitable."[13]

After the suspension the available options to the Treasury Department to meet expenditures were: a) raise money from taxes, b) borrow from suspended state banks, c) borrow money from abroad, d) issue more U.S. notes but suspend their feature of being redeemable on demand but designate them as legally acceptable for all debts.

Taxes were not the solution, as there was no time to belatedly raise them in sufficient amounts to meet the government's pressing need. State bank currency was only $150 million on January 1, 1861, while the demand for the war effort alone was far greater. In addition, leaning on this source for loans would have created a scarcity of bank notes. State banks would have had to print an amount of notes leading to uncontrollable inflation, creating further financial distress. Foreign credit was not an option. Though partaking in the initial loans to the government on July 17 and August 5, 1861, by years end European banks no longer purchased U.S. securities. In addition, various New York banks ceased to facilitate the sale of U.S. bonds in coordination with European banks.[14]

As Chase described later, the only apparent option was to issue more treasury notes, not redeemable into specie on demand, but in a form acceptable for payment to contractors, and to circulate as a general currency. He wrote:

> No other mode of providing, with any tolerable degree of promptitude, for the wants of the army and navy, and the necessities of other branches of the public service, seemed likely to effect the object with so little public inconvenience and so considerable public advantage as the issue of United States notes adapted to circulation as money, and available, therefore, immediately in Government payments.
>
> It now became the duty of Congress, not merely to provide the means of meeting the vast demands on the Treasury, but to create a currency with which—until the close of the war at least—loans and taxes might be paid to the Government, debts to individuals discharged, and the business of the country transacted. Nothing less would satisfy the need of the time.

In accord with this Administration decision, Congressman E. G. Spaulding of New York introduced a bill to make the demand notes issued in 1861 a legal tender. The House took up the bill on January 22, 1862. A long debate took place over the expediency and constitutionality of the measure in both houses of Congress.[15] Congress passed the Legal Tender Act on February 25, 1862, authorizing $150 million of legal tender "United States notes, $50 million of which were in lieu of the demand notes issued the July prior, which had stopped circulating after the suspension of the banks.[16] The Act also authorized $500 million in 6% 20 year bonds, callable by the government after 5 years. Despite the Administration's previous action of withdrawing most of their reserves many of the largest banks appeared before Congress in support of the bill. They cited the inability to accept the Treasury's notes on demand, or to aid the government, if a legal tender quality was not given to its notes.

Chase described the notes as an "evidence of indebtedness when the expenditures of the nation exceeded its receipts." The notes would remain outstanding until they could "be redeemed either in specie, or vested in a more permanent form of indebtedness, absorbed in taxes or withdrawn."[17] Chase later wrote in 1863, that by "putting a large part of the debt in the form of United States notes, without interest, and adapted to circulation as money," the burden of the necessary war debt was reduced as low as possible.[18] By means of the legal tender treasury notes, payments made to manufacturers for the requirements of the war, and other indispensable services, were made in a credit able to be used for all other transactions. The series of transactions made first to contractors, and by contractors to others, enabled general business to be conducted. The new means of payment restored economic activity at a critical time. It revived domestic commerce, manufacturing, production of mines and furnaces, and farm investment. Interest rates decreased from 15-20% to 5-8%, allowing debtors to pay off loans and reinvest in their businesses. Tax receipts increased as did purchase of government bonds. The legal tender notes served as a successful means of turning the products of labor and industry into currency, and within a year established a uniform currency.[19] The bill achieved its purpose to a greater degree than had been hoped despite the provision to pay duties in specie having proven to be a mistake. See Appendix I.

In addition to the authorization of the legal tender notes and 5-20 bonds, the Act of February 25 also included a temporary loan provision for $25 million. Chase had proposed that in order to extract further benefit from the debt created by the legal tenders, he "desired authority to receive temporary loans in the form of deposits reimbursable after a few days notice." These were short-term deposits made by the public with the Treasury, for which they could receive 5% interest. This made available more funds to the government at a very small cost, since they could pay back the owner at virtually any time. The amount of temporary loans authorized was further increased to $100 million in July 1862.[20]

On July 11, 1862, a second issue of $150 million of legal tender U.S. notes were authorized by Congress and signed by Lincoln, $50 million of which were reserved to pay off temporary loans in case of emergency. By December 1862, the amount of U.S. notes then in circulation or in the Treasury was $223 million. However, as state banks continued to operate without federal regulation, many state banks used the legal tenders as a replacement for reserves in order to continue leveraged issues. Lincoln was deeply concerned about this practice and addressed it in his State of the Union speech that year.

Chapter 14
Banking & Funding Strategy 1863-1865

At the end of 1862, with the legal tender expedient in place, the Lincoln Administration outlined in greater detail its national banking plan. In their December addresses, both Lincoln and Chase made the national banking plan their number one issue.[1]

On December 4, 1862, Chase communicated more of the details and reasoning behind the national banking plan from the year prior. The plan, he wrote, "contemplates gradual withdrawal of bank note circulation, and proposes a United States note circulation, furnished to banking associations."[2] The system would provide a currency uniform in value throughout the nation, "upon the foundation of national credit combined with private capital." The currency would be representative of the growing capital of the country, its amount limited only by capital, and brought into existence according to demand.[3] Backing the notes by U.S. bonds provided a safety to the nation's banks which had not been in place previously. The banks would pay specie on demand for their notes as before, once resumption of specie payments took place. In cases they were not paid by the individual bank, they would be redeemable by the Treasury's sale of the bonds held on security for the notes. In addition, unlike the state banks, all national banks would be required to receive at par, for any debt or liability to the bank, any notes or bills of other national banks. These considerations would make the banks much safer depositories of public money than state banks had been from 1834-1846. Importantly bank assets would be more certain security for their liabilities should they be met with a sudden demand for redemption.

The demand created for U.S. bonds to form banking associations promised to raise the value of U.S. bonds while establishing uniformity in their price. Since banking associations would make a profit both as holders of the bonds, and on their circulation, demand for bonds would be created. As during the beginning of the Washington Administration, these were important considerations for a Treasury in peril. Eventually, in the distant future, Chase saw the promise of a "reduction of the public debt to the amount required as a basis for secured circulation." His view was that outstanding U.S. government debt would be necessary only in proportion to capital required by the national banking system.

He also spoke of the nature of the banking law to the close union of the states. A United States note circulation issued by banks would supply a "firm anchorage" to the union of the States by the greater permanence and stability connecting their economic transactions. Chase went so far as to state that the lack of economic unity might have prevented secession:

> Had the system been possible, and had it actually existed two years ago can it be doubted that the National interests and sentiments enlisted by it for the Union would have so strengthened the motives for adhesion derived from other sources that the wild treason of secession would have been impossible?[4]

In their addresses that year, Chase and Lincoln also explained that while legal tenders had been highly beneficial and successful, they were only necessary as an interim measure until the national banking system was established. Chase said the withdrawal of coin from circulation, $250 million of it, had created a vacuum only partially filled by the legal tender United States notes. The legal tenders did not, he said, "fully meet the demand for increased circulation by the increasing number, variety, and activity of payments in money."[5] Instead of continuing with more legal tenders, he believed the vacuum should be filled by national bank notes. Chase wrote:

> The issue of United States notes . . . if exclusive, is hazardous and temporary. The security by national bonds of similar notes furnished to banking associations, is comparatively safe and permanent; and with this may be connected, for the present, and occasionally, as circumstances may require, hereafter, the use of the ordinary United States notes in limited amounts.

This issue had required clarification, since the success of the legal tender act had led some to propose that all currency could be issued and deposited with the government. Chase explained that government bills of credit (the legal tender notes) were superior to the notes of unregulated state banks but were not capable of meeting all the needs of a long-term national currency. In addition to the danger of corruption, excessive expenditures, and fraud in management, he suggested it was unwise for the Treasury to be responsible for the circulation of the whole country for two primary reasons. The amount would prove insufficient for the needs of the economy since the only means for legal tender United States notes to be put into circulation was in the disbursement of appropriations, at times when expenditures were greater than revenues. The exception to this rule would be if the government wanted to loan new issues directly, which would entail, he said, "all the complications and hazards of making the Treasury into a bank." In accord with this view, William Elder, a future member of the Johnson Treasury department, later pointed out that it would not be feasible for the Treasury department to supplant the function of banks, since the determination of the correct amount of currency and credit is something achieved on a local level. He said if attempted by the federal government it would require a bureaucracy of impossible size.[6]

In the same month, on December 1, President Lincoln advocated the national banking plan in his annual message to Congress. He reviewed the previous year's extraordinary financial developments, stating that the suspension of the banks had made "the large issues of United States notes unavoidable," with no alternative means available to pay the troops and meet other demands so cheaply. He commended Congress for making the U.S. notes legal tender for all debts, enabling them to be received for loans and internal taxes, and referenced their success in serving as a universal currency. They "satisfied, partially at least, and for the time, the long-felt want of an uniform circulating medium, saving thereby to the people immense sums in discounts and exchanges," in contrast to the cost of the 1850s described earlier.

Lincoln then clarified the Administration's long-term policy with respect to the nation's currency, qualifying his support for legal tender notes. "A return to specie payments, however, at the earliest period compatible with due regard to all interests concerned should ever be kept in view," he wrote. Lincoln cited the need for a currency free from wide fluctuations in value.[7] To achieve this he expressed his preference for a banking currency based on the security of U.S. bonds:

> Convertibility, prompt and certain convertibility, into coin is generally acknowledged to be the best and surest safeguard against [fluctuations in the value of the currency]; and it is

> extremely doubtful whether a circulation of United States notes payable in coin and sufficiently large for the wants of the people can be permanently, usefully, and safely maintained. Is there, then, any other mode in which the necessary provision for the public wants can be made and the great advantages of a safe and uniform currency secured? I know of none which promises so certain results and is at the same time so unobjectionable as the organization of banking associations, under a general act of Congress, well guarded in its provisions. To such associations the government might furnish circulating notes, on the security of United States bonds deposited in the treasury.[8]

Congress debated the Administration's plan in January. Lincoln spoke again to Congress that month, recommending his banking plan and warning of the dangers of unregulated state banking paper. An Act, "To provide a national currency, secured by a pledge of United States stocks, and to provide for the circulation and redemption thereof," was passed on February 25, 1863. Banks received a value of notes equal to 90% of the value of their bonds deposited. In January 1, 1863, there were 1,466 state banks in operation in the U.S. with a capital of $400 million and a circulation of $238 million.[9]

1863-1865 Treasury Funding

The Legal Tender Act of February 25, 1862 had authorized a sale of 6% 5-20 bonds (bonds callable by the government after 5 years or payable in 20 years). In 1862, these bonds fared poorly and by March 31, 1863, only $60 million had been sold. This was in part due to the fact that there were much better options available for using legal tender. In December 1862, $223 million legal tenders were in circulation out of $300 million authorized.

The Treasury's December 1862 report noted the enlarged demands upon it arising from increased war expenditures and the prices of goods. Prices had increased due to an increase of taxation on articles of consumption and a shortage of labor, the latter having been drawn from productive pursuits into the war effort. There was still a budget deficit of $276 million for the year 1862, and $622 million for 1863. Therefore, on March 3, 1863, Congress authorized a third $150 million of legal tender notes to meet this demand, along with other interest bearing treasury notes. The total amount of legal tenders in circulation reached $430 million by June 1864.[10] The quantity was more than double the paper money in circulation prior to the war.[11]

In May of 1863, another attempt was made to sell the 5-20 bonds authorized in 1862 by employing the American banking house Jay Cooke & Company. Editors of newspapers and others were enlisted, and it ultimately proved a very popular loan, taken in large and small sums from $50 to $1000 by all classes of citizens, counties, and states. This new success rested upon strong patriotism to aide the government and the fact that a sufficiently large amount of legal tenders had been introduced into circulation by this time. In addition, a rise in the price of gold made government bonds paying coin interest more attractive.[12] By July 1, 1863, $168 million of 5-20 bonds were taken up, and by the first of October following $278 million. This amount grew such that by January 1, 1864, there were $500 million outstanding.[13]

By means of the sale of the 5-20 bonds it became clear that the government would not need to inflate the currency with legal tenders in order to meet the needs of the government. The bonds furnished its $1.5-2 million in daily expenses. In 1863, 5-20 bonds were considered the most successful form of funding by the Treasury in its history. They financed almost the entire cost of the Civil War.

In Secretary Chase's last report to Congress on December 10, 1863, he outlined the course he had taken in the previous years, and how his bond and currency policies would continue to guide the nation toward prosperity. He remarked on the success of the 5-20 bonds, that:

> The Secretary is unable to perceive in what better or more effectual mode the important object of distribution could be accomplished. . . . Real and great advantages are derived from the wide diffusion of the debt among the people, through business transactions, and through the exertions of the officers of the departments, and agents for loans already noticed.[14]

National unity and strength were among the benefits he had in mind, since the holders of the notes and bonds had "a direct interest in the security of national institutions and stability of national administration." The Continental Monthly of February 1864 likewise wrote:

> The most signal triumph of Mr. Chase's whole system of finance is to be found in the truly marvellous success of his favorite five-twenty bonds. Even at the present time the public enthusiasm for these securities seems to be unabated, and it is more than probable that the whole amount authorized to be issued will be taken up quite as rapidly as the bonds can be prepared or as the money may be required.[15]

In addition to the 5-20 bonds and the aforementioned temporary loans, Chase issued one year 6% interest bearing treasury notes, called "certificates of indebtedness," in amounts of $50 million in 1862 and $150 million for each of the years 1863 and 1864. Chase explained his use of various short-term debt instruments rather than more long-term bonds, stating that "the object of future controllability was prominent." Along with these various forms of borrowing, using interest and non-interest treasury notes and bonds, the increasing and unpredictable demands of the war led the Treasury to adopt new techniques and designs for an array of taxes.[16] The taxes were not as oppressive as expected due to the increases in economic activity, and they remained only a small part of public income.

Chase saw a continued use of temporary loans after the war as a method for the government to absorb excess currency. For this purpose, in December 1863 he proposed an expansion of the temporary loan program beyond the $100 million already authorized. Congress, he wrote, could "fund the whole or any part of the temporary debt in bonds having a very moderate interest, and redeemable at the pleasure of the government after very brief periods, or perhaps at any time after their issue." Chase continued:

> Such an arrangement the Secretary inclines to think would operate beneficially by increasing the amount of currency when unusual stringency shall require increase, and reducing its amount when returning ease shall allow reduction.[17]

The 1864 Bond failure

In 1864, due to the pressures of the war, the slow progress of the national banking system's establishment, and his own convictions to extend the government's borrowing profile, Chase attempted to fund the government deficits with 5% bonds, instead of 6% bonds used the previous year. These were known as the 10-40s, redeemable at 10 years instead of 5, with an outer limit of 40 years instead of 20. On January 21, 1864, Chase attempted to borrow $200 million in this form, hoping for the same success of the 5-20s the previous year. However, the market did not bear the decreased interest rate, only $73 million were sold in the subsequent five months. The general public had come to expect and deal in the 6%, 5-20 bonds as a new standard, and the 5% 10-40 bonds did not meet their expectations.[18]

Due to the failure to raise money from this source, Chase sought recourse to various other short-term debt instruments to fund the government deficits. He made use of interest bearing legal tender treasury notes that had been authorized on March 3, 1863, issuing $150 million 1-2 year legal tender treasury notes at 5% interest, and 3 year 6% legal tender compound interest notes. Much of this short-term treasury debt also circulated as additional currency.[19] The funding system became complicated and unpredictable, decreasing the government's credit with the public.

While in 1863 it appeared currency was redundant enough to float 6% bonds, in 1864 it was not the case for a float of 5% bonds since holders of currency had better use applying it to other purposes due to profit opportunities created by the war. Had state banks been able to serve as fiscal agents to the Treasury in the transition in establishing the national banking system, it is possible this miscalculation could have been avoided as they would have had a much better reading of the market for the bonds and the public's alternatives at the time.[20] In contrast to this view, the subsequent Treasury Secretary, William Fessenden, who assumed office in July 1864, defended Chase's failed attempt to lower the borrowing terms. He said that with the unpredictability of the war, the varying confidence of victory, and general insecurity at the time, it would be employing the benefit of hindsight to have forecasted a failure of the loan. Another factor was the volatility in U.S. bond prices due to the large speculation in gold in 1863 and 1864 that had filled the newspapers with warnings regarding the government's currency and bonds. See Appendix I.

To regain control over the credit of the country and the funding system, in June 1864 Congress authorized Fessenden to issue 7.3% interest bonds. Of these, $200 million were sold immediately. In response, Fessenden said it once again proved that the U.S. public could lend all that was required for the government and demonstrated entire confidence in the nation's securities. He felt that it showed that there had been an accumulation of capital and production sufficient to lend the government its daily expenditure as well as bear taxes sufficient to pay the interest on the amount lent.[21] He wrote:

> After nearly four years of a most expensive and wasting war, the means to continue it seem apparently undiminished, while the determination to prosecute it with vigor to the end is unabated.

To fund the government through the end of the war, Fessenden utilized the 7.3% issue, along with 6% compound interest notes, certificates of indebtedness, and additional 5-20 bonds. Ultimately the funding of the extremely large and unpredictable demands of the war were lofty achievements by Chase and Fessenden.

National Banks Established

After 135 national banks were organized in 1863, by the spring of 1864 it became certain that a large proportion of the surplus capital of the nation would become invested in U.S. bonds and in the stock of national banks. During the year ending November 25, 1864, 282 new banks were organized and 168 state banks had been converted into national banks, for a total of 584 national banks then in existence. These banks held a capital of $109 million and deposited $82 million of bonds in the Treasury to secure a circulation of $66 million. The states of Pennsylvania and New York headed the list, the former with 109, and the latter with 100 banks.[22]

In his December 6, 1864, Fourth Annual Message, Lincoln summarized the progress of the national banking system for the public:

> Changes from state systems to the national system are rapidly taking place, and it is hoped that very soon there will be in the United States no banks of issue not authorized by Congress and no bank-note circulation not secured by the Government. That the Government and the people will de-

> rive great benefit from this change in the banking systems of the country can hardly be questioned. The national system will create a reliable and permanent influence in support of the national credit and protect the people against losses in the use of paper money. . . . It seems quite clear that the Treasury can not be satisfactorily conducted unless the Government can exercise a restraining power over the bank-note circulation of the country.

After the war, it was determined that revenues from taxes and customs duties would pay for the expenditures of the government and the interest on the national debt. The only borrowing required would be to pay for the principal. The national banks became agencies for this purpose, selling $335 million in government securities during 1865.

The national banking system provided a uniform currency free from most of the disturbances and inconveniences experienced under state banks. Congress had demonstrated and exercised its power to regulate the money of the country and to fix its value. It was an accomplishment that merchants and banks had desired for years but never thought possible.[23] In the 1840s, 1850s, and early 1860s, the trust in the solvency of distant banks had become so compromised that the idea of a bank note from one part of the country being received in a distant place at par was considered a miracle. The restoration of stability for credit within the financial system was one of the Lincoln Administration's greatest achievements.

However, though the National Banking Acts restored uniformity to the currency and provided better security for bank notes, they did not address the impact of negative trade balances on bank reserves and were overly focussed on lawful money reserves for notes at expense of the deposit functions of banks. Two clear omissions in the national banking legislation were discount rate controls on the withdrawal of gold by over traders of imports, and the separation of banks into deposit departments and banknote issue and redemption departments. See Appendix II.

Part V

The Challenges and Problems of the National Banking System

Overview

When the Civil War ended on April 9, 1865, there were clear improvements that needed to be made to the financial system in order to support the post-war economy. With minor changes and proper implementation, the National Banking System was sufficient to provide a stable currency that could expand with the demands of production and enlarge its capital base in the same proportion.

Notwithstanding repeated recommendations for improvements to the National Banking System by numerous Treasury officials between 1865-1871, the government did not remedy the growing number of problems that arose.

Due to the artificial limitation imposed on national bank notes, there was no increase in national banks between 1866 and 1870. As a consequence, there was always more legal tender notes in circulation than national bank notes, and the latter were not redeemable. The distribution of banks that were in circulation by 1866 was predominantly in the East and North, leading to severe regional discrepancies in credit and national banknote availability.

The result was an expensive, inflexible, and often insufficient currency, in discord with economic demand and supportive of speculation rather than continued investment in new capital. There was a lack of currency and credit where it was needed and a concentration of it where it was not. Rather than loans of capital, the growing tendency was to lend the same deposit multiple times in concentrated regions of the country.

These problems were augmented by the ability of national banks to meet their cash reserve requirements by depositing part of them in financial centers. Idle cash accumulated, and periods of speculation with bank reserves followed by shortages became increasingly common. The resulting financial instability and speculation led to the historically notable financial crisis of 1873.

During the depression of 1874-1879, the banking policies of the United States were largely caught in a struggle of partisan wrangling and theory. Instead of improving upon the National Banking System with legislation to address the causes of the financial crisis of 1873, government action was largely that of creating new obstacles to its success. Despite the belated lifting of the limitation on national bank notes in 1875, other Congressional actions led to a decline in national bank currency and a rise in state and private banks.

In the 1880s, the development of a prolonged period of government surplus and repayment of government debt led to a large premium on government bonds. The national banks' profits declined while their circulation decreased by 50%. The Independent Treasury system greatly contributed to this decline due to its method of handling government surpluses. In place of national bank notes, the circulating currency became supplied by large amounts of silver and treasury notes backed by gold and silver. These did not deliver the same multiplier effect to credit in circulation.

Financial instability and a dependence on foreign capital led to another major financial crisis in 1890 and again in 1893, the latter driven by excessive amounts of inelastic government currency. Both crises brought attention to the inability of obtaining national bank circulation on demand in times of crisis in order to prevent contractions in the money market from leading to full blown panic and depression. In 1900, attempts were made to remedy the liquidity problem with new legislation that greatly increased national banking facilities. However, as in the 1880s, the Independent Treasury system absorbed a large amount of the new bonds authorized to secure national bank note circulation. The economy grew into the new limits, and familiar stresses in the financial system led to the panic and crisis of 1907.

Chapter 15
Circulation Limitation and Other Errors of Implementation 1865-1870

Regardless of its flaws, the national banking system was a major improvement and ready to fulfill its purpose in 1865. As designed by the Lincoln Administration, it was to be limited only by demand and capital, and secured with U.S. bonds. After the war, this required addressing the original limit of national bank notes that could be authorized, which was set at $300 million on February 1863.

It would appear from Chase's reports that this limit was meant to be temporary, and after the economy grew into the limit the next Congress was supposed to raise it to an amount necessary to support economic activity. Indeed, in 1865, Comptroller Freeman Clarke asked that the limit be raised to $400 million by swapping out $100 million in legal tender notes with $100 million in national bank notes. He proposed that $100 million of the 6%, 5-20 bonds be authorized to secure the additional circulation, and the subscription to the bonds to be paid in legal tender notes, which would then be retired.[1]

Lifting the limit on national bank notes would drive the economy toward more production and new exports, bringing the balance of trade more in favor of the U.S., restoring the gold reserve. This would make a return to specie redemptions easy Clarke wrote, and the demand for gold would "be confined to the healthful and legitimate adjustment of balances with foreign countries." If the South were supplied with banking facilities necessary for the production of staples, their export of goods would reduce the export of gold. If the demands of business and the needs of trade and industry required more banks, they should be authorized. Economic demand for capital would then determine the size of the circulating currency, and naturally bring down legal tender notes as they were removed from circulation with new national bank notes authorized in their stead.

The stable picture of growth Clarke described, reflective of the Lincoln Administration's outlook, seemed promising. However, Congress did not raise the limit, neither that year, nor any other year until 1870. The authorized limit was reached in October 1866 and the effects were notable.

Sectional Credit Availability

As comptroller of the Currency in 1864 and Treasury Secretary beginning March 1865, Hugh McCulloch had been very conservative in the formation of new banks. He hoped to prevent inflation by keeping the total amount of currency of bank notes and legal tender notes low. He discouraged the creation of new banks in favor of conversions of state banks. On March 3, 1865, an Act of Congress said that 50% of the $300 million maximum of national bank notes would be distributed according to the population of the states and 50% distributed according to existing banking capital and resources of the states. The apportionment was not precise and became a struggle of influence, with the less populated states receiving less, and the more established states receiving more.

In 1865, 875 new national banks were successfully organized, as their number reached 1,513 by October. Their capital stock tripled from $135 million to $393 million. Bonds deposited with the Treasurer to secure circulation reached $276 million. This growth was promising; however, nearly 80% of the new national banks formed were conversions from existing state banks.[2] The formation of new banks was needed in the growing west and south. Capital became consolidated in the established banking centers, and an unequal distribution of bank capital became a substantive problem for western and southern states requiring new banks for growth and reconstruction. Also, the conversions of state banks diminished the aggregate bank circulation. This is due to the fact that the national currency was not delivered until its former amount of state bank notes were reduced.[3] When Clarke had proposed an increase of national bank notes in December 1865, this problem was already apparent.

Once the $300 million limit had been reached in 1866, it was no matter if those with capital to invest wanted to form a bank to assist their region. They could gain a charter, but they would not receive any notes to issue for discounts, one of the key forms of profit for banks, and a necessary requisite for western and southern regions. Consequently, the total number of national banks in the United States did not go up, its number remaining at about 1,640 banks between 1866 and 1870. By 1870, 14 populated states had $80 million more than their share, while 30 states had less than they were entitled.[4]

Making matters worse, a 10% tax on state circulation was instituted in 1866, leaving the South and West with even less local capital to borrow or notes to use as a medium of exchange. After state bank notes were taxed out of existence, state banks in the South and West were compelled to rely on aid from eastern banks for national bank notes through their issuance and subsequent deposit of them in the southern and western banks. The West and South became dependent on the East and North, the former borrowing on collateral and delivering joint commercial paper for rediscount in eastern banks. However, many small banks provided with sound assets were unable to make a direct official request on the central city banks for rediscounts. In this way they ended up paying tribute to larger banks for the use of money. This arrangement led to an increasingly expensive system of liquidity maintenance. Interest costs in the South and West were twice those of elsewhere. As large city banks were often short of currency themselves, struggling to meet the 25% cash reserve requirement of the National Banking Act of 1864, they could ill afford to send bank notes to the regions in need.[5]

This regional discrepancy was made more dramatic by the fact that in the 1860s the need for a medium of circulation in the states west and south of New York grew seven times more rapidly than in the East. This was because less populated regions made payments from three to ten times more often with notes than with checks on banks, due to the distance involved in these regions and a lack of convenient bank locations.[6] Lastly, the reintroduction of millions of men into the workforce as producers, formerly operating as soldier-consumers of goods in battle tended to increase the competition for credit. The Southern states also required a replacement for their Confederate currency. The cost for returning soldiers to obtain circulating notes and credit should have been decreased, but in fact increased.

The Lack of Redemption & the Inflexibility of the Currency

Another major problem was that the currency of legal tender and national bank notes became inelastic. Without national bank notes being increased after 1866, their amount remained less than the stock of legal tender notes. Chase and Lincoln had proscribed in 1862 and 1863, that once the National Banking system was established, the proper place of the legal tender notes would be to serve as a lawful money reserve, one used to redeem the national bank notes until the banks had regained sufficient specie reserves. But for legal tender notes to be a reserve, there needed to be fewer legal tenders than national bank notes. Hiland Hulburd, Comptroller of the Currency from 1867-1872, conservatively described this role for legal tenders:

> If the proper mission of legal tenders were fully understood, and the necessity of placing our currency on a permanent basis—either of specie or legal tenders, which stand as the substitute for specie—were properly appreciated, there would be no difficulty in providing for the proper reduction of legal tenders so as to leave room for a very moderate increase of national currency.[7]

Instead, the opposite took place. From 1863 to 1873, there were always more legal tender notes than bank notes. Though they had benefited the country during the Civil War, they became extremely problematic afterward as the combined aggregate of legal tenders and national bank notes became an inflexible and rigid currency.

Legal tenders were inflexible in that they remained in circulation or as deposits in banks and a source for loans by banks, regardless of whether they were needed or not. They were a sum of money permanently available, at times in great excess of need, and at other times in shortage. In 1865 and 1866 Comptroller Freeman Clarke and Deputy Comptroller Hiland Hulburd described the significance of their failure to fluctuate and expand and contract with the normal demand of commercial interests. When business was slow, legal tenders accumulated in the financial centers as excess reserves and were liable to be used for loans to speculative enterprises. Then, when the general business of the country accelerated, a scarcity of currency was often experienced. Given the limitation on the new bank notes, this scarcity was impossible to supply.[8] In comparison with national bank notes, legal tender notes became, ironically, very comparative to specie, since they did not adapt with the seasons of trade, as the promissory notes of banks had previously.

It was not only legal tenders that had this inelastic tendency. The whole currency, both legal tender notes and national bank notes, were incapable of increasing and decreasing as required. Since specie payments had not been resumed for lack of sufficient gold reserves and legal tenders continued to remain larger in amount than national bank notes, the latter were therefore not redeemed, neither in gold nor legal tenders.

As legal tenders were of no greater value, there was no point in redeeming bank notes into them.

In 1865, Clarke proposed that "all the banks be required to redeem their notes in New York, Boston, or Philadelphia," the largest cities in the U.S., and the locations which debts between cities could be extinguished.[9] If there were redemptions in these cities, the large banks could accumulate surplus notes and redeem them. Competition would make it unprofitable for too many banks in the field. Ultimately this proposed redemption law was not passed by Congress.[10]

The Errors of McCulloch and the Congress 1865-1869

A major factor in determining Congress's inaction as to the limitation on national bank notes was the opposition of Treasury Secretary McCulloch. In addition to having had reservations about the formation of new banks, he felt that no new note issues should be authorized until a general resumption of specie payments had taken place.[11]

McCulloch's reasoning was based on a view that the quantity of currency rather than its quality was responsible for prices. Since his priority was reducing prices, McCulloch said the legal tenders should simply be decreased without simultaneously increasing national bank facilities. He argued that by decreasing the currency, prices would decrease, exports would increase, and specie reserves would increase.[12] When specie reserves increased, then, he said, an increase in national banks would be warranted.

This view proved to be in error. Increasing national currency did not require first reducing the legal tenders or waiting until specie payments resumed. Increased exports could be achieved through financial system stability with more local capital formation and less duplication of deposits between regions. More national banks and their notes would stabilize the banking system by making redemptions in legal tenders possible once there were more bank notes than legal tenders in circulation. This would allow currency in circulation to fluctuate with demand. The ability for banks to redeem their notes in specie would have resulted as a consequence of the free establishment of banks where they were needed. By limiting the subscription of capital to new banks, there would be less idle currency and deposits available for speculation. In other words, the absolute amount of the currency was not as important a factor in determining prices as the distribution and interface with legitimate demand. Congress sided with McCulloch and it became the Administration's policy.

In this context, the Treasury's funding of short-term debt, which would not have been a problem, became an issue. When Hugh McCulloch took over the position of Treasury Secretary on March 1865, he set about providing for the principal of the outstanding debt quickly and rapidly converted short-term debt into long-term debt. While U.S. creditors were more interested in the stability of the financial system, McCulloch argued for quick payment of war debts. By December 1867 he had funded into 5-20 bonds most of the short-term debt payable on demand or short notice. This short-term debt included the six month temporary loans, one year certificates of indebtedness, and one to three year Treasury notes bearing interest of 5-6% as well as Treasury notes bearing 7.3%.[13]

Unfortunately, these 5-20 bonds were not used for the incorporation of new banks. The effect of the conversion was to exacerbate the problems created by the national bank shortage in the West and South. This was related to the fact that some of the interest paying Treasury notes were used for circulation in addition to being used as bank reserves for loans. Some banks were therefore forced to contract.[14] In addition, in April 1866, Congress expanded McCulloch's authority for funding interest bearing obligations to include non-interest debt, i.e. legal tenders and demand notes.[15] They were retired at a conservative reduction of $4 million a month. From June of 1866 to November 1867, legal tenders contracted from $400 million to $357 million.

As described in previous pages, by the summer of 1867, the combined shortages of paper currency in the West and South became very acute. Though the economy was expanding, the means of payment had contracted. Interest rates increased and prices fell. The pinch radiated throughout the manufacturing sector. Bills of exchange increased from 5-7% to 8-10% in 1867, and then to 15-20% by 1868. The shortage of money was blamed by many on the policy of contraction of legal tender supply. However, the true culprit was the shortage of overall banking facilities. When Congress met in December 1867, it responded to the crisis by halting the contraction of greenbacks. As debate on a bill passed to halt contraction took place on February 1868, one Congressman remarked, "No further contraction will be made when industry is in a measure paralyzed." Congress generally focused on legal tenders, and failed to address the limit on new bank formation.[16]

Banking Suggestions and the Vote of 1870

The currency issue did not go away and under the Ulysses S. Grant Administration. Comptroller Hiland Hulburd was explicit in setting forth his view that an unlimited expansion of national bank circulation was warranted. He told Congress that the amount of currency should not be theirs to determine but should continually fluctuate with demand. He wrote:

> If Congress limits the amount, there will always be those who will be dissatisfied, and who will seek legislation either for the purposes of contraction or expansion. And so long as the volume of currency depends upon legislative enactment, uncertainty and instability will pervade all financial operations.[17]

There would be no danger of excess bank formation in areas where banking facilities were already established. Excess banks would create a competition for lawful money as reserves, diminishing the amount available and increasing the cost of redemption. Lifting the limit would also provide for western and southern regions then suffering from lack of paper money, and in great need of the facilities provided by banks. He wrote:

> While in other sections destitute in whole or in part of banking facilities for the legitimate demands of business, the necessity for banks and currency would justify the increase of bank circulation, notwithstanding the fact that by such increase the burden of its redemption would also be enhanced.

Hulburd had disagreed with McCulloch's opposition to new banks from 1865-1868. He now argued with greater force that the tendency of the new banks would be to speed up redemption by creating more bank notes than legal tender notes, bringing the value of legal tenders back to par with gold:

> Free banking may thus be established with safety, anterior to specie payments, conditioned only upon the withdrawal and cancellation of a legal tender dollar for every dollar of bank currency issue, free banking may be permitted without delay and with equal safety.

In 1870, Congress eventually did respond to the free banking debate and enacted legislation on the subject.[18] "Open wide the door to the organization of national banks to any extent," said Senator John Sherman, one of the bill's sponsors, provided "an equal amount of greenbacks shall be retired as the new notes are issued." This meant an increase in the authorized national bank currency by $357 million, i.e. the amount of legal tenders outstanding. This would more than double the amount of national bank currency, and belatedly fulfill the Lincoln Administration's original intention. Sherman continued:

> The only limit on it is the amount of greenbacks now outstanding, and when they are exhausted, it will be for Congress to determine whether we shall go further. As bank notes are issued, United States notes will be retired, thus changing the burden of resumption from the U.S. to the banks by their voluntary consent.[19]

However, the original bill for free banking was voted down and a significantly curtailed version was passed. The ostensible reason for the no vote on the original was that it included a provision to exchange the bonds held by the banks with bonds of lower interest, benefiting the government at the expense of the banks. The new circulation authorized for the banks was to be based on these new bonds. This proposal was an unnecessary penalty on would-be banking corporations in terms of their right to circulate bank notes on deposited bonds. The banks opposed it and influenced many in Congress to vote against the bill. Had the banks supported the original bill it would have likely have led to more profit than was lost. Instead of free banking, the final Act of July 1870 allowed for an increase of only $54 million national bank notes, and a withdrawal of $25 million notes from eastern banks to be distributed to new western banks. The 1870 increase led to the formation of 145 new banks by 1871, providing some relief in western and southern states, but none for eastern and middle states.[20]

The blunder of 1870 was an anticlimactic end to a long struggle on the issue, and would prove fatal for the national banking currency. By the time free banking was finally authorized in 1875, a combination of other issues, addressed in the subsequent chapters, resulted in the national bank currency declining rather than expanding.

Chapter 16
Speculation and the Crisis of 1873

A growing issue for the Grant Administration was speculation using bank reserves along with the increasing cost of obtaining a reliable means of payment. The National Banking Act of 1864 designated seventeen cities as financial centers. In these locations national bank associations were required to hold 25% lawful money reserves against their total notes and deposits. National banks in these cities could deposit up to half of these reserves in national banks located in New York City. National banks outside of these seventeen cities had reserve requirements of 15% and were permitted to deposit three-fifths of those in a national bank located in one of the financial centers.

As depositories of the reserves of country banks, the financial center banks accumulated more reserves than they could employ in their normal business. They often lent the excess reserves out for speculative investment purposes. This money was more often than not demanded when money became tight, commonly at harvest time or when prices fell and credit was in high demand. During these periods competition for these deposits also rose. Banks in the financial centers began offering interest on deposits to induce country banks to select them. The bidding up of interest necessitated reinvestment with riskier investments in order to make sufficient profit to pay the higher deposit rates. Anticipation of tight money periods led many banks in the country to lend their excess reserves temporarily rather than invest their excess reserves in capital. When business was dull they would lend their money to eastern city banks as a way of making interim profits. Since few had use for short-term money of this kind, the New York banks would in turn lend it to investors or stockbrokers at low rates of interest. The deposits lent out for speculation were then unavailable in times of stress, and when country banks made simultaneous demands for their deposits panic would break out at city banks.[1]

During this period fluctuations in business activity often generated financial difficulty for the banks due to their inability to supply their debtors and communities with sufficient cash when required. Without the ability to create notes or a central institution devoted to the purpose, banks were unable to turn their liquid assets into a means of payment when most needed. The result was an unstable basis for the banking system, which could easily be pushed to a breaking point when unanticipated factors intervened.

To address these problems, Comptroller Hulburd proposed in 1868 that a clearinghouse agency should be established that would ensure redemptions of excess notes and centralize reserves. The central redeeming agency would prevent the reserves from being lent out to speculators and stockbrokers. It was to be a reservoir that would distribute reserves wherever they were needed for domestic exchange, facilitating debt settlements between cities. This agency would redeem national bank notes in gold. These measures would make the currency better able to contract and expand in response to supply and demand. However, only the redemption component of this agency would be established and not till much later.[2]

Reviewing the assets and liabilities of the national banks from October 1866 to October 1873, it can be seen that loans on deposits increased in an unstable fashion. While the capital to deposits ratio stayed roughly the same, loans on deposits increased from $323 million in 1866 to $605 million in 1873, an increase of 87%. At the same time the deposits themselves increased from $564 million to $622 million, an increase of only 10%. In the same period, the capital stock of the national banks increased marginally from $415 to $491 million. As these figures show, the growing tendency was to lend the same deposit multiple times across various regions of the country. The law prohibiting the formation of new banks was a factor in this, as more loans based on new bank capital would have been possible. The consequent inflation was a burden on the rest of the economy. In addition, the increase in loans and deposits increased the required reserves of the banks, tying up even more of the circulating medium of national bank notes and legal tenders. Currency was therefore taken out of circulation and shifted away from needed investment while inadvertently supporting speculative investment activity.[3]

1871 Recommendation from the Comptroller

In 1871, Comptroller Hulburd recommended more drastic proposals towards reducing speculative activities and to provide security for the financial system to foster steady growth. First he called for "the extension of the national banking system wherever capital and trade may invite, withdrawing, if it should seem desirable, United States notes, as fast as bank notes are issued." Redemption would soon be possible under this plan, and its cost would be a check on the issues of the banks. Every hundred thousand dollars of bank notes issued would accelerate resumption of specie payments in a gradual process. The small savings in the western and southern regions that lacked banks would be pooled together in new banks to provide a much needed means of payment.[4]

This time, Hulburd addressed the underlying assumption that had originated under Hugh McCulloch: that free banking was not safe unless all banks had resumed paying specie on demand. He explained the difference between the solvency of banks and the convertibility of paper into coin:

> Ultimate solvency is of far greater importance to the community than convertibility, and the liberal and judicious use of credit is of far more value in the commercial world than the instant command of gold and silver.[5]

As long as banks were solvent (the condition of assets exceeding liabilities), commerce would be supported through bank credit. By insisting on the convertibility into gold and silver at the expense of an adequate number of safe institutions, banks had in fact become insolvent by over extending themselves to meet demand. On the other hand, if the solvency of banks were well provided for and the banking system was allowed to grow of its own accord, whether or not all notes were at par with specie, convertibility could be expected to take care of itself.[6]

Hulburd was adamant that the banking system needed to grow before waiting for the time when banks had accumulated specie reserves. For this purpose, he recommended a means to accomplish both, mainly by limiting specie conversion of bank notes only but not deposits. National currency would be redeemed by national banks in legal tender or coin, but deposits adjusted by private contract. For their deposit customers, banks would only pay in the same kind of money deposited, or "current funds" as Hulburd put it. If this were done, he said, "it would be practicable to place the currency on a specie basis long before it would be possible to place the entire demand liabilities of the banks on a similar footing." He continued:

> If specie payments are to be resumed, let the effort be concentrated upon the currency, and leave deposits and all other currency debts to be adjusted by private contract. As the first step in this direction, the Associated banks in all cities should be required to settle balances through their clearing-houses, in current funds.[7]

As it was, the obligation to pay specie on deposits only came up during crisis, when the system was least able to meet the demand. If banks were authorized by law to settle their deposit balances through clearing houses in the same type of funds they received, it would facilitate resumption of specie payments, satisfying those requiring specie payments before authorizing new bank notes. This would remove the larger risk within the banking system. In New York, for example, it would have been easy to provide for the redemption of $34 million bank notes. But according to the established practice, to provide specie on demand meant provision for over $200 million deposits. "It is this practice," he wrote, "which renders the finances of the country so unsteady and unreliable, to wit, the false principles which underlie the financial management of the money centers." The check and regularity provided by a currency at par should not have been made to depend on a few major large banks, with large deposit businesses. He added:

> To the people the establishment of the currency on a sound and solvent basis is the one important thing, it makes no difference to them whether depositors in the large cities are entitled to receive specie for deposits made in currency.[8]

Further, Hulburd noted that in the period of 1866 to 1871, though there had been no major crises, the banking system had "more than once been on the verge of a panic which threatened the most disastrous consequences." On "three occasions," he wrote, had New York banks been forced to pay specie on their deposits, they would have had to suspend withdrawals. This despite the fact that the rest of the country could have maintained specie payments for the amount they required. For those who understood banking and the needs of business, the clear fact was that these deposit businesses in the major money centers were almost never made in specie. Their businesses consisted of one large balancing act of payments on credit. It was therefore all the more untenable that a requirement of specie reserves for the large banks should prevent the rest of the banking system from possessing a measure of flexibility. Hulburd was harsh, knowing the consequences of maintaining the status quo in this regard:

> If any substantial interest were sacrificed, or any valuable principle violated, by the abandonment of this dogma, there might be some reason for taking the risk; but if deposits could be made payable in kind, that is, in current funds, lawful money, or gold, as the case might be, the depositor could have no just ground of complaint, while one great obstacle to the resumption and maintenance of specie payments would be removed.[9]

Hulburd's suggestions were not implemented. The failure to respond to these issues between 1865 and 1871 by comptrollers and others led to a building pressure. Ultimately the crash of 1873 can be traced to this inaction. While the impetus for events in 1873 was a steep drop in bond prices, the problems were systemic and simply waiting for an event to trigger a crisis. The financial system was then based on multiplied bank deposits rather than a more diverse capital base. A financial panic commenced in 1873 with the failure of the Jay Cooke and Co. His associated banks fell victim to the collapse of several major railroads they were financing. Distrust of the banks led to withdrawal by depositors. Suddenly similar demand broke out at country banks putting pressure on their reserves. The on-call loans that they relied upon were unavailable. Collaterals shrank and financial center banks were unable to provide relief. Between September and December 1873 deposits fell from $622 million to just $540 million.[10]

In the middle of the crisis, New York banks authorized the issue of clearinghouse loan certificates to any member upon its "bills receivable" and other good assets. These took the place of cash in the settlement between banks and were essentially a loan of the credit of the association to the banks. These were effective, and within two months confidence was restored to the banks. The economy however did not recover and would not do so until the end of the decade. The use of clearinghouse loan certificates became a general practice in subsequent crises.[11]

Chapter 17
Partisan Wrangling and the Decline of National Bank Circulation

In the year after the crash of 1873, some in Congress belatedly spearheaded a move for free banking. They introduced a bill calling for the repeal of all laws limiting the aggregate amount of national bank circulation as well as the complicated laws for the redistribution of circulation from east to west. In their place, the bill authorized unlimited issue of circulation to banks organized under the national banking law. It added a conservative retirement of legal tender notes to the amount equal to eighty per cent of the additional national bank notes issued. The bill proposed a single unified and flexible paper currency with a broad capital base, distributed according to the economic demand of each region. This Act passed on January 14, 1875.[1]

But the free banking Act for the National Banking System did not live up to its promises, as the measure required an accompanied action that was not taken. A sufficient premium on the U.S. bonds that national banks held, or would purchase for their new circulation, was not adequately taken into consideration. The value of U.S. bonds had increased significantly due to a funding plan of the Grant Administration, but the national banks were not allowed to issue a value of notes equal to the effective market value of their bonds holdings. In other words, as with the original National Banking Acts of 1863 and 1864, the banks still could only issue notes in an amount equal to 90% of the value of their deposited bonds in the treasury. This was the case even if the bonds were worth $115 in 1875. The total premium on the $360 million in bonds the banks then held was estimated to be $64 million. The value of the notes they issued at 90% was $325 million. Therefore, in November of 1875, with the bonds plus premium worth $425 million, the banks would experience a loss of over $100 million on their asset value. Unless Congress increased the amount of notes the banks could issue to the market price value of their bonds, the banks were incented to sell their bond holdings into the market rather than retain them to create bank circulation. Instead of securing a sound currency for the nation, party politics and populist opposition to national banks led Congress to take a hard line on valuation, rendering the Act ineffective.[2]

The banks began to deposit legal tender notes in the Treasury to claim and sell their bonds. A previous act in 1874 had made it easy for them to reclaim their bonds for sale, as a redemption agency had been established at the Treasury allowing banks to withdraw their bonds and retire their notes, provided they deposited legal tender notes in their stead. The potential profits to be made by selling their bonds increased as the government's funding plan continued and bond premiums increased further. More and more national bank notes were taken out of circulation. By November 1876, the cumulative new note authorizations and retirements resulted in a net decrease of $30 million of national bank notes. The total amount of national bank notes outstanding was by then $292 million. Meanwhile, the stagnation of business continued and was reflected in currency held by the banks in the principal cities, where reserves increased to 33%.[3]

In effect, the bond premium issue nullified the long anticipated arrival of free banking. The real profit to be made on bank circulation after accounting for the difference in the value of the bonds was not enough to attract sufficient capital in national bank stock. By 1879 the profit fell to 1.3% on the invested bonds. The number of national banks actually declined from 2,086 to 2,052 banks from 1875 to 1879. In 1879 there were 1,005 state banks and 2,600 private banks, numbers reflective of the fact that banking had become more profitable outside the national banking system.[4] The lack of profit on circulation also forced national banks into more risky activities with their deposits in an effort to make up for the lost profit.

The failure to increase circulation for banks on their bonds reflected an anti-bank ferment that increased during 1874 and 1875 in the wake of the crash of 1873. The causes of the speculative build-up and over extension were not adequately addressed. After 1875, banking reform fell to financial debates dominated by partisan disputes and abstract notions. Movements for greenbacks and silver along with arguments regarding specie redemption formed the bulk of the discussion with respect to the financial system. Little was discussed with respect to methods for improving and strengthening the National Banking Acts.

Specie Resumption Debate

The Specie Resumption Act was passed in 1875, setting 1879 as the period when banks would be compelled to redeem national bank notes and legal tenders for gold. It was true that specie redemptions of deposits were a major weakness of the design of the banking system, and should have been remedied. However, specie demands during normal times were not a threat to the stability of the financial system, as specie was not utilized or demanded save during crisis and for foreign trade. Many opponents of specie resumption argued that banks would contract as people rushed to redeem their currency in gold.

In 1877, then Representative James Garfield presented facts to allay concerns, showing a report he had requested from Comptroller Hulburd in 1871 as Chairman of the Committee on Banking and Currency. The report showed what had become increasingly true since the 1850s as cities became more populated. Of all bank payments, only 12% were received in cash, i.e., specie and bank notes, while 88% of payments were received in checks, drafts, and commercial bills.[5] Comptroller Knox provided his own figures to make the same point:

> Deposits consist chiefly of bank credits and are derived largely from the discount of commercial paper, and are paid mainly by transfers on the books--not with either coin or currency. Throughout the country all large payments are made, not with money, but with checks. In the principal cities these payments are accomplished by the operations of clearing houses.[6]

Knox went on to state that from 1854-1878, $454 billion in payments were made on credit and less than $19 billion with money. The average daily exchanges made by bank balances were $61 million while only $2.5 million were made with bank notes and lawful money, or four cents to every dollar. The holders "had not lost one dollar through the use of bank notes," he wrote, and therefore they were not at risk of suddenly declining to receive bank notes and instead demand gold.[7]

A number of factors had also helped to prepare the Treasury and banking system for the belated resumption of specie payments. Agricultural output had accelerated between 1875 and 1879, bringing the balance of trade in favor of the U.S. It was $79 million in 1876, $150 million in 1877,

$257 million in 1878, and $294 million in 1879.[8] In addition, the Treasury became a member of the New York clearing house association in 1878, resuming relations with banks for select payment purposes. They were no longer solely reliant on the Independent Treasury method of receiving and paying in specie. Banks agreed to receive U.S. notes for their ordinary balances, as well as in the payment of interest upon the public debt and other obligations officially receivable in coin. When the time came for resumption in 1879 there was no sudden demand for gold and few withdrew more than needed for commerce, nor did the banks present legal tenders to the Treasury for redemption. As for the national bank notes, people preferred the notes to coin, just as holders of legal tender had found that medium of exchange more convenient. Specie resumption for deposits was a liability during crisis, but not so during normal operations.

The Legal Tender Movement

In 1876, a movement for government currency became very prominent. Many saw the benefits of the legal tender paper currency so great that they urged the government to become the source of circulating notes. These groups began to promote government currency not merely as a war-time solution but as a replacement for banking. The movement's proponents made arguments that were quite similar to those of President Martin Van Buren, speaking of "the duty of effecting an utter and final divorcement between the government and the banks."[9]

President Andrew Johnson's Treasury official and economist William Elder pointed out that the consequence of abolishing the National Banking Acts would be to return the control of the nation's currency to the state banks, as in the 1810s, and the 1840s through the 1850s. The necessity of banks to provide discounts for commerce would remain, and the replacement of national bank notes with legal tender notes would simply mean a currency of legal tender notes issued by state banks. There would be less security to the notes and convertibility would no longer be assured. The alternative, wrote Elder, would be if the government attempted to become the lender of all the needed currency of the country. But if the government attempted to supplant all of the banks and determine the exact amount of currency needed, it would require an unmanageable institutional presence. The best form of currency and credit had been proven to be one reflective of the exchange of products and industry and which came into existence equal to this demand. Determining this demand was the purpose and function of local banks.[10]

Chapter 18
National Bank Difficulties and Financial Crisis 1879-1907

In 1879, Comptroller of the Currency John J. Knox made a number of familiar proposals to improve the national banking system. He said the system was worth improving, as it gave protection to depositors, had safe and unimpaired capital, a large surplus, cash reserves, and had secured circulation. He proposed substituting legal tender notes with national bank notes and other legislation to restore profitability to national bank circulation. He proposed laws to modify regulations on bank notes so the banks could furnish the required money of the country and to account for the problems of having the currency issues depend solely upon U.S. bonds.

Just as Hulburd had warned prior to the crash of 1873, Knox expressed concern about the rigidity of the system and the inability of credit to expand and contract with demand. Since legal tenders were the dominant currency, they would accumulate during dull times and lead to speculative activities. When the business economy would then pick up legal tenders were often tied up in speculation, leading to shortages of credit. The limitation of national bank notes made it impossible for them to expand credit availability in such circumstances. To break this cycle he proposed increasing the gold reserve so that legal tenders would be redeemed in economic slowdowns, rather than to support speculation. Though a gold reserve for this purpose would be at first expensive, having an elastic currency would be cheaper in the long run. But instead of regulation that would have allowed for an increase in the circulation of notes of national banks, the opposite occurred.

In the 1880s, the growth of government surplus led the Treasury to pay off $1 billion of its outstanding bonds, raising their price to a sustained premium of around 25% on average. National banks continued to sell the bonds that secured their circulation throughout the decade as their sale became more and more profitable. From 1878 to 1892, national bank circulation fell from $303 million to $146 million.[1] The high premium on government bonds was certainly a leading cause for the reduction of national bank notes, but it would not have been so rapid were it not for the government's policy with regard to silver and silver backed treasury notes. A movement for silver coinage had begun after the Specie Resumption Act of 1875. In 1878 the Treasury was directed by Congress in the Bland-Allison Act to purchase and coin silver at $2-4 million a month. Silver certificates began to fill the place of national bank currency. Then, in 1890, Congress authorized an additional paper money, called "Treasury notes," in the Sherman Silver Purchase Act. By 1892, there were $325 million silver certificates and $116 million Treasury notes in circulation, an increase of $450 million.[2] National bank currency was edged out by government currency. Despite this, the number of national banks continued to grow during the 1890's, by making up for lost profit in currency with profit in discounting deposit credit in checking accounts, similar to what state banks had done at the end of the 1860s.

The 1880s also saw the worst defects of the Independent Treasury system brought forward by large surpluses in the Treasury. Payments into the subtreasuries by banks on behalf of taxpayers resulted in a withdrawal for the same amount from their reserves, since lawful money was being transferred from the banks. This led to a decrease in loanable funds in the proportion of their reserves to liabilities. At that time this meant roughly $6 of decreased liabilities for every $1 taken from their reserves being paid into the Treasury. To avoid this effect, national banks were allowed to retain the money to be paid to the government on deposit instead, provided they purchase U.S. bonds for the same amount and deposit them in the Treasury as security for the government deposits.[3] However, this attempt to mitigate the direct reduction of loanable funds reduced the total amount of U.S. bonds outstanding for national banks to purchase for their circulation. This reduction in turn negatively impacted liquidity in bank notes.

In 1884, a panic took place driven by commercial failures. In 1890, a much larger crisis resulted from the dependency of the financial system on foreign capital and its exposure to foreign crisis. Foreign money had fueled a rapid expansion of western agricultural production, new railroads, and recapitalization of U.S. manufacturing. A movement of capital to the western states deprived eastern states of loanable funds for their own manufacturing when capital migrated west into speculative real estate. In the summer of 1890, banks in the West were caught unduly extended when a financial crisis in Europe cut off the money supply. In addition, a sell off of U.S. securities held by foreigners resulted in a withdrawal of gold from U.S. banks. Gold demand in New York and other large reserve cities rapidly increased. From February to May, 46 national banks in New York suffered a loss of deposits amounting to $44 million.[4]

In 1893, one of the worst financial crises took place in U.S. history. This time it was caused by the enormous inelasticity of government currency, and the similarly fixed amount of national bank currency. The volume of government currency had become so large that the Treasury was almost the sole source of paper currency. In April of 1893, the ability of the government to maintain gold payments to redeem its paper came into doubt, and depositors began to withdraw their deposits. Banks had to call in loans and discounts under the force of these withdrawals in 1893. Withdrawals led to a shrinkage of deposit liabilities from $1.8 billion to $1.5 billion in a few months, making it difficult for banks to extend loans to their wholesale customers. During the panic national bank notes were difficult to secure. The financial machinery became dysfunctional and business slowed to a halt while 158 national banks failed.[5]

As was the case in 1873, again in 1893 the associated banks in the major money centers issued interest bearing clearinghouse loan certificates to settle clearing house balances and prevent the banking system from freezing up. They were issued to any member of the association, "on the deposit of bills receivable and other securities." They provided banks relief and facilitated the inter-bank settlement of balances resulting from daily exchanges.[6]

In each of these crises, in addition to the usual pattern of country bank demands for their reserves that had been lent out by city banks, an increasingly significant factor was the growing tendency of national and state banks to invest their assets in investment securities. In the 1820s and 1830s, the involvement of state banks and the Bank of the United States in long-term investments had been key to the growth of roads and canals. Savings banks also developed during this time. In the 1840s and 1850s, eastern banks began employing the balances of unused funds from their financing of western agriculture in longer-term investment. The National Banking Act of 1864 did not address the involvement of banks in investment operations or how much of their short-term funds could be used in the purchase of long-term securities and bonds. Its aim was a uniform currency with security for general commercial operations. As a consequence, the state and national banking systems developed after 1864 were generally free of limitations on their engagement in investment banking. National bank support for investment was important but it was not adequately regulated, and uneven maturities of liabilities and assets became a problem. After 1875, stock savings banks and private investment banking houses became somewhat more formalized, and loan and trust companies developed after 1884. Investment banking developed a tendency to divert funds of commercial banks into speculative causes, but the use of commercial funds to support the investment market did not become recognized as a problem until about 1885. By the middle of the 1890s, large industrial consolidations brought the investment banking sector to prominence and the issue began to impact the entire financial system.[7]

After the crisis of 1893, when the Cleveland Administration attempted to make bonds available for national banks to secure circulation, long delays in implementation brought the ineffectiveness of the system to light. A number of experts came up with ideas for security behind national bank notes other than U.S. bonds, subsequently referred to as the "Baltimore Plan." Many experts discussed the need for a more elastic currency that came into existence based on commercial paper rather than being limited by bonds, one that could more quickly respond to financial pressures.[8]

In the campaign of 1896, discussion of bank currency reform became secondary to debates on bimetallism and deflating debt, particularly for farmers. After the election of William McKinley, Congress focused on securing gold standard legislation along with modest changes to the National Banking Acts. In 1900 the Gold Standard Act made gold the standard of payment rather than silver, and provided for a minimum gold reserve in the Treasury of $150 million for legal tender notes, among other considerations. The Act also provided for a number of legislative changes to banking arrangements in order to facilitate the creation of national bank note currency. Outstanding bonds were refunded into 2% bonds for new national bank currency, the minimum capital for new banks was lowered by 50% from $50,000 to $25,000, and the proportion of national bank circulation allowed on deposited bonds was finally increased from 90% to 100% of their value. The removal of the restrictions led to rapid growth in national bank note circulation and the number of national banks. By 1905 there were 5,528 national banks. Nearly 2,400 national banks with capital less than the previous minimum had joined by 1907. Many state banks converted to national bank status. National bank note circulation grew from $332 million in 1900 to $666 million in 1908.[9]

The Crisis of 1907

At the end of the 1890s, the Treasury had begun to develop a surplus, which grew large after 1900. When taxes were withdrawn from the banks into the subtreasuries, the withdrawals limited bank accommodation. As in the 1880s, the Treasury opted instead to use the national banks as depositor banks, increasing their number to 1,400 by 1904. But as the Independent Treasury laws required the banks to purchase and deposit bonds in the Treasury in order to secure government deposits, the result was that by 1906 and 1907 all of the 2% bonds authorized in 1900 had been absorbed and deposited in the Treasury, either to secure notes or protect public deposits.

Since it was not the practice of Congress and the Treasury to authorize bonds for national banks during surplus periods, the national banking system was once again trapped within legislative limits instead of those determined by economic demand and capital supply. As the limit on 2% bonds to secure deposits was reached, and no further surplus could be deposited in the national banks, the excess surplus from taxation was transferred from the banks to the subtreasuries, reducing the volume of credit in the economy. Despite its surplus condition, the Treasury then broke standard protocol and borrowed for the Panama Canal in order to supply new bonds for the banks as a basis for note issues, switching the new bonds for those securing existing government deposits. However, this measure was not sufficient to relieve the credit shortage.

By the beginning of 1907 banks were experiencing a liquidity shortage. Banks had a surplus of illiquid and speculative credits on their books.[10] Banks had lent all they could and had bought all the bonds they were authorized to purchase. There was no federal institution to loosen the reserve requirements or discount assets to generate liquidity and the Treasury was unable to relieve the banks through deposit of the surplus as nearly all of the bonds had been used against existing government deposits. The expansion of national bank note currency to meet the expanded liquidity needs was not possible. Circumstances deteriorated rapidly.[11]

As in previous bank crises, clearing house loan certificates were utilized. Treasury Secretary George Cortelyou and Comptroller William Ridgely took action to enlarge the volume of bonds for new national bank notes by ruling that other securities could release the bonds for the purpose of new notes. However, as banking expert, H. Parker Willis later wrote, "the assistance came too late to do very much good," and the general inability to increase national bank circulation in the crises led to another economic depression in the aftermath of financial crisis. The financial system was not organized to unwind the dangerous elements of financial investment while maintaining growth and stability. The economic depression that followed was widespread.[12]

Part VI

The Federal Reserve and the Credit Modifications of the 1930s-1940s

Overview

After the crash of 1907, decades of discussion regarding fundamental oversights of the National Banking System came to the fore, leading to the Federal Reserve Act of 1913. Its new centralized reserve requirements for banks belatedly acknowledged the domination of bank credit over the use of cash. The Independent Treasury System was overturned, artificial restrictions on note creation for liquidity purposes were removed, and the Reserve Banks were given centralized credit control powers to supervise the money markets.

The dominant theory underlying the original Federal Reserve Act favored an automatic reaction to the market rather than the use of discretionary powers. This aspect of the Act, combined with large government borrowing for World War I, led to an institutionalized system of discounting promissory notes of member banks backed by government bonds for the purpose of providing long-term credit as well as security investments. In the stock market boom of the 1920s this technical discounting requirement facilitated excesses. In this regard the Act did not succeed in fulfilling previous hopes of creating appropriate monetary tools necessary to control periods of rapid speculation.

After the crash of 1929, the portfolios of most banks were filled with assets that had lost substantial value. However, many banks still had a large amount of loans on their books made to sound enterprises. Due to the discount provisions of the Federal Reserve Act, most of these assets, of both short and intermediate maturities, were not acceptable for rediscounting at the Fed.

As the rate of bank failures increased and the depression worsened, this issue became widely debated in the early 1930's. Congressional action was taken in February of 1932. The question of which assets should be given liquidity support by the Fed became one of increasing legislative initiatives during the period of 1932-1950. A number of approaches were explored with varying degrees of success.

In 1932, the first action was to expand the types of assets the Fed could rediscount for member banks. This was largely unsuccessful due to a combination of economic conditions and its limited nature. The second action in the spring of 1933 liberalized the legislation of 1932 and was moderately successful. However, neither was sufficient to create a widespread change in the pattern of bank lending. The types of loans that industries and businesses needed for the economy in order to emerge from the Great Depression were called into question. Institutional studies on the subject concluded that the types of loans most needed were for intermediate duration credit and working capital.

This led to inter-agency discussion between January and March of 1934 to create a parallel bank structure within the Federal Reserve districts that would be devoted to the purpose of providing intermediate credit for industry, directly and jointly with member banks. This plan led to additional discount and loan powers for the Federal Reserve banks and the Reconstruction Finance Corporation. Debated in 1935 were more general modifications to Section 13 of the Federal Reserve Act that would allow for Federal Reserve Board discretion in determining which types and maturities of assets were safe to rediscount.

After the recession of 1937, the need to increase bank loans for small and medium sized businesses became a continued subject of legislation. Numerous bills were put forward in 1938 and 1939 to improve the ability for banks to employ their excess reserves and surplus toward purposes not technically eligible for rediscount at the Federal Reserve. During World War II the Federal Reserve and the Reconstruction Finance Corporation issued loan guarantees and made direct loans. After the war a number of proposals came forth to retain the successful aspects of the Federal Reserve's loan guarantees for working capital and intermediate credit and to improve the previous amendments to Section 13 put in place since 1932.

Chapter 19
The Federal Reserve System and its Beginnings

Experts and scholars had been considering the systemic problems within the banking system since the 1880s and earlier (as reviewed in Part V). The financial crises of 1907 provided an opportunity for these ideas and discussions to take center stage.

The system had failed during periods of weak reserves, tight or loose credit, and inadequate currency availability. A consensus emerged among policy makers and scholars that the severity of the financial crises during the previous decades was due to the inability of the national banking system to provide liquidity in deposits or currency in times of crisis. The existing system could not support normal growth of commerce due to an outdated and decentralized reserve structure and an inefficient Treasury. While a last attempt was made in 1908 to salvage the national banking system by addressing note currency with the stopgap Vreeland-Aldrich Act, a complete overhaul of the banking system had become unavoidable, culminating in the Federal Reserve Act of 1913.[1]

A major factor in the severity of previous bank crises was a lack of a satisfactory reserves in the system from which banks could augment their own.[2] This had led them to repeatedly raise interest rates during periods when credit was needed, or worse cease making loans while suspending payments. Liquidity needed to be maintained to prevent the perpetuation of crises due to structural inadequacies. As historian H. Parker Willis put it:

> The reserve system planned to obviate these old fashioned panics by permitting the banks at such times to transfer their best assets to reserve institutions, thus getting into a position where they could make additional advances of credit without forcing rates up to ruinous levels.[3]

Under the 1913 Act, national banks subscribed to the capital stock of a Federal Reserve Bank with 6% of their capital and surplus. Once banks became stockholding members of the Federal Reserve, they operated under a new set of reserve requirements. Unlike the National Banking Act's requirement of gold and legal tender reserves, the reserves of the Federal Reserve banks acknowledged modern banking methods. While the national banking system was formed under the assumptions of the 1850s and focused on controlling the issue of currency, the Federal Reserve Act was formed under the understanding of the primacy of bank credit and its impact on credit supply.[4]

Since the 1840s and 1850s, as cities became more densely populated, the preferred means of payment by commerce and industry had increasingly become checks and bills of exchange, transferred by means of bank deposits. The main function of banks had long been that of dealing in credits for their customers and not accumulating and lending out money. By the 1890's over 80% of all business was carried using credit instruments.[5] It was only rational that reserves should consist of the same type of assets in which banks mainly dealt. Therefore, demand credit, the deposits of banks, originated largely in the discount of commercial paper and securities & loans, became the basis for their reserves.[6]

Member banks were required to transfer a portion of these deposits to Federal Reserve banks. The National Banking Act of 1864 required lawful money reserves of 25% for banks in financial centers and 15% for country banks. The Federal Reserve Act required member banks in central reserve cities to maintain 18% of their deposits with a Federal Reserve bank, this amount being 15% in reserve cities, and 12% in country banks. These amounts were later modified to 13%, 10%, and 7% respectively.[7]

With these reserves having been established the reserve banks could rediscount commercial paper and U.S. securities in order to create currency. It was hoped that the creation of currency would therefore be more elastic than the bond secured currency of 1864-1913, and fluctuate with economic demand. National bank notes were replaced with Federal Reserve notes. These were issued by the reserve banks and secured by commercial paper and gold. There was no artificial limit placed on the note currency beside economic demand and need for adjustment of the country's gold supply with that of other nations.[8]

The theory was that by discounting commercial paper, the rate would then become determined by the needs and demands of commerce. Banks would be able to obtain a liquid means of payment for their liquid assets.

When banks needed to lend more, they could raise their reserves by bringing eligible assets to the Fed for discount, rather than contract or raise rates as in the past.

Under this structure, the Federal Reserve banks could ease or restrict credit for the banks of the country in three main ways: first, by changing the discount rate, thereby increasing or decreasing the cost of credit for member banks; second, by changing reserve requirements, thereby expanding or contracting the amount of loans and discounts which member bank could make; and third, by open market operations, buying securities of the U.S. government and other securities, thereby increasing or decreasing the total amount of assets held in the reserve banks and credited to the banks. These open market operations would also influence the discount rate, and amount of loanable funds.

The Federal Reserve Act replaced the archaic Independent Treasury system that had been based on cash transfers from banks with a modern system of deposit credit. Reserve banks were designated as legal depositories for federal funds and did away with the subtreasury system founded under Presidents Martin Van Buren, John Tyler, and James Polk. The government became a depositor with the Federal Reserve banks and could receive and make payments along with the rest of the country. For the first time since 1836, taxes, duties, and public dues were paid in bank credit. The collection of taxes was no longer impacting the supply of credit to the economy. Checks of taxpayers were deposited in the Fed, resulting in the transfer of credit from the accounts of depositors to the government. Underlying reserves were no longer disturbed, and the sudden expansions and contractions of bank liabilities was eliminated. Due to entrenched interests in the subtreasury system that by then had become a bureaucracy, these entities sought to maintain profitable control over the nation's funds, and subtreasuries were not fully abandoned until 1920.[9]

Other important changes were check clearing provisions for parity of exchange among banks and the ability to prevent the exportation of gold.[10] Each of these was an important cost saving element that improved upon costly money brokers that existed when trust of bank paper over greater distances did not exist.

The Act's Original Commercial Preference

According to historian H. Parker Willis, a central motivation of the Federal Reserve Act in the wake of the 1907 crash was a means to not only prevent crisis, but to protect the commercial banking system from speculation while creating more facilities for ordinary business. He wrote:

> The Federal Reserve Act had been adopted in an effort to maintain the self-dependence of the commercial banking structure of the United States, and to avoid the absorption of too large a proportion of commercial bank's funds in connection with speculation."[11]

This purpose, wrote Willis, guided the action to lower the quantity of reserves and the formulation of its original rediscounting features. The lowering of reserve requirements from the levels that existed under the National Banking Act, he wrote, was an attempt at "dividing the then existing fluid funds of the community between commercial and investment banking." Apparently, with these additional funds, it was thought that the investment banks would be left to themselves, and the reduction would quell the fears of certain banking interests that central banking was going to "prevent diversion of funds into investment banking channels." After this provision of funds was made, the rediscounting provision was then explicitly written to serve only commercial operations.[12] The Federal Reserve Act stated that no such paper was to be discounted, "covering merely investments or issued or drawn for the purpose of carrying or trading in stocks, bonds, or other investment securities, except bonds and notes of the government of the U.S."

This same line of thinking was expressed in the statement of Representative Carter Glass, when announcing the bill drafted by the House of Representatives on September 9, 1913. He emphasized that it would create a joint mechanism "for extension of credit to banks with sound assets who desired to liquidate them for meeting legitimate commercial, agricultural, and industrial demands."[13] According to this view, its main functions were to head the money market and reduce the cost for business arising from an inefficient banking system. It was to have little relation with investment bankers and the capital market, and be limited to maintaining liquidity, protecting commercial banks, supervising the development of specie reserves, and conserving the assets and liquidity of institutions involved in commerce.[14] Intentions existed prior to 1929 of separating commercial and investment banking.

In summary, the Federal Reserve Act of 1913 addressed banking issues that had been ignored in the National Banking Act, revived powers that had not been employed on a national scale since the second Bank of the United States, and brought the U.S. banking system up to what were then modern standards. While it shared many of the technical credit controls and fiscal functions of the second Bank of the U.S., the Federal Reserve System possessed much less discretionary power over loans and discounts. Many of the original features required years to implement as both political and moneyed interests initially opposed them. Other elements were abandoned, modified, or amended in subsequent legislation.

WWI and the 1920s

In the first years of the Fed, the slack initially provided by the lowered reserve requirements made its rediscounting features largely dormant. Member banks required no assistance in order to lend all they desired. The Fed was therefore unable to set the discount rate. By the time this slack was used up in 1917, government borrowing for World War I had begun in earnest. This borrowing became the determining factor for interest rates, as the Fed would rediscount government bonds purchased by member banks needed to correspond to the rate on the bonds. This rate was set at 3.5%.

Beginning in 1918, bonds issued by the government were purchased by the member banks and subsequently rediscounted at the Fed. "Soon after the opening of the war," wrote H. Parker Willis in 1922, "it seemed that the portfolios of reserve banks might come to consist almost entirely of so called war paper." The Fed could not distinguish whether the proceeds of its rediscounts of government bonds for the member banks were going toward the purchase of more bonds to support the war effort or toward investment securities and other longer-term loans that did not strictly meet the eligibility requirements of commercial paper.[15]

In 1916, the Fed gave assent to allow member banks to borrow from the Fed "upon their own direct notes with eligible paper used as collateral instead of discounting the paper in the usual way." Since U.S. bonds were among the eligible paper there was a large increase in the use of member bank obligations, secured with government bonds as collateral. This procedure became the standard method for member banks to receive credit by the end of the war. After the war, with $27 billion in U.S. bonds outstanding and widely distributed throughout the bank networks, reserve banks were under pressure to continue discounting the promissory notes of member banks based on government bonds, regardless of the purpose of the loan.[16] During the war liquidity in the financial system was based on the support of the government in purchasing and holding government bonds. Now the Fed became a dealer in government bonds and advanced funds to member banks for any purpose they desired, provided they were secured by government obligations.[17]

The original theories of elastic currency and a system defined by the needs of commerce were not being utilized in practice. Federal reserve notes and reserve credit was based on government securities and increasingly being utilized for longer-term investments, not short-term commercial financing.

From 1920-1929 member banks were operating based on interaction developed during wartime with respect to their loan portfolios. At the same time, investment banking and stock exchanges had grown significantly since the 1890s to serve the expanded industrial sector that came to prominence during World War I.[18] Stock market speculation developed in the 1920s as a result of excessive involvement by member and state banks in direct purchases of long-term securities and lines of credit based on securities portfolios. There was also excessive involvement in "broker loans" (advances made on stock exchange securities as collateral), in the extension of consumer credit based on installment plans, in guarantees of commercial paper, and in lines of credit on real estate.[19]

The Federal Reserve banks were less responsible for this speculative build up than they were enablers of it. By continuing to advance funds to member banks on their promissory notes secured by government bonds, with the proceeds increasingly being used for speculation, they were injecting excess liquidity into the system. This was to some degree a result of Federal Reserve President, Benjamin Strong's policy of keeping U.S. interest rates low in order to assist British, French and German central banks in reconstruction and gold reserve retention.[20] The reserve banks came to be defined by the capital market rather than institutions limited to defining the money market. Willis wrote:

> The outcome was to make the Reserve banks dependent quite as truly as any other banks upon the ability of the

> community to purchase, pay for, and hold or absorb issues of bonds, stocks and other securities."[21]

When the crash of 1929 occurred the Federal Reserve banks themselves were compromised as the bulk of their loans had been made against long-term paper. Their liquidity was largely dependent on the liquidity of the stock market.[22]

Chapter 20
Fed Discount Limitation Problems and the Amendments of 1929 -1933

During the Great Depression many banks deserved to fail and be closed due to speculative activities. But a great number of banks still had a majority of sound assets yet these were unsaleable as the market for them had declined precipitously. Due to the discount constraints of the Federal Reserve, most of the loans banks had made for productive purposes were of no greater use to them in maintaining their liquidity positions than were the speculative loans. As the depression settled in and economic conditions deteriorated, the Federal Reserve's rediscounting provisions became a subject of increasing frustration.

Outside of government bonds, the Federal Reserve banks were only able to rediscount short-term commercial paper of the "self-liquidating" variety, i.e. promissory notes and bills of exchange related to transactions of commerce, industry, and agriculture up to three months in duration and up to six months for agriculture. This limitation put the Reserve system at a distance from much of the economy. As Federal Reserve board member Menc Szymczak put it,

> They were not authorized to make advances on a wide range of other assets which made up an important part of the total earning assets of banks. These included real estate loans, securities other than those of the United States Government, and loans to businessmen which did not meet the requirements of the narrowly-defined eligible commercial paper.[1]

The short-term commercial paper that qualified for borrowing from the Fed, wrote Szymczak, had "constituted a constantly decreasing proportion of the total assets of member banks ever since the System was established."[2] Banks had become much more invested in longer-term assets than simple commercial paper.[3] In 1929, short-term commercial paper eligible for borrowing at the Fed accounted for only 12% of total loans and investments of member banks, and by 1934, only 8%. During the crisis, the Fed's credit was therefore of little use to the banks in the event they needed its support for their loans and other assets.[4] Since the Fed could not discount longer-term assets of the banks, forced sales and liquidations of sound capital perpetuated the banking collapse of 1931 and 1932. Though many banks held sound assets, they could not gain assistance from the Federal bank structure. Szymczak wrote:

> When the great liquidation occurred, many banks with assets which were good but technically ineligible for borrowing at Reserve banks, were obliged either to dump them on a falling market, suffer severe loss and contribute to the deflation in values or to close their doors.[5]

Another writer in 1930s stated:

> During the banking crisis [the technical provisions of eligibility] failed to protect the banking structure from complete collapse. When help was most urgently needed to prevent the progressive spread of the rot of cumulative destructive deflation many banks possessing otherwise sound assets were unable to receive adequate relief from the Federal Reserve for lack of the eligible variety.[6]

In 1931-1932 bank closures spread panic and banks did not want to extend loans for which they would not be able to gain assistance at Reserve banks. The Fed's restrictions intensified a deflationary process that had begun with the stock market collapse in 1929. Banks sold off assets on the cheap, and these sales further depressed the value of other assets. Banks held onto the little eligible short-term commercial paper they had in fear of lacking resources to meet the demands of their depositors. A panic to find eligible short-term paper that Reserve banks would acknowledge "reduced the volume of deposits and the liquidity of the banks to the point where the banking structure had been so much liquidated as to have become entirely frozen."[7] This severe banking crisis cut the business community off from its normal lines of credit.

The Fed Discount and Loan Amendments of 1932

The bank failures of 1931-1932 led Congress to attempt to unfreeze the banking system by temporarily permitting the Reserve Banks to provide credit to member banks on other assets. Congress passed emergency legislation on February 27, 1932. In addition to measures to securing the stability of the banking system, a new section was added to the Federal Reserve Act. Section 10b gave the Federal Reserve banks the power, for the first time, to make advances to member banks on the basis of promissory notes which the Board decided were secure, whether or not they were technically eligible for rediscount.

However, the Act as passed was very limited: The authority to make such advances was to expire a year later. The power was limited to "exceptional and exigent circumstances." The bank had to be a member bank with relatively small capital of under five million dollars. Each advance required the approval of five members of the Federal Reserve Board (FRB), not simply an authorization in the district. The bank needed to have exhausted its otherwise eligible paper. The bank was required to prove it could not otherwise obtain credit. In addition, the FRB could limit the types of assets accepted as security for the advances. Only fifty such advances were made, for a total of thirty million dollars.[8]

In July, there was another attempt to use the Fed to assist in the crisis. With the continuing depression Congress passed the "Emergency Relief and Construction Act" of July 21, 1932. Along with adding powers to the Reconstruction Finance Corporation (RFC) to assist in bridge, highway construction, and the support of agriculture, the Act included another amendment to the Federal Reserve Act.[9] President Hoover had vetoed an earlier version of the bill which had given the RFC the power to make loans to individuals and corporations. In its place, an amendment to Section 13 of the Federal Reserve Act was included in this July bill, giving the Federal Reserve powers "in unusual and exigent circumstances" to discount credits for individuals and corporations for up to ninety days. This was the first time in their history that reserve banks were given authority to provide credit assistance directly to individual corporations, and some members of Congress spoke in opposition. The amendment was utilized sparingly, and was more restrictive than Section 10b.[10]

Fed Amendments and Bank Lending Issues of 1933

The Federal Reserve discount and loan amendments of 1932 were ineffective in changing the course of the depression. In March 1933, the incoming Franklin Roosevelt Administration addressed the ongoing crisis in the banking system, including the specific question of advances to member banks.

The Administration first acted to stabilize the banks, declaring a bank holiday on March 5, and the Emergency Banking Act was passed on March 9. Since the Fed was unable to serve as the vehicle to recapitalize the banking system, the RFC was utilized instead. Banks issued preferred stock, which the RFC purchased. Part of the Act authorized bank conservators to conduct an orderly reorganization of the nation's banks, writing off bad assets and resizing capital amounts. Other emergency actions included accepting U.S. bonds as collateral for Federal Reserve notes to be issued to banks for operating liquidity. This was necessary as gold that had formerly backed a portion of the notes was hoarded or exported.

In addition, the March 9 Act loosened and eliminated some of the restrictions of Section 10b of February 1932, authorizing advances to member banks by the Fed and allowing member banks to utilize a greater proportion of their remaining assets. Senator Carter Glass opposed the Act, stating that the provisions were "so broad and so liberal that no friend of the Federal Reserve System, in ordinary times, would tolerate them for a moment"; and that under the bill, member banks might bring their "cats and dogs" to the Federal Reserve banks and have them discounted.[11] In Roosevelt's first fireside chat of March 12, 1933, he focused on the banking crisis. Roosevelt made reference to this liberalization of Section 10b towards assisting banks:

> Remember that the essential accomplishment of the new legislation is that it makes it possible for banks more readily to convert their assets into cash than was the case before. More liberal provision has been made for banks to borrow on these assets at the reserve banks and more liberal provision has also been made for issuing currency on the security of these good assets. This currency is not fiat currency. It is

> issued only on adequate security—and every good bank has an abundance of such security.

In addition to the modification of Section 10b, an additional power was added to Section 13, authorizing direct advances to individuals or corporations, including non-member banks for ninety days on notes secured by U.S. bonds.[12] The measure contained few restrictions and introduced a departure from the view that Federal Reserve banks should only act as bankers' banks. Some opposed the Act, including Senator Glass, who said in response that: "It broadens in a degree that is almost shocking to me the currency and credit facilities of the Fed System to non-members." In the House, Chairman Henry Steagall described it as "a simpler and broader authority for loans by federal reserve banks upon securities and collateral not eligible under the general authority of the Federal Reserve Act."[13] However, the provisions of the March 1933 Bank Act to expand the facilities for short-term lending did not achieve significant results.[14]

As 1933 came to a close, industry, commerce, and business remained stagnant, and working capital had been depleted by the depression. Small and medium sized businesses were unable to gain relief from their local bank. "Banks are not extending enough new credit," said Jesse Jones, the chairman of the RFC, on February 5, 1934. Having been turned away by banks, industries applied to the RFC, but to no avail, as it was not authorized to accommodate these loans. Jones reported that the RFC was receiving industrial loan applications on a daily basis that were perfectly sound even though they would take more than ninety days to liquidate. These could be made by local banks and liquidated if the borrowers were provided reasonable notice. The FRB later explained this situation to regional banks:

> There were a considerable number of commercial and industrial enterprises, particularly in the smaller categories, that were in need of additional funds to meet their current operating needs which they had not been able to obtain from banks, although they might have sufficient assets and earning capacity to justify the advance of such funds provided they were given an adequate time in which to work out their problems.[15]

Commercial banks were only lending on short-term–ninety day notes–and did not want to make loans where the time required for repayment would be longer than permitted under the requirements of eligibility for rediscount at the Federal Reserve banks. Without "quick assets in the statements of the borrowing companies," banks were not willing to lend.[16] The large commercial banks stated that bank examiners would classify as "slow" and "doubtful" and "unsafe," loans merely due to their extended maturity.[17] However, most of the economy's businesses and industries were not in possession of the types of short-term collateral demanded by banks and the FRB. Eugene Black, Chairman of the Board of Governors of the Reserve said, "Small industries have never had a chance to get working capital anywhere" and are forced to build it up from earnings.[18] Most business and industry had depleted their reserves and had only plant and machinery to offer as collateral.

The Section 10b emergency bank credit amendments of 1932 and 1933 were for short-term credit loans to banks to assist them during crisis conditions. Credit to a member bank seeking to lend did not translate into new economic activity if that member bank did not have the backing of the Fed to use its capital for the purpose of long-term loans.

The year 1933 also saw the passage of a major Banking Act in June, popularly known as the Glass-Steagall Act, the first national legislation to address the use of commercial banking funds for investment banking purposes. The interconnections between the two fields had become increasingly complex since the 1880s, reaching their most advanced form in the late 1920s. The broad structural changes made to the banking system took many years to implement. This 1933 Act also created the Federal Deposit Insurance Corporation(FDIC).[19]

Chapter 21
Credit Supply Initiatives of 1934-1935

The methods of the previous year to encourage bank lending had largely failed. New steps were taken in 1934 to provide member banks the support required to make the longer-term loans necessary for a recovery. At the February 7, 1934, meeting of the FRB, Governor Eugene Black said that ongoing considerations were being granted by the Treasury Department regarding the extension of credit to industry. He reported on President Roosevelt's request for a study on the subject "as well as a study of possible amendments to the Banking Act of 1933."[1] Black said one of the proposals for meeting the crisis was to organize "intermediate credit banks" to meet the demands of industry.

That same day, a column by a Washington insider was published stating that a solution outside of the existing framework was needed, making mention of the new plan:

> The setting up of an intermediate credit system of banks which would issue their own marketable debentures and use the proceeds to make capital loans to small companies has been urged for several months and various plans are under consideration . . .[2]

Black circulated a memorandum the next day with a number of points as to how these intermediate credit banks in each Reserve district could be organized.[3] On February 23, the matter of such banks "within the Federal Reserve System" was discussed again, referencing a request from President Roosevelt for a bill to be drafted. Black had obtained the approval of the plan from nearly all of the Fed Governors. The following day they discussed details such as the matter of the section of the bill which would allow the credit banks to issue preferred stock. On February 26, a draft bill was unanimously approved by the Board and sent to the Secretary of the Treasury.[4]

The bill proposed a nationally coordinated depository and stock-issuing bank structure with a branch in each Federal Reserve district lending to industry, and to assist and cooperate with member banks for the same purpose. In order to aid banks for long-term lending, the industrial credit banks were to rediscount for commercial banks and lending institutions for those purposes, make joint loans, or purchase the loans from the banks. Long-term credit transactions with industrial concerns would be facilitated. If in sudden need of cash, the member bank would be able to rely on the industrial credit bank in its district to take the loan onto its balance sheet.

The U.S. government was to provide funds for the Fed to capitalize the intermediate credit banks. In addition, the credit banks were to sell preferred stock to banks, institutions, companies, and individuals, allowing others to share in the profits of long-term industrial growth.[5] Their design was more similar to the Bank of the United States than the RFC. They would leverage their capital by borrowing up to five times its value and serve as depositories for revenues of the government on which they could lend. Unlike the RFC, the bonds would be used to raise additional capital not backed by the U.S. government, making them an independent banking facility. While the existing Fed locations and coordination facilities were to be utilized, this independent banking structure was to be uniquely devoted to directing credit to industry.

On March 5, Black reviewed his conferences with the President, the Secretary of the Treasury, the Director of the Budget, and representatives of the Reconstruction Finance Corporation and the Federal Deposit Insurance Corporation. There was broad agreement that industrial credit "should be made available through credit banks of the kind contemplated by the bill."[6] The FRB explained their position on this matter to Congress:

> In the judgment of the Board, there exists an undoubted need for credit facilities for industry and commerce beyond those that are now being supplied through the commercial banks or that can be supplied through the ordinary operations of the Federal Reserve System acting within the limitations of the Federal Reserve Act. In brief, the need is for loans to provide working capital for commerce and industry, and such loans necessarily must have a longer maturity than those rediscountable by Federal reserve banks.[7]

That first week of March, the Treasury and the Board circulated a survey of credit needs to banks and chambers of commerce.[8] Results of the survey were completed by 5,000 banks and 1,000 chambers of commerce showing the need for working capital by smaller industries. Later that summer, more thorough studies were made, investigating the problem of commercial banks refusing loans for industry. The results of a July 1934 study done by the Bureau of Census at the request of the Department of Commerce found that 45% of borrowers reported credit difficulties. In September, another study showed that of 1,788 applications for industrial loans in the seventh Federal Reserve District only 374, or 20%, were approved, despite the sound position of the firms.[9]

Before the final bill was introduced into the Congress, a lengthy article was published on March 15 celebrating the proposed backing for investment:

> If a commercial bank knows that at any moment it can get 80 per cent of its funds back by depositing with the intermediate credit division of the Federal Reserve banks all the notes which it has received from business for long-term credit, there will be a disposition to make such loans to businessmen in the first instance . . .
>
> In other words, self-liquidating loans, which hitherto have been by banking practice limited to ninety days with a renewal or two, dependent on conditions at each renewal date, will be supplanted by longer term commitments on credit.[10]

On March 19, President Roosevelt sent the draft bill along with a letter to Duncan Fletcher, Chairman of the Senate Banking Committee, referencing the results of the survey of banks and chambers of commerce. The results of those surveys supported the need for the proposed credit institution to serve mid-sized industrial interests.

However, by April 20, the FRB minutes reported on a meeting with President Roosevelt, Glass, and Fed Governor Black regarding a revised bill. Black and Glass only agreed to "provide for the extension by Federal reserve banks of credit for the purpose of furnishing working capital to industrial and commercial concerns."[11] This was seen by some as a deviation from the bill's original intention. One newspaper journalist lamented on March 12 that someone had "poured a counter proposal in [Roosevelt's] ear . . ." He continued, "They ask . . . why not amend the Federal Reserve Act to permit its key banks to make five year loans? (as it is they now have authority to make short-term loans and aren't doing it–but that's another question.)"[12]

The resulting bill was debated in the Congress until June 19, 1934, known as the "Industrial Advances Act."[13] Instead of an industrial bank structure in each Fed district, powers of industrial lending were given to the Federal Reserve banks themselves, along with a similar list of powers given to the RFC.

Industrial Loan Powers of the Federal Reserve and the RFC

The Industrial Advances Act of June 19, 1934, added a new section to the Federal Reserve Act, 13b, giving the Fed the power to directly lend to established industrial and commercial businesses for up to five years. They would back up banks and other financing institutions in making such loans by making joint loans or be on call to take over a loan.

The law limited the funds available for advances and commitments by the Federal Reserve banks to their total surplus that in July 1934 was $140 million. In addition, the Treasury matched the amount with its own funds, increasing it to $280 million.[14] Despite the availability of a $280 million revolving fund, the Fed had lent little more than $88 million by May 1935. Meanwhile, the banks held $2 billion in excess reserves, leaving an enormous amount of lending capacity that could be put to use. In Chicago, Szymczak told the banks that if they would "decide to lend, a little more freely to comparable enterprises, it [would] be a distinct advance toward putting bank funds profitably to work."[15] He pointed out that the billions of idle bank funds were instead being put to use by government credit through the sale of its bonds to banks, bridging the gap between idle men and idle money. He urged them to make these loans themselves and jointly with the Fed under Section 13b. Szymczak gave one example of how the Reserve had "come closer to the public in a tangible and concrete way" under Section 13b, reading from a letter the Reserve received in 1935:

> We wish to thank you for having permitted the Federal Reserve Bank to make loans to individuals, as the banks that we do business with have refused to help us; had it not been for the Federal Reserve we probably would have been at a great handicap, that is, our farmers would have had to go on the relief.

A fair amount of lending by the Reserve did occur for two years after the passage of the Industrial Advances act, but the RFC became the central instrument to carry out the purpose of industrial credit facilitation.[16] The Emergency Relief and Construction Act of July 1932 had authorized the RFC to loan to companies involved in constructing specific bridges, highways, waterworks, and other projects. However, as stated, the RFC was not authorized to make general industrial loans prior to the Industrial Advances Act of 1934, when it was then made a vehicle for this purpose. In June 1934, the RFC was amended, giving the corporation the power to "make loans to any industrial or commercial business" when credit was not available for the business at prevailing bank rates for the type of loan the business required. The loans were to be "adequately secured" and could be made either directly by the RFC or in cooperation with banks and other lending institutions. The maturities were not to exceed five years.

The RFC made loans directly or in cooperation with banks for the purchase of labor and materials, new business enterprises and expansion, the purchase of new machinery, or for the financing of industrial construction. In addition to this new power, the 1934 Act authorized the RFC to extend or renew earlier loans related to the Emergency Act of 1932. This was specifically for corporations involved in highways, bridges, rail, and water works projects, towards ensuring the success of the original loans. The RFC could adjust their claims by accepting new securities with different interest rates and maturities. Additional loans for the proper functioning and completion of projects were authorized in order to increase assurance that the borrower would be able to repay the entire investment to the RFC.

In January 1935, Steagall chaired a week long House hearing on a bill to extend the RFC's functions. The bill set 1945 as the final date for all maturities, allowing ten years instead of five for loans. In addition, the 1934 provision of "adequate security" for loans was reworded to read "secured as to reasonably assure the repayment of the loans," the former provision having been more restrictive than the Federal Reserve's industrial loan provision that had resulted in few loans being made.[17] Corporations and industries were then able to obtain credit on reasonable assurance of the loan being repaid. The RFC operated off budget, borrowing from the U.S. Treasury according to limits set by Congress. All loans made through the RFC, as loans, and not appropriations, were to be repaid.[18]

Echoing the method of the Bank of the U.S. in the 1820s-1830s, the credit of the RFC allowed economic cycles within the private sector to be offset for a time in order to effect a transfer and sale of goods and commodities. This prevented the ruin of many important manufacturers and industries along with the chain of businesses dependent upon them. Also like the Bank, it increased the overall indirect and direct long-term credit available to the economy. Unlike the Bank the RFC was not a depository institution for United States revenues and thus could not lend them as a source of credit to banks. Also, the RFC did not receive private subscriptions to its capital stock as had been proposed for the original March 1934 credit bank plan.

The 1935 Sound Assets Plan

In 1935, further attempts were made to mobilize the surplus capital within the banking system. Under Chairman Steagall, the House version of the 1935 Banking Act proposed that banks receive loans on any "sound assets" of commerce, industry, and agriculture. Previously only short-term paper met the technical requirements for self-liquidating eligible paper.[19] Szymczak described this House version in June, before the final bill was passed in August. The bill was to replace the "elaborately defined and restrictive rules" about the maturities and character of commercial, agricultural, and industrial paper allowed for rediscount by the Fed. Instead, the FRB would be given discretion to regulate what would be eligible. In addition, member banks would be able to "make advances to any member bank on a promissory note secured by any sound asset of such member bank." This proposal was, according to Szymczak, "the greatest departure in the bill" from the prevailing views held in 1913 when the Act was first established.

In a hearing on the 1935 Banking Act, Federal Reserve Governor Marriner Eccles stated that in periods of crisis, banks tended to refrain from making loans except on paper eligible for discount. A bank conducting business on this theory was not able to serve their communities adequately, and "would neglect its local responsibilities." Eccles proposed a change to Section 13's discounting function in accord with the House version of the bill that would "place emphasis on soundness rather than on the technical form of the paper that is presented." Similarly, echoing former Comptroller Hiland Hulburd in 1871, Chairman Steagall stated that discounting on the basis of soundness would allow the Fed to operate on "principles of solvency rather than technical requirements."

Some members of the hearing said that short-term credits were not necessarily safer than long-term credits, and in some cases less sound. Representative Clarence Hancock declared that "the old idea of commercial paper or such paper as can be liquidated almost overnight" had been "the greatest curse to business activity." The statement of the House Banking and Currency Committee on the bill passed out of the House summarized the substantial change in the general credit policy of the Federal Reserve with respect to member banks that it proposed.[21] The Committee said the purpose was to remove the strict technical limitations on what type of commercial paper could be used to obtain credit from the Fed. It hoped to assure member banks that they could obtain the short and long term funds they need for their regions. It was especially focused on the latter type of investment in order to spur on the recovery of business. The amendment would, the Committee explained, "encourage the member banks to invest their savings deposits, which are essentially capital funds, in longer-term loans." The term "soundness of assets" would have been a new term in the Federal Reserve Act. The Committee saw this general term as "a greater safeguard to the banks than short maturity of loans or the particular form of the underlying transaction."

This original version was defeated in the Senate, and some changes were included in the Bank Act of 1935, though it was more limited. The emergency clause, Section 10b, giving four month advances to member banks, was restored and added as a permanent power of the Fed with its restrictions removed.

Chapter 22
Fed Lending Powers and Proposals 1939-1950

In 1938, the problems of the banking system with respect to long-term credit and economic instability remained. Few banks made five year loans to small and medium sized business and industry.[1] They rarely utilized the RFC for joint loans, a fact which Jesse Jones addressed at a hearing early that year:

> Many industrial loans are good that would not necessarily be desirable by a bank, because payment of the loan will depend too usually upon the profitable operation of the borrower. This is the type of loan that we would like the cooperation of the banks in making, where employment will be provided and the security will reasonably assure ultimate liquidation of the loan.[2]

On April 12, 1938, Congress passed another amendment broadening the scope of the RFC's activities, permitting it to grant loans on whatever maturity it judged appropriate, up to ten years or more. In the last three quarters of 1938, following the amendment, authorizations increased from $4 million a month on average to $40 million a month, drawing forth the potential which had existed for long-term investment in the productive sectors of the economy.[3]

While the RFC was successful in its own sphere, credit needs required systemic changes to the banking system itself. This problem was addressed in a number of ways the following year. In 1939, Senator James Mead introduced a bill making it easier for banks to make long-term loans. A series of illustrative news columns were published describing the bill by Washington journalist David Lawrence. In February, one of his columns was published under the heading, "Congress Studies Credit System as Recovery Measure, Country in Need of Intermediate Plan."[4] The column described an effort by Senator Mead of New York and Representative Allen of Pennsylvania to renew 1934 proposals to establish an "intermediate credit system" for business that was integrated throughout the private banking system. The plan was to insure private loans made by banks "when such loans would enable business 'to increase its production, extend its operations, or modernize its plant and equipment.'" He said the subject had been an ongoing debate in Congress but generally confined to using government funds. He wrote:

> Actually, the power to make loans to industry has been given to the RFC and the Federal Reserve System, but such loans are restricted to what is known as temporary accommodations. There has been no way by which long-term loans of from seven to ten years could be obtained at moderate interest rates from the banks.

Lawrence said the new proposed bill was unique in that instead of government money being lent to industry the plan would activate "the private funds now lying idle [in] the banks." This would give banks a chance to increase their loans and earn a decent interest. Lawrence reported on the bill to insure bank loans again in May, stating that if it was passed "a spurt to American business of unprecedented proportions might easily result," putting billions in private banking capital to work:[5]

> The loans are to be made eligible for rediscount at the Federal reserve banks, so they could hardly become frozen assets or impair the standing of a bank because they could quickly be turned into cash . . . The proposal is broad enough to open up the whole credit system and thus put to work through established channels of private banking the billions of dollars of idle deposits accumulated in the nation's commercial banks.

In June 1939, Lawrence reported that "A movement has begun in Congress looking toward insurance of business loans," reviewing the opposition that had blocked the ability to obtain "workable legislation" on the subject since 1934. Lawrence then wrote:

> For several years, there has been need of an intermediate credit system in America. Commercial banks were never designed to furnish intermediate credit, and, when bankers

> talk about credit, they usually mean short-term credit for businesses. They do not think of "mortgages" for construction as a form of bank credit, because they customarily think of 90-day loans and even nine-month loans as the type of bank credit that is used by business.[6]

The bill for loan insurance available to private banks was not adopted. Another attempt to address the credit needs of the economy with respect to the banking system was made in October of 1939. A bill was introduced to establish a corporation dedicated to making industrial loans with branches established in each Federal Reserve district. Similar to the industrial credit bank plan of 1934, each regional Fed's surplus would be used to create lending capacity.[7] In effect, the plan was to move the Federal Reserve's Section 13b industrial loaning provision outside of the Federal Reserve banks themselves and into a special purpose corporation. It was proposed that the loan corporation be limited to the surplus and capital of the Fed rather than dependent on joint funds with the Treasury Department, as was the case with the Fed's Section 13b industrial loan powers. Local banks would then make joint loans with the Fed, similar to the arrangement with the RFC. Its measures were proposed to make the Fed's lending powers less restrictive and more efficient than Section 13b in preparation for war build up. This corporation was not established, and WWII was instead financed through loan guarantees, both by the Fed and the RFC.

An Executive order on March 26, 1942, authorized the guarantee of loans for purposes of war production contractors. Government guarantees were made through the Federal Reserve banks and RFC. To facilitate participation by the Reserve banks, the 1942 loan program made the execution of its industrial loan powers in Section 13b more flexible. The Reserve banks were granted discretion with respect to the credit standing of companies without a long process of paperwork. They were also empowered to set discount rates and interest charged on the loans at each district Reserve bank, without prior authorization by the FRB in Washington. The war brought the Federal Reserve's industrial lending potential near to that of the RFC during the depression of the 1930s. In 1942, the Reserve approved applications under its industrial lending powers for $128 million, nearly the amount authorized in the preceding eight years since the power was obtained.[8]

However, the guarantee aspect of the Fed's wartime programs was the most important change in supplying credit to the economy. As of September 30, 1946, it had processed 8,771 guarantees, aggregating to nearly $10.5 billion dollars, with losses having been less than the fees collected for the guarantees. On March 26, 1947, the war department wrote to Fed Chairman Eccles describing its appreciation for the Federal Reserve System's execution of the guaranteed loan program to assist war production contractors. It said the program was based on using "not only the funds already in the commercial banks of the country," but also "the existing credit machinery." Federal Reserve banks had been appointed fiscal agents of the War Department for that purpose.[9]

From 1944-1951 various attempts were made to improve upon Section 13b of the Federal Reserve Act to establish independent or semi-independent financial institutions fulfilling the same purpose as the RFC.[10] One such proposal was made by Senator Charles W. Tobey on April 17, 1947, to use the surplus of the Federal Reserve as a source of loan security. It was modeled on the success of the wartime Fed loan guarantee program with which financing institutions were already accustomed.[11] Tobey's bill would have repealed the special industrial loans provision of Section 13b of the Federal Reserve Act. In its place, Section 13 would be modified, with a new paragraph making involvement in such loans a permanent function of the Fed:

> Any Federal Reserve bank may guarantee any financing institution against loss of principal or interest on, or may make a commitment to purchase and thereafter purchase from a financing institution, any loan made to a business enterprise which has a maturity of not more than ten years.

The Fed would utilize its own funds for the guarantees, the amount of which was not to exceed the surplus at the Fed, and they were to be of maturities not more than ten years. The FRB was highly in favor of the bill, citing their special qualification to provide financial assistance to business enterprises through the commercial banking system given their existing reserve and discounting facilities along with their regulation of banking activities. They supported repealing the lending provision of 13b which had allowed the Fed itself to make direct loans, since the broader purpose was to ensure adequate credit to private business in time of need. By its repeal the Fed would be taken out of direct competition with banks. In addition, the FRB explained that this system of guarantees with its own funds would be preferable to loans from government agencies. As they wrote:

> Since the Federal Reserve Banks are permanent institutions with experienced personnel, the Board feels that whatever financial assistance is to be provided under governmental authority for business enterprises through commercial banks should be extended by the Reserve Banks.[12]

The architects of these referenced plans of 1944-1951 saw great need for a banking structure more capable of interfacing directly with the economy in its entirety. They sought to create the means for the private sector to engage in longer-term investments. Though government agencies such as the RFC could influence the structure and efficiency of the financial system, they could not solve credit problems as readily as permanent modifications to the banking system.

Conclusion

In this book we have explored the development of the U.S. financial system as a response to the ongoing challenge of credit supply. Insufficient means of exchange and the lack of access to loanable capital have repeatedly been limiting factors for commerce, trade, business, industry, agriculture, and the development of infrastructure. Repeated efforts have been made to deal with this central issue. Successful innovations in credit supply involved ensuring a currency based on credit and generated by economic demand. Successful innovations included an adequate source of capital to serve as the basis for loans and discounts and provided economic entities the ability to obtain credit for goods and services in the process of production and sale.

In 1687 Boston attempted to authorize a bank that could turn pledged capital and other property into a means of exchange and loans, whose notes would possess sufficient credibility to circulate. Failing the development of banks of this kind, the demand for a sufficient means of payment and a basis for loans was instead met through the use of government bills of credit and loan offices. This facilitated sustained growth in the colonies in the 1730s-1760s. After the Declaration of Independence one of the key issues in forming a union among the states became how to solve ongoing currency and credit crises. When the Continental Currency of the Revolutionary War period became discredited, a joint government and private investment company, the Bank of North America, was authorized in 1781 to create a non-depreciating means of payment through discounts of promissory notes of trade and commerce and making loans. It represented the successful establishment of what had been attempted in an early form nearly one hundred years before in Boston. However, the long-term solution required a banking system integrated with a government empowered to use the resources of the nation in order to turn debt into capital. Otherwise, banking capital based on scarce specie reserves restricted growth. By funding the war debts with sufficient taxation, new loans, and other measures to pay the interest and principal, government debt became a capital equal to money. The Bank of the United States and state banks were adequately capitalized to meet the demand for credit and create a currency plentiful enough to support economic growth. The second Bank of the United States followed the model of the first. It once again demonstrated the success of a bank-based funding system. It showed the benefits of a public private institution whose capital stock was based on subscription paid in government securities, that could utilize deposited government revenues as a source of capital, and whose purpose was to ensure a safe, adequate, and cheap credit supply for the economy. When the Bank was successfully managed it facilitated low cost commerce and trade, aided in the efficient collection of taxes and revenues, directly and indirectly aided infrastructure projects, and supplied industry, agriculture, and other sectors of the economy with banknotes and deposit credit through loans and the discount of promissory notes.

In the late 1830s, however, the federal government abandoned this functioning system and required that payments to and from the government be made in gold and silver. The Independent Treasury system was out of touch with business and trade that utilized payments almost entirely on credit in the form of banknotes and increasingly by transfer of deposit credit from account to account via checks. State banks and private brokers attempted to fill the void created by the government's withdrawal from federal credit and currency management. The disconnect introduced between the method of payment demanded by the government and that of the rest of the economy led to instability and a great increase in the cost of exchanging goods and services in the 1840s-1850s.

The National Banking Acts of the 1860s established uniformity and a banking system based on government securities. But the Acts were overly fixated on specie reserves and contained artificial restrictions on the amount of capital that could be pledged to create currency. During the civil war the void in credit supply from a sound banking system was filled by the use of government bills of credit. Though successful in their original purpose, the artificial limits on capital for lending under the National Banking System led to a sustained demand for the treasury to fill the void and supply a means of payment. This led to a disjointed and inflexible hybrid currency and credit structure, one based on a growing use of state banks and their deposits over more secure national banks and inelastic government currency over national bank currency. Additional friction between the Independent Treasury and the National Banking System constrained credit. Economic growth continued but under conditions of great financial instability, repeated crisis and depression, and high costs in obtaining credit.

The demise of the second Bank, the Independent Treasury, and the problems of the National Banking System demonstrated the consequences of serious differences between the government and the needs of commerce and industry. They showed the importance of meeting the demand for credit supply by authorizing institutions able to respond efficiently to real economic demand and the need to avoid imposing artificial restrictions on credit creation based on theory.

The Federal Reserve created in 1913 was a banking system that could operate based largely on deposit credit reserves instead of specie reserves. This brought the banking system more closely into line with payment and financing methods of business. However, the abuse of the Fed's provision for rediscounting government securities contributed to speculation in the 1920s while the Fed's inability to rediscount loans made to business and industry after the crisis left banks without liquidity support, worsening the depression. The Fed lacked the power to turn sound assets and intermediate and longer term credit instruments of industry and business into a means of payment and a basis of credit. The demand for credit of this kind led to an expansion of the powers of the Reconstruction Finance Corporation (RFC). The RFC generated profitable growth in meeting this demand but not on the scale the private banking system could have had if it incorporated similar mechanisms.

This book demonstrates that adequate credit supply is essential to economic growth and that people will search out ways to access credit and supply it. If not through the banking system or other well established systems on a national level then credit will be supplied through other less efficient methods. Given the economic demand and need for credit there is great value in meeting it with general policies integrated throughout the financial system rather than through methods unable to interface fully with demand. The successful examples of credit supply reviewed in this book indicate that an essential role of government is to create the means through which sufficient credit can be exchanged and capital can be borrowed. It is vital that institutions have sufficient powers to ensure adequate quality of credit as well as quantity.

The financial system will continue to evolve over time as a varied expression of how the government and private sector choose to meet the ongoing challenge of credit supply.

Appendices

Appendix I
The Causes of Inflation and Increases in the Price of Gold 1862-1865

A review of the economy during the Civil War would not be complete without addressing high levels of inflation in the prices of goods and commodities during those years. Its main causes were the increased demand of a war economy coupled with errors on the part of Congress related to the Legal Tender Act which led to an unprecedented demand for gold, followed by outright speculation in gold.

Demands of the war were clearly a leading cause of price increases. The war led to a scarcity of supply in southern goods. The removal of men from normal occupations increased the wages for those who remained working in the civilian ranks. As wages went up, already scarce commodities increased in price and wages then rose further with the increased prices. With a rising demand for labor, the power of laborers and farmers to name their wages increased. As raw materials advanced in price manufactured goods followed suit. In this way, the war created a continuous increase in prices for three years. At the same time, great fortunes were made by speculators in commodities and by companies in the fulfillment of large army contracts. The rapid circulation of currency from large public expenditures stimulated increased consumption, further affecting prices. A new array of taxes also increased prices. In addition, some traders held goods off the market for the purpose of driving up prices.

Some blamed legal tender issues for the rapid price increases. It was true that the amount of paper currency in circulation was greater than it was at the beginning of the war, but the increased currency demand for supplies and business activity was also much greater than before. In December 1862, while addressing the causes of increased prices, Chase showed that because of the vast increase in demand for payments, the country required all of the government's increase in paper currency. In fact, at that time, prices for many articles of consumption such as wheat, pork, corn, hay, beef, and other staples actually declined or barely increased in 1862. Many people found it difficult to obtain legal tender notes when attempting to subscribe to a government loan. This indicates a shortage of currency, not an excess.[1]

A year later, in December 1863, under similar commodity price increases, Chase again addressed the issue of price increases being laid on an increase in legal tender notes. He said that even if it had been possible to borrow coin to pay for the war efforts instead of creating a debt of legal tender notes, the same increase in prices would have occurred. If coin had been paid out to fortunate contractors with the same shortage of labor, prices would have still increased. As Chase explained:

> Prices too would have risen from other causes. The withdrawal from mechanical and agricultural occupations of hundreds of thousands of our best, strongest and most active workers, in obedience to their country's summons to the field, would, under any system of currency, have increased the price of labor, and of consequence, the prices of the products of labor; while the prices of many things would have risen in part from other causes, as, for example, the price of railroad bonds from vast increase of income through payments for military transportation and the price of cotton from deficient supply.[2]

In 1864, Treasury Secretary William Fessenden made similar observations. Though there had been various circulations of interest bearing treasury notes and greenbacks, there remained a scarcity of circulation. His view was that this made it difficult to obtain loans, indicating again that the supply of currency was fully employed. The growing war economy was requiring a greater amount of notes for making payments. Comptroller Hugh McCulloch said that while expenditures of the government did expand the currency and contributed to price increases, the same would have occurred with a gold reserve based currency.

Congress Creates an Artificial Demand for Gold

Prior to 1862 banks were paying specie on demand and the price of gold was fixed as it could be obtained for currency at par. Under the suspension of specie payments gold became a commodity and its price fluctuated with demand, as would any other article of trade. Beginning in 1862, the price of gold began to rise due to speculation. This speculation was caused in large part by two interconnected tactical errors made by Congress in 1862. Prior to the war gold had been in demand only for export payments and any advance in currency exchange.[3]

The Senate version of the 1862 bill added that the interest on U.S. bonds would be paid in coin. Many in the Senate saw the promise of coin interest in gold as a way to uphold the credit of the nearly bankrupt nation. However, while legally payable in specie bonds were almost always paid domestically in notes of banks offering a specie guarantee. Few required or demanded specie under most conditions. The second error was that of the conference committee of the House and Senate adding a measure demanding duties to be paid in coin. Again, prior to 1862, duties could be paid in the currency of banks offering a specie guarantee. Since banks had suspended that guarantee, common sense would have dictated a course of allowing duties to be paid in legal tenders until banks resumed specie payment. Instead, $50 million annually in duties were required to be paid in gold. As this could not be obtained from banks it was necessary that it be purchased from dealers, allowing them to influence the price of gold.[4] The promise of interest payments in gold created a distinction between United States treasury notes and gold, unfavorable to the former. Though the government had made its own currency legal payment as good as coin this provision created the perception that they were no longer equal. These decisions created an environment where speculation in gold became a profitable pursuit. Without this government legislated demand for gold, it is doubtful the speculation that followed could have been sustained.[5]

Speculation in Gold

When specie payments stopped, gold made a small advance due to people hoarding gold supplies. This was to be expected. However, when dealers in gold realized that government policy had created demand for gold its price began to advance to much higher levels. The largest source of price increase was coin demand on the part of importers. Speculators and sympathizers with the rebellion took advantage of merchants and importers needing to obtain gold for their duty payments. High duties in gold on hundreds of millions of dollars worth of foreign goods formed the bedrock of speculative activities.

As Comptroller Hugh McCulloch wrote in 1864, one source of the gold price came from a "hostility to the government and agents of rebellious states and sympathizers with the rebellion." There was an explicit effort to increase the cost to the U.S. government in the commodities needed to purchase for the war. This influenced price controls in the U.S. during wartime. "Whether loyal importers and manufacturers of the East or enemy of the republic, they had the same desire to raise the price of gold," McCulloch wrote. When the price of gold went up, sellers of commodities used it as a pretext to increase the prices charged for payment with legal tenders.[6] Increased activity of U.S. industry from war demand and an adequate supply of currency increased the market for foreign goods, which entered American ports with great speed. It was in the interest of importers to have high prices for their goods, so they could pay the increasingly costly duties in gold.[7]

High prices in gold were also driven by those dealing in commodities markets that the government had entered for its war goods, including pork, beef, flour, oats, etc. These traders made large purchases that were put into storage in these markets, driving up prices. They then claimed that the high price of gold was the cause of increasing commodity prices, knowing the government demand was inelastic to price. Commodity traders, knowing the duties and interest were to be paid in that medium of exchange, also stored gold supplies.

At the same time many leading capitalists and members of the aristocracy in England and France expressed support for the rebels. Journalists in those countries took on a deprecating tone towards the Union's chances of surviving. This tended to frighten holders of U.S. securities resulting in foreign selling of U.S. bonds with the proceeds used to buy gold. Of this Chase wrote: "Taking advantage of these and other circumstances tending to an advance of gold, speculators employed all the arts of the market to stimulate that tendency and carry it to the highest point." On October 15th, 1862, gold sold in the market at a premium of 37% to legal tender notes.[9]

As the price of gold rose, investors in U.S. bonds receiving gold interest payments could double their money. The payment of interest on bonds in coin, an amount in itself far below that paid out due to speculation in gold, had, as Fessenden acknowledged "facilitated the operations of those disposed to enhance the price of gold for speculative purposes."[8] In addition to buying bonds, many heartily lent their money to the sources of speculation just described on which their gains in bonds depended. In

1864 the premium of gold to legal tenders became so high that $357 in gold would purchase $1000 of legal tenders.

The overall result was demand for gold that exceeded anything seen over the previous century. However, at the war's end many counted the losses sustained to the government by speculation as a necessary cost. The rise in the price of gold had also contributed to the sale of 5-20s in 1863, therefore serving as a blessing in disguise. As Stephen Colwell put it, "great evils sometimes carry compensation with them." In addition, the high price of manufactures, agriculture and labor, were regarded as a boon to many classes of people, helping them reconcile the taxation they were made to pay.[10] Ultimately the Union victory was realized but at a higher cost than might have been the case.

Speculation in Gold vs Depreciation of Legal Tenders

During the same period, some of the opponents of legal tenders circulated arguments that the price of gold was not rising due to speculation and rather, was a measure of the depreciation in legal tender notes. Chase, Fessenden, McCulloch, and others made detailed arguments showing that the fluctuations in the price of gold were not correlated with the increased amount of legal tenders, and that there was no excess of the latter.

In December 1862 Chase first noted that while it was true that legal tenders were no longer at par with the value of gold, it was also true that the Legal Tender Act had made them a substitution for coin and convertible into bonds. He went on to point out that since gold was no longer used for money it had been demonetized. It "became an article of merchandise, subject to the ordinary fluctuations of supply and demand, and to the extraordinary fluctuations of mere speculation," he wrote. Chase also showed that the quantity of currency was not excessive in light of legitimate demand: from November 1861 to November 1862, United States notes had increased from $15 million to $210 million, while state bank corporate notes had increased during the same period from $130 million to $167 million, for a total increase of $232 million of currency. However, it was in fact not an increase but a substitution for the $210 million in coin that had been in circulation as of November 1861 but was no longer in circulation in 1862. By November 1, 1862, "the coin had been practically demonetized and withdrawn from use as currency or as a basis for currency." Therefore, the aggregate circulation, Chase wrote, only increased from $355 to $377 million, or by $22 million.[11]

Turning to the theory that gold prices were a result of a redundant legal tender circulation, Chase noted the non-correlation in their prices. During the period when the price of gold had fallen 7%, the currency had increased by several million. In 1864, Treasury Secretary Fessenden and Comptroller Hugh McCulloch illustrated the non-correlation between the volatility of gold and the amount of legal tenders in circulation, pointing to speculation as the root cause of gold's price volatility. At the end of 1862, with a total currency in circulation of $300 million, the gold premium was at 33%. Three months later, the currency remained at roughly the same volume yet the premium rose to 71%. In July 1863, the currency increased to $400 million while the premium on gold fell to 24%. At close of 1863, the currency rose to $500 million, but the premium was at 51% well below its highs of February the year before.[12] In 1864, gold volatility was extremely high with exchange rates in greenbacks of $1.50 to $2.85, back down to $1.87, and back up to $2.50 in a matter of months. The price of gold at that point appeared to have little relationship to paper money or credit availability. Fessenden wrote of these figures in December 1864:

> The experience of the past few months cannot have failed to convince the most careless observer that, whatever may be the effect of a redundant circulation on the price of coin, other causes have exercised a greater and more deleterious influence.
>
> It is quite apparent that the solution of the problem may be found in the unpatriotic and criminal efforts of speculators, and probably of secret enemies, to raise the price of coin, regardless of the injury inflicted upon the country—or desiring to inflict it. . . . All such attempts should be indignantly frowned upon by a patriotic community, and the efforts of all good citizens invoked to counteract such nefarious schemes.

Hugh McCulloch reviewed similar figures for the rise and fall of gold. He added as further proof that while gold was high the price of real estate in legal tenders was no higher than it had been on a coin basis before 1862. He concluded that it was clear by looking at the gold market in New

York from 1861-1864 that "its value has been regulated by other causes than the inflation of the currency."[13] He concluded:

> Nothing can be more conclusive of the incorrectness of the opinion that gold is always the standard of value, and that the high price it has commanded in the United states during the progress of the war is the result of an inflated currency, than this brief statement of its variations in the New York stock market.[14]

After the war, the demand for gold remained exceedingly high for the payment of import duties and for government gold interest payments. By 1867, the demand for gold to pay import duties was one half million per day, higher than at any previous time. Gold had become a disruptive factor as a speculative commodity and a contributor to inflation. Since lawful money reserves were a part of the National Banking System, the government's responsibility was to reestablish redemptions of banknotes in lawful money, either specie or legal tender. Under normal conditions, restoring specie payments had meant having an adequate reserve available for trade balances. Banks could not accumulate sufficient gold reserves unless the artificial demand for gold was eliminated and its value brought down to the value of the legal tender notes in circulation. Making the paper currency equally acceptable to gold would also have assisted in bringing prices down. Restoring specie reserves would have been a simple contribution to establishing uniform banking institutions. Additional security could have been brought to the banking system by limiting payment of specie on demand to national banknotes, not deposits, allowing deposit redemptions in kind.[15]

Appendix II
Oversights of the National Banking Acts of 1863 and 1864

In the period leading up to the National Banking Acts, state banking legislation focused on securing banknote circulation through enforced redemption at the expense of laws addressing the other functions of banks. The provision for bonds to be held in the Treasury for the redemption of national bank notes was clearly an improvement to a security dependent on the reserves of individual banks. The uniformity in value it made possible had a universally beneficial effect on commerce. However, the main activities of the banks associated with deposits did not receive sufficient attention in the Acts. The chief activity of the banks in the decades before the National Banking Acts was not that of issuing banknotes. It was firstly the creation of deposit accounts from which payments could be made for domestic trade. The secondary function of banks was to facilitate "domestic exchange," specifically the balancing of credits and debts between cities.

Banks created a fund of deposits for payments through the purchase of promissory notes and bills of exchange for individuals and companies in order to provide deposit credit for the notes. Credits of this kind made up 90% of the deposits in banks. Most commercial debts were paid utilizing this fund of discounted commercial paper between parties. The amount of credit created in this fashion supported an amount of transactions that circulating banknotes and coin were simply unable to achieve.[1] The other main function of the banks was in balancing credits and debts between major cities in the wholesale market for commodities. These larger transactions were mostly conducted through bank ledgers, balancing accounts on books without transport of specie or banknotes.

In comparison with these two functions of the banks, the issue of banknotes, either in discounts or loans, accounted for a much smaller portion of their overall activities. This was particularly true in larger eastern cities. In 1864, the ratio of bank notes to bank deposits in the Mid-Atlantic states was $82 million banknotes to $267 million bank deposits, a ratio of 1 to 3. Amongst the Associated of Banks New York, Boston, and

Philadelphia, the ratio was 1 to 12. Due to the speed with which the credit of deposits in banks could be transferred to make payments in comparison with banknotes, payments with deposits accounted for nearly all of the yearly payments made by banks nationwide. In 1864 it was estimated that over $100 billion in payments annually cleared banks nation-wide. Of this amount, the paper circulation of the country accounted for just one half of a percent, the remainder being accomplished by balancing the credits and debts of customers on the books of the banks.[2]

Despite the importance of these other functions of banks, and their role in securing deposits, security for the redemption of bank notes received the lion's share of attention from legislators. The following are a number of proposals for improving the National Banking Acts from this standpoint, put forward in 1864 and 1867 by Stephen Colwell, a former official of the U.S. Mint and commissioner for the Treasury. His proposals would later be echoed by Comptroller of the Currency, Hiland Hulburd, in his reports of 1868-1871.

Removing Redemption Risk from Deposits

As stated, the discount of individual and corporate paper with sixty to ninety day maturities accounted for 90% of the deposits of the country. However, despite the maturity of the corporate paper, the deposit credit given for them became an immediate liability for the bank in specie (and legal tender notes after 1862). Accordingly, the banks held liabilities redeemable on demand many times the value of their reserves in lawful money.[3] However, the ultimate security of bank notes and deposits was the commodities for which they were issued in discount of commercial paper, i.e. the solvency of the debtors, not specie reserves. Reserves were a security in the sense of promoting uniformity, but not a security against major crisis. Though the demand to redeem deposit credit and bank notes into specie was rare, the danger was lying in wait in periods of crisis when banks were least able to redeem, as in 1857.[4]

One possible method for reducing this risk in the National Banking Acts would have been to separate payments that required the use of specie or banknotes from those that did not and were simply a method of adjustment. Deposits would no longer be withdrawn in specie and would only be redeemable in kind. Depositors would withdraw the same forms of credit they deposited, i.e. bills of exchange, national banknotes, promissory notes, and other forms of commercial paper.[5] In other words, the issue department of the bank would be separate from the deposit department, with the former redeeming notes in coin and the latter in the paper it initially received. Under this arrangement, National bank notes secured by bonds could have been issued for the value of a deposit without danger. Unlike state banks national banks could issue only a limited number of notes.[6]

Security Against Import Driven Specie Drain

Foreign exchange was similar to the domestic exchange market, a system of debt cancellation between distant points, performed between different countries rather than different cities. In lieu of sending actual money, a bill of exchange was purchased either for imports or exports. However, when exports declined rapidly there was often an insufficient amount of bills of exchange on export products that could be purchased to pay for imports. The cost for those scarce bills of exchange rose, leading many importers to pay for goods with specie. It was at this point specie reserves of the banks came under pressure. Importers turned to the banks, which were legally obliged to redeem their notes and deposits to meet the specie demand. In self-preservation, the banks would curtail loans. What generally followed were falling prices and increased rates of interest that in turn impaired domestic trade. Another foreign driven source of specie drain on the banks occurred when a foreign crisis led to a necessity for foreigners to sell their U.S. bonds and state securities simultaneously.[7] Upon sale of the bonds for bank notes, the bank notes were presented for redemption, leading to heavy draw on U.S. bank reserves.[8]

To address these problems, the National Banking Acts could have included a central method to penalize those overtrading in foreign goods. Under the Bank of the United States, these excesses were possible to manage with proper oversight, and the Bank's resources were often used to put pressure on importers and exporters of specie.[9] Banking legislation could have forced overtraders to pay the market price for gold instead of being allowed to redeem their notes at par.

Another method to reduce the threat of the gold demands during crisis would have been the creation of a bullion bank to manage the country's gold reserves and foreign exchange balances, setting debts due to and from foreigners. The bullion bank would have controlled the penalty rate for those requiring gold in foreign trade during periods of negative trade balances. If gold were demanded, banks would transfer their deposits of gold by issuing drafts on the bullion bank. The gold would be accessible in an emergency, and individual banks would be relieved of the threat of being pressured to give gold to their customers during crises. The bullion bank's discount rate for borrowing gold would not impact the rest of the country's normal rate.[10]

Acknowledgements

Among those who contributed to the realization of this book I would like to especially thank my cousin Michael Litt. In addition to catching general drafting errors, his editing of the manuscript significantly improved the clarity and precision of a great number of sentences and word choices. He also made a number of extremely valuable suggestions and proposals for additions. These suggestions led to a handful of crucial finishing touches. In the latter vein I am similarly indebted to Dr. Rosemarie Zagarri for making a number of invaluable book recommendations for Part II and for spurring me on to incorporate them into the final manuscript. I am indebted to Dr. Paul London for his careful editing of a number of key pages of the text. In addition, I am grateful for his review of the near final manuscript and providing valuable feedback. All readers of this book have benefited from his and Michael Litt's recommendation to add further clarification in the text for a number of uncommon but important and frequently used terms. I express my gratitude to John Wagner for spending the time to review an early draft. His professional comments helped affirm the book's overall readability. I thank Dr. Lee Willis for his audience early on while writing four of the chapters. This was critical to shaping the book's tone. His encouraging remarks and review were a timely and welcome confirmation of the book's relevance. I thank my friend Leandra Bernstein for her valuable writing suggestions and encouragement. I would also like to thank Professor Frank Manheim for reading my previous writings and encouraging me to write the book. I express special gratitude to my family for their support in this endeavor, but in particular, my parents, Joyce and John. For my sources I thank the creators and managers of the Internet Archive; the Federal Reserve Archival System for Economic Research; Google Books; the librarians facilitating the Interlibrary Loan System of Virginia and Wisconsin; Princeton Theological Seminary Libraries Special Collections; the Department of Special Collections at the University of Wisconsin Madison and University of Notre Dame; the American Philosophical Society and Yale University for their creation of franklinpapers.org; the National Archives for founders.archives.gov; and Dr. Jan Kregel for a conference discussion that reminded me to read the work of H. Parker Willis.

Notes

Part I: Early American Banking and Credit

Chapter 1. Blackwell's Bank of 1687 and the First Colonial Bills of Credit

1. John Woodbridge, "Severals Relating to the Fund," in *Colonial Currency Reprints with an Introduction and Notes, 1682-1751*, edited by Andrew McFarland Davis, Vol. I (Boston: John Wilson & Son, 1910), 109-118; Benjamin Franklin, "A Modest Inquiry Into the Nature and Necessity of a Paper Currency," in *Colonial Currency Reprints*, Vol. II, op. cit., 335-357.
2. "The Comparative Value of Money between Britain and the Colonies," *Coin and Currency Collections*, Department of Special Collections University of Notre Dame Libraries, www.coins.nd.edu; Andrew McFarland Davis, Introduction to *Colonial Currency Reprints*, Vol. I., op. cit., 16-21.
3. John Blackwell, "A Discourse in Explanation of the Bank of Credit," in *Colonial Currency Reprints*, Vol. I, op. cit., 121-146.
4. The son of the founder of Massachusetts Bay, John Winthrop Jr. was a scientist, chemist, an explorer and discoverer of mineral and mine deposits in Massachusetts and Connecticut, and a co-founder of one of the first ironworks in Massachusetts in 1633. While Winthrop's writings on the subject are few, they are seen in his correspondence with Samuel Hartlib, with whom he discussed numerous scientific and other topics. Apparently no remaining copy of Winthrop's original paper exists.
5. In that period, the use of the term money signified specie, i.e. money in coins, made chiefly of gold or silver.
6. James Hammond Trumbull, *First Essays at Banking and First Paper-money in New-England*, American Antiquarian Society (Worcester: American Antiquarian Society, 1884), 8-9.

7. Potter expanded on this point, writing, "There is not at all any true worth in the best money or metal that this earth can afford, further then as by being generally accepted for things of real value. It gives to him that so accepts thereof, security for obtaining some other commodity of like or greater value." William Potter, *The Key of Wealth*, (London: R.A., 1650).

8. "Though though money be but ten times more than formerly, their trading shall be near one hundred times more than formerly: for if this multiplied stock of moneys, would in this case revolve about in near the tenth part of that time, as their former small stock would have done; . . . being ten times greater than the former; each revolution thereof . . . causeth full ten times as great a sale of commodity, that is full ten times as great a trade, as each revolution of the former small stock would have done." Potter, op. cit., 6; *Dictionary of Political Economy*, edited by Robert Harry Inglis Palgrave, Vol. III (London: Macmillan and Co., 1910), 177.

9. Potter, op. cit., 38.

10. Ibid., 45.

11. Potter, op. cit., 46-79; *Dictionary of Political Economy*, op. cit.

12. Woodbridge, op. cit.

13. Further, by the deposit of wrought metal in the bank, the mine owner was to pay interest on the bank bills or obtain more credit with which to pay out wages. Other tradesman could pay with the value of their goods. By serving as a clearing house the bank would benefit manufacturers, since they would be "always furnished with credit." Blackwell, op. cit.

14. The comparative superiority of the bank credit currency to the scarce gold and silver was made: "None of these advantages may be expected out of the small pittance of cash that now is, ever was, or likely will be in this country, unless assisted in trade and enriched by the help this bank proposes." Ibid.

15. Adolph Oscar Eliason, *The Rise of Commercial Banking Institutions in the United States* (Minneapolis: University of Minnesota Press, 1901), 10; Blackwell, op. cit.

16. Davis, Introduction to *Colonial Currency Reprints*, Vol. I, op. cit., 10-12.

17. The council wrote further: "And for that it is not visible how the same may be remedied unless some other medium be approved than the species of silver, which very injuriously hath been transported into other parts hence." Joseph Felt, *An Historical Account of Massachusetts Currency* (Boston: Perkins & Marvin, 1839), 46-47.

18. Randolph, Edward, *Edward Randolph: Including His Letters and Official Papers,* Vol. II (Boston: Prince Society, 1898), 21; Davis, Introduction to *Colonial Currency Reprints,* Vol. I, op. cit., 16-21.; Davis, Andrew McFarland, "Was It Andros?" *Proceedings of the American Antiquarian Society,* New Series, Vol. XVIII (Oct. 24, 1906-Oct. 16, 1907): 346-361.

19. Another factor was the hostility of secretary Edward Randolph to Blackwell, whose prospective role as executive of the Bank was likely seen as a threat to the authority of Andros. Blackwell left the colony at the time the Bank plan was aborted. Davis, Introduction to *Colonial Currency Reprints,* Vol. I, op. cit. 16-21.; Davis, "Was It Andros?," op. cit.; University of Notre Dame Libraries, op. cit.; Charles H. J. Douglas, *The Financial History of Massachusetts* (New York: Columbia University, 1892), 47.; Eliason, op. cit., 10-12.

20. Cotton Mather, "Some Considerations on the Bills of Credit," in *Colonial Currency Reprints* Vol. I, op. cit., 189-195; John Blackwell, "Some Additional Considerations on the Bills of Credit," in *Colonial Currency Reprints,* Vol. I, op. cit., 197-206.

21. John Blackwell also pointed to the unpredictable nature of silver as money. "Silver in old England is like the water of a swift running river, always coming, and as fast going away; one in its passage dips a bucket-full, another a dish or cup-full for his occasions; but if the influx of plate from the West-Indies be stopped but for a little while, and the efflux in returns for England continue will not the mill-pond be quickly drained." Blackwell, "Some Additional Considerations on the Bills of Credit," op. cit.

22. "Money . . . is but a countermeasure of men's properties and instituted means of permutation," he wrote, then stating that the use of metal as money had been excusable while under an earlier ignorance of writing and arithmetic, but could now be removed from traffic. Mather, op. cit.

23. For further detail and historical context of the 1690 bills of credit see, Charles H. J. Douglas, 1892, op. cit.; Eliason, op. cit; and Dror

Goldberg, "The Massachusetts Paper Money of 1690," *The Journal of Economic History*, 69, no. 4 (December 2009): 1092-1106.

24. John J. Knox, *A History of Banking in the United States* (New York: Bradford Rhodes & Company, 1900), 15-24.; "Essays on Colonial Currency," University of Notre Dame, www.coins.nd.edu.
25. "Some Considerations Upon the Several Sorts of Banks," *Colonial Currency*, Vol. I, op. cit., 336-348.
26. "Some Proposals to Benefit the Province," *Colonial Currency*, Vol. II, op. cit., 97-107; "The Distressed State of the Town of Boston Considered," *Colonial Currency*, Vol. I, op. cit., 398-408. In some degree the concepts being put forth presaged the role that U.S. Treasury securities began to fulfill under Secretary of Treasury Alexander Hamilton on the balance sheets of the Bank of the United States and other state banks.

Chapter 2. Expanded Uses of Bills of Credit in the 1720s-1760s

1. C. W. MacFarlane, "Pennsylvania Paper Currency," Annals of the American Academy of Political and Social Science 8 (Jul., 1896): 51.
2. Benjamin Franklin, "The Legal Tender of Paper Money in America," February 13, 1767, franklinpapers.org.
3. "A Modest Inquiry Into the Nature and Necessity of a Paper Currency," Colonial Currency, op. cit, Vol. II, 335-357. Franklin argued that land was a better basis for a stable currency for the colonies than specie. In making his case for land, he showed that the measure of value or the wealth of a country should "be valued by the quantity of labour its inhabitants are able to purchase, and not by the quantity of silver and gold they possess." Since the value of land was more closely connected to the quantity of labor, as well as population growth, and could be controlled by the colony, unlike gold and silver, Franklin argued that land was a more reliable basis for a colonial currency. If the value of land was falling, he said, the legislature could take action to prevent the bills from falling with it. It would be more likely that the value of land would rise with population, he wrote. This rise would be prevented by providing that all taxes are made in the bills, and that "interest, as it is received, may be again emitted in discharge of public debts." By circulating back,

he wrote, "it returns again into the hands of the borrowers, and becomes part of their future payments." This would prevent a lack which would increase its value above the original value of the land on which it was emitted.

4. "An Act for Reprinting, Exchanging and Remitting all the Bills of Credit of this Province" in MacFarlane, op. cit.

5. John Russell Bartlett, Records of the Colony of Rhode Island and Providence Plantations, in New England, Vol. 5, (Providence: A. C. Green, 1860), 11-12; Bray Hammond, Banks and Politics in America from the Revolution to the Civil War (Princeton University Press, 1957), Chapter 1.

6. McFarlane, op. cit.

7. Franklin, "The Legal Tender of Paper Money in America," op. cit.; Benjamin Franklin, "Remarks and Facts Relative to the American Paper Money," March, 11, 1767, The Pennsylvania Chronicle, May 25–June 1, 1767, The Pennsylvania Gazette, June 4, 1767, founders.archives.gov.

8. Thomas Pownall, Governor of Massachusetts Bay from 1757 to 1760 praised Pennsylvania's paper money, writing, "there never was a wiser or a better measure," "never one better calculated to serve the uses of an increasing country . . . more steadily pursued or more faithfully executed." MacFarlane, op. cit.

9. In 1896, author C. W. MacFarlane examined the records and wrote that "Franklin's claim, that there had been no advance in the price of the necessaries of life, is reasonably true up to 1750." After this time, a great increase in export demand took place which increased prices. MacFarlane, op. cit.

10. Franklin, "The Legal Tender of Paper Money in America," op. cit.

11. Hammond, op. cit. 15-25.

12. Franklin, "The Legal Tender of Paper Money in America," op. cit.; Hammond, op. cit., Chapter 1; Davis, Introduction to Colonial Currency Reprints, op. cit.

13. Referring to his joint plan with Franklin, Pownall wrote, "It was, by us, jointly proposed to the government, under successive administrations, in the years 1764, 1765, 1766." The Administration of the British Colonies, 4th Edition (London: 1768), 231-253; Thomas

Pownall, "A plan proposed for a general paper currency for America, to be established by the British government," The Administration of the British Colonies, 5th Edition, Vol. I (London: 1774), 198-221; "Scheme for Supplying the Colonies with a Paper Currency," franklinpapers.org; Farley Grubb, "Benjamin Franklin And the Birth of a Paper Money Economy," philadelphiafed.org.

14. Franklin, "The Legal Tender of Paper Money in America," op. cit; Franklin, "Remarks and Facts Relative to the American Paper Money," op cit.

15. While this 10% was stated as a depreciation of paper currency by that much, he made a comparison with banknotes of England, stating that an increase demand for silver was never stated as a depreciation of the bank notes.

16. McFarlane verifies these statements of Franklin. McFarlane, op. cit.

17. Bills of exchange and promissory notes were financial instruments that allowed merchants to pay for their purchases on credit. They postponed the time of payment and served as a medium of payment. While a promissory note allowed one person to purchase from the other based on the promise to pay in the future, a bill of exchange allowed a merchant to purchase from a second based on the debt owed to him from a third party. In this regard a bill of exchange was very similar to a bank check, but unlike a check a bill of exchange was payable by any third party, usually not a bank but a merchant. In addition, unlike a check a bill of exchange was payable to the holder at a specific future time, usually sixty to ninety days or longer from when it was drawn for the purchase of goods, not payable on demand. Though this definition is sufficient for the purposes of this book the following extended illustration is provided for the interested reader. A first merchant who had recently sold goods to a third party on credit, for a certain amount of money, could use his creditor status with the third party to purchase goods from a second merchant for that amount. The bill of exchange was effectively a promissory note between two parties that was then signed over to the seller (the second merchant) by the purchasing merchant. When a bill of exchange was drawn, it stated that the third party who had promised to pay the first merchant would now pay the second. Bills of exchange served as a primary agency to enable the buying and selling of goods without coin. Coin would be effected at the time of final settlement of the bill of exchange by the

third party (the debtor), or, the third party would pay the creditor with another credit instrument. Domestic bills of exchange were used between distant cities while foreign bills of exchange were used between countries. Since merchants were constantly buying and selling between cities, large debts and credits between many parties accumulated. Buying a bill of exchange drawn on (payable in) a distant city was equivalent to settling a debt in that city and removed the need to send coin to the creditor. In a similar way, foreign bills of exchange were purchased by importers to remove the need to send specie abroad for payment. Just as domestic bills of exchange were a way to adjust debits and credits created between merchants of different cities, foreign bills of exchange were used to balance debits and credits between importers and exporters of respective countries. The source of foreign bills of exchange was exporters, who would draw up bills of exchange with purchasing merchants. As the amount of exports went up the price of a foreign bill of exchange went down since the number of bills of exchange being drawn increased. If the amount of imports went up, the price of a bill of exchange increased, since there was then a greater demand to settle debts abroad for the imports purchased. When exports dipped far below imports, a supply shortage of foreign bills of exchange would cause the rate of foreign exchange to rise. This would eventually make it cheaper to send specie abroad to pay for imports than to purchase a foreign bill of exchange to pay for imports. The use of the term bills of exchange occurs frequently in Part III of this book. Stephen Colwell, *The Ways and Means of Payment*: A full Analysis of the Credit System, with its Various Modes of Adjustment, 2nd edition (Philadelphia; T.B. Lippincott & Co., 1860), 205-212.

18. For details regarding the economic and military actions by Britain with respect to the colonies in the 1760s to 1773 see Ron Chernow, Washington: A Life (New York: The Penguin Press, 2010), Chapters 9-16.

Part II: The Bank of North America, the Bank of the United States, and the Development of the Funding System

Chapter 3. Designing a Currency with Credit

1. John J. Knox, A History of Banking in the United States (New York: Bradford Rhodes & Company, 1900).

2. Franklin had apparently proposed a method to Congress that would have prevented the depreciation. Benjamin Franklin to Josiah Quincy, Sept 11, 1783; "I lament with you the many mischiefs, the injustices, the corruption of manners, etc., etc., that attended a depreciating currency. It is some consolation to me that I washed my hands of that evil by predicting it in Congress, and proposing means that would have been effectual to prevent it if they had been adopted. Subsequent operations I have executed, demonstrate that my plan was practicable. But it was unfortunately rejected."

3. Max M. Edling, A Revolution in Favor of Government (London: Oxford University Press, 2003), 151.

4. "Letter to ____ December-March 1779-1780," The Papers of Alexander Hamilton, Vol. II (New York: Columbia University Press, 1987). The letter is likely directed to Philip Schuyler, see Forrest McDonald, Hamilton (New York & London: W. W. Norton & Co., 1982), notes II, no. 24; "Hamilton to James Duane," September 3, 1780, "Hamilton to Robert Morris," April 30, 1781, Papers of Alexander Hamilton, Vol. II, op. cit.

5. Ibid.

6. Charles J. Bullock, The Finances of the United States From 1775 to 1789 (Madison: University of Wisconsin Press, 1895), 158.

7. Knox, op. cit., 15-24.

8. Articles of Confederation, 1781, Art. VII.I

9. Jack N. Rakove, The Beginnings of National Politics (New York: Alfred A. Knopf, 1979), 303.

10. Rakove, op. cit., 301.

11. Roger H. Brown, Redeeming the Republic (Baltimore and London: Johns Hopkins Univ. Press, 1993), 150.

12. "Hamilton to Morris," April 30, 1781, Papers of Alexander Hamilton, op. cit. Hamilton's 1781 plan was for an authorized capital stock of 3 million pounds (six shillings to a pound), one-third in specie and the rest in land, and "European funds," to start at half that amount at least. In 1791, Hamilton would later elaborate on the error of this idea of uniting land and specie as capital in the bank because of the conflicting interests and difficulties of converting land into money. This would be driven by the expectation of banknotes to be redeemable in gold. Blackwell's Bank of 1687 based on land and other property had no such expectation, nor did Franklin's successful colonial currency of Pennsylvania based on land. Hamilton said it was the combination of land and gold which made land as part of the stock a problem.

13. Gouverneur Morris later served as a delegate to the Constitutional Convention of 1787. There he participated as one of its most active members in addressing the body and wrote the final draft of the U.S. Constitution.

14. Robert Morris, The Papers of Robert Morris, 1781-1784, edited by E. James Ferguson, "February 7-July 31, 1781" (University of Pittsburgh Press: 1973), 79.

15. Ibid., 85-86.

Chapter 4. The Bank of North America Takes Action

1. Brown, op. cit., 25; "Morris to Franklin," November 27, 1781, franklinpapers.org.

2. The Bank did not want all of its funds tied up in government loans and asked for repayment. Morris sold the government's stock in the Bank for this purpose beginning that fall until July 1783. Robert Morris, A Statement of the Accounts of the United States of America During the Administration of the Superintendent of Finance, Commencing with His Appointment on the 20th Day of February 1781, and Ending with His Resignation on the 1st Day of November 1784 (Philadelphia: 1785); Knox, op. cit., 25-50.

3. William Graham Sumner, Robert Morris: The Financier and the Finances of the American Revolution, Vol. II, (New York: Dodd, Mead, & Co., 1892), 33-35.
4. James Wilson later served as a delegate to the Constitutional Convention of 1787 where he debated more topics of the convention than any delegate except Gouverneur Morris. Through his knowledge of political theory and law his influence at the convention was second only to James Madison. Wilson was chosen to organize all of the resolutions and debates of the Convention into the first draft of the Constitution and formal language of law. Clinton Rossiter, 1787: The Grand Convention (New York: W.W. Norton, 1987), 202; Gordon Lloyd, "The Constitutional Convention," teachingamericanhistory.org.
5. James Wilson, "Considerations on the Bank of North America, 1785," The Works of the Honourable James Wilson L. L. D., Vol. III (Philadelphia: Lorenzo Press, 1804), 397-427. Morris had foreseen this circumstance when he wrote in a letter to Hamilton in May 1781 "we must expect that its ruin will be attempted, by external and internal foes." He cited this fact as a reason against Hamilton's plan for land to be included in the capital stock of the Bank.
6. Morris, A Statement of the Accounts, op. cit.
7. Hammond, op. cit., 56-58.
8. "H to Vicomte De Noailles, April-June 1782," Papers of Alexander Hamilton, Vol. III, op. cit., 83-86.

Chapter 5. The 1782-1783 Origins of the Bank-Based Funding System

1. Edling, op. cit., 56-57.
2. Woody Holton, Unruly Americans and the Origins of the Constitution (New York: Hill and Wang: 2007), 26-27.
3. Holton, op. cit., 136, 213-215.
4. Rakove, op. cit., 303, 311-313.
5. Georgia was still under British occupation, and therefore only Maryland and Rhode Island's compliance was needed.

6. Hamilton continued to correspond with Morris throughout the summer and fall, and proposed ways for the tax receivers to induce the people to circulate Morris's bills of credit. They were only being used to make payments, not fulfilling their intended purpose as a currency. James Kent, Commentaries on American Law, Vol. 1 (New York: E. B. Clayton, 1840), 207; John C. Hamilton, The Life of Hamilton, Vol. I (New York: D. Appleton, 1840), 405.

7. Brown, op. cit., 25; Oberholtzer, op. cit.

8. Rakove, op. cit., 316.

9. Jonathan Elliot, The Debates in the Several State Conventions on the Adoption of the Federal Constitution, Vol. I (Washington: 1901), 100-106. "Continental Congress Motion on Payment of Interest on the Domestic Debt and on Sending a Deputation to Rhode Island," December 6, 1782, founders.archives.gov. It was feared that Pennsylvania would appropriate its money to satisfy claims of its citizens against the U.S. rather than meet the congressional requisition. A permanent fund for discharging the public debt was discussed in November and December to prevent these creditors from taking needed state funds.

10. Fitzsimmons was a merchant and co-founder of the Bank of North America, delegate to the Constitutional Convention of 1787, and author of the July 4, 1789 Act of Congress to provide import duties.

11. The congressional statement said there could be little confidence in decisions based on thirteen separate entities. It called for security in the nation's credit based on a pledge by all the states to each other in such a way that it could not be revoked without a violation of the compact. This would later be the character of the Constitution and the ratification process of 1787-1790, that no state could secede from the Union without compliance of all the states. John Quincy Adams, The Jubilee of the Constitution: A Discourse, (New York: Samuel Colman, 1839).

12. Elliot, op. cit.

13. Rakove, op. cit., 316.

14. "Franklin to Robert Morris," December 23, 1782, franklinpapers.org.

15. The Papers of Robert Morris, op. cit. 368; Ellis Paxon Oberholtzer, Robert Morris, Patriot and Financier (New York: MacMillan Co., 1903), 192-194.

16. Papers of Alexander Hamilton, Vol. III, op. cit., 245-247.

17. Rakove, op. cit., 319-320.

18. Journals of the American Congress from 1774 to 1788, Vol. I (Washington: Way and Gideon, 1823), 153-156. Hamilton pointed out the likely economic reasons for the opposition of Virginia and Rhode Island: the former stated it had little share in the debts to and from the U.S., and the latter was levying a tax on all goods purchased by Connecticut, whose merchants were opposed to any competition from Congress for its duties.

19. The amount Congress was to levy was $900,000, less than 50% of the required $2.4 million to pay the annual installments of the interest on the $42 million of debts of the United States in 1783. Except for the the impost of $900,000, the Act did not designate the sources of taxation the states would collect, leaving it to them to determine. Collectors were to be appointed by the States rather than Congress. The Resolutions of Congress of the 18th of April 1783 (New York: Carroll & Patterson, 1787).

20. Rakove, op. cit., 323.

21. "Hamilton to George Clinton," May 14, 1783, founders.archives.gov. He also objected to the lack of designation of funds for state collection, as they would be improperly chosen and in a haphazard way. The result would be a revenue that would not increase in proportion with the growth of the country.

22. The committee repeated the explanation of benefits of a fund made from an impost, distributed equally through the economy according to consumption, as opposed to other forms of taxes.

23. The Resolutions of Congress, op. cit.

24. Hamilton had warned of this effect in his May 14 letter to Governor Clinton, that while the Act "was framed to accommodate it to the objections of some of the states… this spirit of accommodation will only serve to render it less efficient, without making it more palatable." Hamilton to George Clinton, op. cit. In June, Hamilton wrote

"A Vindication of the Congress," addressing the clamor against Congress' unpaid debts.

25. Rakove, op. cit., 325-329.

26. Hamilton was not opposed to emitting bills of credit of any kind, but emitting "unfunded paper as the sign of value," a distinction which had also separated successful and unsuccessful colonial bills of credit in the previous century. Hamilton later put this into more concrete terms as his maxim in his reports on Public Credit as Treasury Secretary of 1790. He also objected that the Articles did not provide Congress the power with "a general superintendence of trade," necessary for regulation and revenue, and the ability to promote or discourage certain manufactures. The Articles had granted the United States the sole power to regulate the coin of the nation, but not that of foreign coin in circulation. One was essential to the other, he explained, "as there ought to be such proportions maintained, between the national and foreign coin as will give the former preference in all internal negotiations."

Chapter 6. The Economic Path to the U.S. Constitution

1. Wilson, op. cit.

2. McDonald, op. cit., Chapter 4.

3. Brown, op. cit., 33-37.

4. The Bank of North America had made numerous enemies in Pennsylvania. Rich speculators and Tories began working toward purposes contrary to those of the Bank. In 1783 it had refused to lend the legislature $500,000 for a plan of speculators to refinance the state's debts. The intention had been to obtain control of the market in unfunded Pennsylvania war debt and profit from its price fluctuations. By doubling the value of the debt of the state through the loan, the debt would continue to be open to speculation. The speculators planned to borrow money from the state, buy securities at a third of the value, then turn them over at par for land. After selling the land, and repaying the loan, they would have turned a profit. In another instance, a group of Tories had been lending to craftsmen and labourers at interest rates of 12-18% per month. The Bank entered the market and reduced the rate to 2.5%. These factions successfully won a majority in the legislature in the fall of

1783, and acted on their intent to rid themselves of the Bank. Though it kept its national charter, they revoked the Bank's state charter, and attempted to scapegoat it for the ongoing crisis of the economy and the bankruptcies of merchants. They further claimed it was unconstitutional and a danger to public liberty. Because of these attacks in the legislature in 1784 and 1785, its operations virtually ceased for a period of time, and the Bank's stock price fell precipitously. In 1785, James Wilson, who had been appointed as one of its directors in 1781, wrote an essay titled, "Considerations on the Bank of North America." He demonstrated the power of Congress to have chartered the Bank and described the context which led to its difficulties. He wrote on the subject of delegated powers to the states and those reserved to the federal government in relation to the economy and the place which a national bank had within them. In addition to its constitutional power, he reviewed its necessity during the war in allowing the government to anticipate payments. McDonald, op. cit., 79-82; Wilson, op. cit.

5. The Resolutions of Congress, op. cit.
6. "Morris to Franklin," September 30, 1784, franklinpapers.org.
7. Brown, op. cit., 20.
8. Rakove, op. cit., 339.
9. Morris, A Statement of the Accounts, 1785, op. cit.
10. Edling, op. cit., 155-157.
11. Edling, op. cit., 54-57, 207; Holton, op. cit., 30-31, 267; Brown, op. cit., 37.
12. Edling, op. cit., 155-157, 193.
13. Brown, op. cit., 151
14. Holton, op. cit., 38, 57-61.
15. Ferdinand Bartram, Retrographs: comprising a history of New York City prior to the Revolution; biographies of George Washington, Alexander Hamilton, Nathan Hale, etc. (New York: Yale Publishing Co., 1868), 103-105; John C. Hamilton, Introduction to The Federalist: A Commentary on the Constitution of the United States (Philadelphia: J.B. Lippincott & Co, 1864). James Madison later remarked of the situation: "A nation leaving its foreign trade . . . to regulate it-

self, might soon find it regulated, by other nations, into a subserviency to a foreign interest. In the interval between the peace of 1783 and the establishment of the present Constitution of the United States, the want of a general authority to regulate trade is known to have had this consequence." James Madison, "Madison on the Tariff," Letter II, October 30, 1828, in The Debates in the Several State Conventions, edited by Jonathan Elliot, Vol. IV (Philadelphia: J. B. Lippincott Co., 1836), 605-608.

16. In 1784 and 1785, trade embarrassment led a few states to consider giving Congress the power to temporarily regulate foreign and internal trade in the states. After Virginia proposed a grant to Congress to regulate trade in April 30, 1784, and November 1785, the states of Pennsylvania, Connecticut, and Massachusetts added their approval at the end of 1784 and spring of 1785. Massachusetts' Governor Bowdoin stated in his May 21, 1785 message that Congress should be vested with "all the powers necessary to preserve the Union, to manage the general concerns of it, and promote its common interests." The Massachusetts legislature reversed this decision however, not agreeing on a method of altering the confederation, and instead passed a resolution that no further proceedings on the subject should take place. New York wanted to fight Great Britain's trade policy and enable Congress to do so, but this power was not granted until 1786, with a provision to forbid any collection of revenue without its sanction. New York began treating Connecticut and New Jersey as foreign powers and laid duties upon the manufactures that came into its ports from those states. In retaliation, New Jersey taxed the light houses owned by New York. The secession of New England and Vermont from the union was discussed. Maine threatened to secede from Massachusetts, Kentucky separated from Virginia, and North Carolina broke in two. John C. Hamilton, Introduction to The Federalist, op. cit; Bartram, op. cit.

17. Holton, op. cit., 65; Brown, op. cit., 19-25.

18. Rhode Island, Maryland, Georgia, and New York had not yet adopted the system either in whole or part and were directed "to pass laws, without further delay, in full conformity with the same." This emergency request received partial compliances from Rhode Island, Maryland, and Georgia.

19. New York had earlier passed an act in April that said all duties in the state could be paid in bills of credit of the state (its paper currency made legal tender). This meant that, according to its supposed compliance in May with the impost, it would collect its own taxes and its collection given to Congress would be in New York's paper currency. By consequence, every other state would be allowed to pay Congress in its own currency. But, while New York's currency was on par, Rhode Island was five to one, North Carolina two for one, South Carolina less than one. The collection would therefore be unsuitable for payment of foreign debts, defeating the purpose. On August 11, Congress passed a resolution stating that it was an occasion "sufficiently important and extraordinary" that they request a special session of the New York legislature to be held to remedy these defects for the dire necessity of the impost system. It was to no avail, as the Governor was not responsive.

20. Hamilton argued that "The principle of the objection . . . would not only subvert the foundation of the Union as now established–would not only render it impossible that any federal government could exist; but would defeat some of the provisions of the Constitution itself." He showed that the Articles clearly had appointed Congress to represent the states and manage the concerns of the union, and asked to what purpose they should exist if they were to have neither legislative or executive authority. He said that the arguments of New York would charge the Constitution with "the absurdity of proposing to itself an end, and yet prohibiting the means of accomplishing that end."

21. The federal domestic debt was then $26 million. This included $11.5 million loan office certificates, $3.7 million final settlement certificates, and $11 million back pay to the continental army. Brown, op. cit., 19.

22. In September of 1786, Hamilton had seized the opportunity of a commercial convention in Annapolis prompted by James Madison of Virginia, to agitate the issue of national power. Though the twelve-person convention accomplished little, its report resolved that a meeting take place at Philadelphia in May of 1787 "to take into consideration the situation of the United States, to devise such further provisions as shall appear to them necessary to render the constitution of the Federal Government adequate to the exigencies of the Union," and to report the final results for confirmation by

the States. By January 1787, neither Congress nor any state had responded to the Annapolis resolution in the affirmative.

23. The New York resolution was moved by General Malcolm and promptly adopted by the assembly, but not taken up in the Senate until the 20th of February. It was obtained after considerable debate, carried with a majority of one, due to Schuyler. "New York and the Federal Constitution," Magazine of American History II, no. 7 (July, 1878): 391-392; John C. Hamilton, Introduction to The Federalist, op. cit.; Henry B. Dawson, "The Motley Letter," N.Y. July 5, 1861, The Historical Magazine 9, no. 3 (March 1871): 177-178.

24. Edling, op. cit., 191-204; Holton, op. cit., 213-215.

Chapter 7. The Bank of the United States and the Funded Debt

1. U.S. Treasury, "Report on Public Credit," by Alexander Hamilton, January 9, 1790, in *Papers of Alexander Hamilton,* Vol. VI, op. cit., 65-123. In his coauthored reports with Hamilton in 1782-1783 and the *Federalist Papers* in 1787, James Madison was in agreement with most of the key financial policies carried out by the Washington Administration. As illustrated Madison had argued for equal treatment to all holders of securities in the 1780s. As late as the fall of 1789 he did not oppose federal government redemption of state bonds. He did oppose these policies as they were implemented in 1790-1795. Holton, op. cit., 258; Chernow, *Washington,* op. cit.; McDonald, op. cit., Chapter 5; John C. Hamilton, Introduction to *The Federalist,* op. cit. Later, as President of the United States and afterward, his own policies became aligned with those of the Washington Administration. See Part III.

2. The new loans were also made more favorable to the government and the nation with a lower interest than the original loans. In his 1790 "Report on Public Credit," Hamilton had written that the rate of interest would, in the coming twenty years, fall to four percent. He proposed reorganizing the debt from 6%, to a portion at 6% and another portion at 3%, as well as other various choices for the creditors, all averaging 4%.

3. U.S. Congress, "An Act to provide more effectually for the collection of the duties imposed by law on goods, wares and merchan-

dise imported into the United States, and on the tonnage of ships or vessels," August 4, 1790.

4. This was proven crucial in the speculative attacks on the debt during the Panic of 1792. McDonald, op. cit.; Cowen, David J., Richard Sylla, and Robert E. Wright, "The U.S. Panic of 1792: Financial Crisis Management and the Lender of Last Resort," Working Paper, Stern School of Business, New York University, October 2006. As its price stabilized the profit of speculation in government debt was removed. Holton, op. cit., 107.

5. McDonald, op. cit; Alexander Hamilton, "The Defense of the Funding System," July, 1795.

6. U.S. Treasury, "Report on the Subject of Manufactures," *by* Alexander Hamilton, December 5, 1791, in *Reports of the Secretary of the Treasury*, Vol. I. (Washington: Duff Green, 1828), 101.

7. U.S. Treasury, "Report on a Plan for the Further Support of Public Credit," by Alexander Hamilton, January 16, 1795, in *Papers of Alexander Hamilton*, Vol. XVIII, op. cit.

8. Robert Hare, *A Brief Review of the Policy and Resources of the United States* (Philadelphia: Bradford & Inskeep, 1810), 76. Edling, op. cit., 160.

9. U.S. Treasury, "Second Report on the Further Provision Necessary for Establishing Public Credit (Report on a National Bank)," by Alexander Hamilton, December 13, 1790, in *Papers of Alexander Hamilton*, Vol. VII, op. cit., 236-342.

10. The government subscribed by borrowing through the Bank for the amount, according to the provisions of the August 4 and 12 Acts of Congress authorizing further loans. The $2 million subscribed by the government was actually never paid into the Bank. While the $2 million was held to be an addition to the specie fund, the money borrowed through the Bank from Holland for the loan was never transferred. Therefore, Hamilton effectively issued a 5% promissory note to the Bank to become a subscriber.

11. Alexander Hamilton, 1795, op. cit., 176.

12. Hare, 1810, op. cit., 53-54; Hamilton, December 13, 1790, op. cit.; Hamilton, January 16, 1795, op. cit.; H. Parker Willis, *American Banking* (LaSalle Extension University, 1916), 207.

13. "Report on the Currency," *The American Quarterly Review*, Vol. XI, (March & June, 1832): 245-248; "On Banks and Paper Currency," by "W.," *Analectic Magazine*, Volume VI (December 1815): 489-518. Two-thirds to three-fourths of sixteen to seventeen million bank notes in circulation equals ten to twelve million units of currency that would have either not been in circulation without the banks or would have cost that much in specie.

14. Hamilton, *Reports of the Secretary of the Treasury*, op. cit. 67.

15. Edling, op. cit., 130-132, 159, 191-212; Hamilton, "The Defense of the Funding System," op. cit.

16. Hamilton, "Report on the Subject of Manufactures," op. cit. Later in 1799, Hamilton urged a similar fund for building canals as a means of more closely uniting the country, following the long work of George Washington and Gouverneur Morris on the subject. "Hamilton to Senator Jonathan Dayton," 1799, founders.archives.gov; Gouverneur Morris was the father of the Erie canal, first suggesting it in 1777. He had vigorously promoted the idea in 1803 after retiring from the U.S. Senate, and was later the chairman of the Erie canal commission beginning in March 1810 until his death. Jared Sparks, *The Life of Gouverneur Morris*, Vol. I (Boston: Gray & Bowen, 1832).

17. U.S. Treasury, *Additional Supplies for 1792*, by Alexander Hamilton, in *The Works of Alexander Hamilton*, Vol. III, edited by John C. Hamilton (New York: John F. Trow, 1850), 326-336.

18. These were proposed by him not only to raise revenue, but to promote manufactures. In addition to their use "as items of revenue," he wrote that several of the duties proposed were "strongly recommended by considerations which have been stated in the report of the Secretary, on the subject of manufactures." A tariff on steel, nails, shoes, and other clothing, and a 15% tariff on pistols, guns, iron, glue, sails, were among those proposed.

19. Hamilton addressed the buildup of the debt that had taken place, writing that "To extinguish a debt which exists" or to avoid increasing it are always favored; but that the payment of taxes for this purpose was always unpopular. He continued: "It is no uncommon spectacle to see the same men clamoring for occasions of expense, when they happen to be in unison with the present humor of the community . . . declaiming against a public debt, and for the reduc-

tion of it as an abstract thesis; yet vehement against every plan of taxation which is proposed to discharge old debts, or to avoid new, by the defraying expenses of exigencies as they emerge. These unhandsome arts throw artificial embarrassment in the way of the administrators . . ." Hamilton, "Report on a Plan for the Further Support of Public Credit," Edling, op. cit., 209.

20. Knox, op. cit., 25-50.

21. These added to the domestic excise taxes already laid yielded well over $6 million annually, while $4.3 million was needed to pay the annual interest and redemption of the public debt. The amount beyond payment of interest on the public debt could then be applied toward the expense of a potential foreign war. Hamilton, 1795, op. cit.

22. Knox, op, cit., 25-50.

23. The importance with which Hamilton viewed the government's stock in the Bank can be seen in his letter to Oliver Wolcott upon its sale, on August 3, 1796 that "I deplore the picture it gives, and henceforth wish to forget there is a bank or a treasury in the United States," writing that not one argument for the sale of the stock or against bonds could not apply just as well to the other. "I shall consider it as one of the most infatuated steps that ever was adopted," he concluded. "Hamilton to Oliver Wolcott," August 3, 1796, founders.archives.gov.

24. "Hamilton to Oliver Wolcott," April 10, 1795, in Henry Cabot Lodge, *The Works of Alexander Hamilton,* Vol. 10 (New York and London: G.P. Putnam's Sons, 1904), 96. For a long period of time, the Treasury, or Exchequer, in England, would issue bills to the Bank of England in an account from which it could then draw upon to make payments before revenue collection had taken place. Stephen Colwell, *The Ways and Means of Payment: A full Analysis of the Credit System, with its Various Modes of Adjustment,* 2nd edition (Philadelphia; T.B. Lippincott & Co., 1860), 605-623.

25. "Hamilton to Oliver Wolcott," June 16, 1796, in Lodge, *Works,* op. cit., 177.

26. "Hamilton to Oliver Wolcott," August 22, 1798, in Lodge, *Works,* op. cit., 317.

Part III: The Second Bank of the United States as an Instrument for Economic Growth

Chapter 8. Currency Disorder and the Finances of Madison's Second Term

1. Nicholas Biddle, Pennsylvania House of Representatives, *Debates of the Legislature of Pennsylvania in the Session of 1810-1811*, reported by William Hamilton (Lancaster: 1811), 28-31.
2. Robert Wright, "Origins of Commercial Banking in the United States, 1781-1830," EH.Net Encyclopedia, edited by Robert Whaples, March 26, 2008, Table 2.
3. U.S. Congress, Committee on Ways and Means. Senate Committee on Finance. *Official documents, &c. in relation to the Bank of the United States.* 21st, 1st session, April 13th, 1830, March 29, 1830 (Steubenville: J. Wilson, 1830), 9-14.
4. McDuffie, op. cit., 1-29. See Note 17 to Chapter 2 for an extended definition of bills of exchange.
5. "On Banks and Paper Currency," *Analectic Magazine,* op. cit.
6. U.S. Congress, *Official documents, &c. in relation to the Bank of the United States,* op. cit., 31-32.
7. "On Banks and Paper Currency," *Analectic Magazine,* op. cit.
8. It should be noted that the majority of the capital of the largest banks was public debt, and therefore, though not paying specie, they still had ample capital on reserve with which to redeem their notes if debt certificates had been authorized for such use. "On Banks and Paper Currency," *Analectic Magazine,* op. cit. James Madison later contemplated this option, writing to Dallas on July 4, 1816, that if the State legislatures would "not enforce the obligations of the banks to redeem their notes in specie, they cannot, surely, forebear to enforce the alternatives of redeeming them with public stock, or with national bank notes . . ." "James Madison to Alexander Dallas," July 4, 1816, in George Mifflin Dallas, *Life and Writings of Alexander James Dallas* (Philadelphia: J. B. Lippincott & Co., 1871), 458.

9. Knox, op. cit., 48; George Mifflin Dallas, *Life and Writings*, op. cit., 129-134; Alexander J. Dallas, November 27, 1814, "Letter from Treasury Department to House of Representatives," in George Mifflin Dallas, *Life and Writings*, op. cit.

10. In addition to these losses, prices had risen due to the war, making the amount borrowed for purchase of government supplies that much less valuable. Knox, op. cit., 50.

11. McDuffie, Wilson, op. cit., 1-29.

12. Dallas, October 14, 1814, in George Mifflin Dallas, *Life and Writings*, op. cit. Alexander Dallas saw a constitutional problem in the federal government's acceptance of notes of suspended banks. While the notes of the Bank of the United States had been made legal money, only coin and treasury notes fell in the same category, not state corporations. When the banks suspended in 1814, a decision in which the Congress had no say, the state bank notes superseded the legal currency of the nation. Congress' power to regulate coin became useless as it had no way to keep paper currencies at fixed values in relation to the value of coin. Dallas wrote that the authority competent to establish national coin is alone competent to create a national substitute, and questioned the constitutionality of banks issuing bills of credit, i.e. suspended banknotes, as they are chartered by state legislatures. U.S. Treasury, "State of the Finances," by Alexander J. Dallas, Communicated to the Senate, December 8, 1815, in *American State Papers: Documents, Legislative and Executive*, Part III, Volume III, No. 454 (Washington: Gales & Seaton, 1834). The issue was also addressed in Knox, op. cit., 22-23.

13. U.S. Treasury, "Support of Public Credit by a System of Taxation—National Bank—Debenture Certificates," by Alexander Dallas, October 17, 1814, In *The Funding System of the United States and Great Britain,* edited by Jonathan Elliot, Congressional Series of United States Public Documents, Vol. 440 (Washington: Blair & Rives, 1845), 588-595.

14. Faced with large discounts, Dallas further explained his proposed system on November 27, 1814 in the course of responding to a House inquiry. He said that the usual test of public credit is the value of the public debt, not the ability to borrow. A desperate man can always borrow at high rates of interest and to stave off the wants of the moment; or land can be sold. But it is only establish-

ing the foundations of public credit, he wrote, that the government can provide for future needs. George Mifflin Dallas, *Life and Writings*, op. cit., 244-248.

15. George Mifflin Dallas, *Life and Writings*, op. cit., 234-243.

16. Knox, op. cit., 52-62.

17. Increased revenues led Dallas and Madison to change their view on treasury notes. Since they would no longer be needed for shortfalls, they contemplated using them instead as a non-redeemable currency to be issued by the Bank, in the period prior to the resumption of specie payments. U.S. Treasury, *Financial Operations of the Late War—Money Matters of 1815—Support of Public Credit—National Circulating Medium*, by Alexander J. Dallas, December 6, 1815, in *The Funding System of the United States and Great Britain*, edited by Jonathan Elliot, Congressional Series of United States Public Documents, No. 86 (Washington: Blair & Rives, 1845), 627-657; James Madison, "Seventh Annual Message," December 5, 1815, millercenter.org.

18. As Madison wrote to Dallas on June 16, 1816, discussing the conduct of banks evading specie payments: "unless the national bank should be both able and willing to afford relief, I see no resource against the existing policy of the State banks, if supported by the State governments . . . but in a treasury paper, with the prerogative of being used in the national taxes and transactions, and an entire exclusion of local bank paper." He may have contemplated, as Dallas discussed in his final report, issuing treasury notes through a national bank. "James Madison to Alexander Dallas," June 16, 1816, in George Mifflin Dallas, *Life and Writings*, op. cit., 453.

19. Dallas, December 6, 1815, op. cit. In this lengthy report, Dallas writes of the coming difficulties in reestablishing a "national circulating medium," and the requirements to obtain the state bank cooperation.

20. Dallas, December 6, 1815, op. cit. A different national bank plan was put forward in December 1815 which sought to incorporate a substantial use of federal bonds as a basis of state bank reserves. In addition to specie, security for redemption for a national bank and state banking system would also be based on 6% public debt certificates. This it proposed, would remove the danger of future suspension, since banks would have the option of redeeming their

notes in public debt certificates as well as the scarce specie. This would provide a means to keep bank circulation in check and prevent future depreciation. It would give greater security to the currency, require much less gold and silver, and link the value of currency to the value of public debt. Once the value of bonds rose above the value of specie, people would prefer the bonds as redemption, and banks would instead redeem notes and deposits in gold, returning specie payments. "On Banks and Paper Currency," *Analectic Magazine,* op. cit. This plan was later cited by the Lincoln Treasury Department as the 1st known proposal prempting the National Banking Act of 1863. U.S. Treasury, "Origin of the National Banking System," *The Historical Magazine* 9 (August 1865): 252-256. A similar plan may have been in mind in Robert Hare's 1810 *A Brief View of the Policy and Resources of the United States,* when he suggested that the first Bank of the U.S. proved the potential capitalization of all banks and insurance companies by up to three-fourths public debt.

21. U.S. Treasury, "Mr. Dallas's Plan of a National Bank," by Alexander J. Dallas, December 24, 1815, in *The Funding System of the United States and Great Britain,* edited by Jonathan Elliot, Congressional Series of United States Public Documents, No. 87 (Washington: Blair & Rives, 1845), 670-676.

Chapter 9. The Bank and the Economic Depression of 1818-1822

1. "James Madison to Alexander Dallas," in George Mifflin Dallas, *Life and Writings,* op. cit., 469-470. There were 110 banks in 1811, and 262 banks in 1817, a number which grew to 339 in 1818. While banks doubled in number between 1811 and 1816, the circulation tripled from $29 million to $99 million. Robert Wright, op. cit; Knox, op. cit., 48-49.

2. Knox, op. cit., 57.

3. Mathew Carey, "The New Olive Branch," *Essays on Political Economy* (Philadelphia: H.C. Carey & I. Lea, 1822), 261-271.

4. Knox, op. cit., 57-58.

5. Govan, op. cit., 51-59; Knox, op. cit., 58.

6. Knox, op. cit., 59.

7. Govan, op. cit., 60-65. John Quincy Adams, *Memoirs of John Quincy Adams,* Vol. IV (Philadelphia: J.B. Lippincott & Co, 1874), 324-325.
8. Govan, op. cit., 60-65.
9. *Memoirs of John Quincy Adams,* op. cit., 382-383.
10. Mathew Carey, *Miscellaneous Essays,* Vol. I (New York: Carey & Hart, 1830), 262-266; Govan, op. cit., 60-65.

Chapter 10. The Bank and the Economic Growth of the 1820s-1830s

1. Previous to this appointment, Biddle's public service had included terms as a Pennsylvania state representative and state senator from 1810-1814, where he was a pioneer in promoting public education and internal improvements. Govan, op. cit., 1-28.
2. Nicholas Biddle, *The Correspondence of Nicholas Biddle Dealing with National Affairs,* 1807-1844 (Boston and New York: Houghton Mifflin Company, 1919), 29.
3. This did not signify keeping an amount of notes equal to its gold and silver reserves, but that they could be redeemed at all places if desired, giving uniformity to the currency, in a ratio of roughly 3-4 dollars of notes per dollar of coin. "On Banks and Paper Currency," *Analectic Magazine,* op. cit.
4. The Bank of the United States, "Report of the Triennial Meeting of the Stockholders," *Niles Weekly Register* 35 (September 27, 1828): 73-74; Govan, op. cit., 84-86. The Bank did make exceptions at some branches to redeeming notes from other branches in later years to protect itself from losses. U.S. Congress, *Official Documents, &c. in relation to the Bank of the United States,* op. cit., 13.
5. "Report on the Currency," *The American Quarterly Review,* op. cit.
6. Some stockholders, in opposition to the Bank's new measures reacted with an attempt in 1826 to control enough of the stock to elect a new President. A speculative attempt was made earlier in 1825 to rival the Bank's influence in New York. Govan, op. cit., 89-90.
7. Govan, op. cit., 85.
8. Hezekiah Niles, *Niles' Weekly Register* 43 (September 22, 1832): 50.

9. The Bank lent $1,000,000 to the C & E between 1826 and 1828; $250,000 to the D & R in 1830; a monthly statement of the Bank of April 1832 shows over $1,000,000 that month to the Union, Schuylkill, C & D, Lehigh, D & H, and D & R. U.S. Congress, Committee to Investigate the Bank of the United States, op. cit., 12, 192-193, 423; "Million Dollar Club," *Neversink Valley Museum*, neversinkmuseum.org; H. Parker Willis, *Investment Banking* (New York and London: Harper Brother, 1936), 225-226.

10. Robert Carlson, "The Pennsylvania Improvement Society and Its Promotion of Canals and Railroads, 1824-1826," *Pennsylvania History* 31, no. 3 (July 1964).

11. Michael Chevalier, *Society, Manners, and Politics, in the United States* (Boston: Weeks, Jordan and Co., 1839), 44.

12. "York County (PA.) Memorial," May 19, 1834, *Register of Debates in Congress*, Part IV of Vol. X (Washington: Gales and Seaton, 1834), 4188.

13. "Report on the Currency," *The American Quarterly Review.*

14. Biddle, *Debates of the Legislature of Pennsylvania in the Session of 1810-1811*, op. cit., 29.

15. "Mr. Biddle's Letter," *Niles National Register* 54 (April 14, 1838): 98-100.

16. Wares remained unsold and labor unemployed, and many projects and industries stood idle since only those with large stores of wealth had the ability to undertake them. The latter were often unwilling to lend their capital out for use and it tended to accumulate as stores of gold and silver. Chevalier, op. cit., 349; H.C. Carey, *Answers to Questions: What Constitutes Currency?* (Philadelphia: Lea & Blanchard, 1840).

17. Ibid., 1-15.

18. McDuffie, Wilson, op. cit, 1-29; Willis, *American Banking*, op. cit., 211-212.

19. This problem also involved a more general complication between banks on the seaboard and interior. Since specie was little used for domestic commerce, and mostly used in facilitating imports, interior banks did not keep as much specie on reserve as seaboard banks involved in foreign trade. However, when seaboard banks

contracted their issues during periods of prolonged negative trade balance, causing excess withdrawal of specie, notes of interior banks become less valuable than seaboard banks, and became a potential liability against them as they were returned in great numbers. In other words, when interior producers were not able to keep pace with the needs of importing merchants to pay for their imports with bills of exchange related to exports, a negative trade balance was extended for a period of time, and interior banks were forced to contract their own issues. Eleazar Lord, *Principles of Currency and Banking* (New York: G. & C. & H. Carvill, 1829), 85-89.

20. Nicholas Biddle, *National Gazette* of Philadelphia, April 10, 1828, extracts printed in *Gouge,* Cobbett edition, 150-156.

21. In 1824-1826, the Bank of England's specie reserves dropped from 14 to 2.5 million pounds, in a period where its liabilities stayed relatively the same amount, from 29-32 million. Carey, *Answers to Questions,* op. cit., 27.

22. Govan, op. cit., 88-99; "Annual Report of the Treasury," by Richard Rush, December 6, 1828, in *The Register of Debates in Congress,* Vol. V, Appendix, (Washington: Gales & Seaton, 1830), 22.

23. Govan, op. cit., 88-99.

24. Rush, "Annual Report of the Treasury," op. cit.

25. Ibid.

Chapter 11. Confirming the Success of the Bank

1. U.S. Congress, Official Documents, &c. in relation to the Bank of the United States, op. cit., 13-17, 37-42; Willis, American Banking, op. cit., 210.

2. Govan, op. cit., 132-159.

3. Thomas Hart Benton, February 2, 1831. Abridgment of the Debates of Congress from 1789-1856, Vol. XI (New York: D. Appelton & Co., 1859), 143-161.

4. Tristam Burges, Memoir of Tristam Burges, edited by Henry L. Bowen (Providence: Marshall Brown, 1835), 337-338. Burges states further that in addition, from 1829-1834, it circulated between $12-

20 million dollars, though it was authorized to circulate the amount of its capital of $35 million. State banks circulated $70 million.

5. In the summer of 1829, the new Administration had attempted unsuccessfully to direct the control of some of the offices of the Bank by claiming certain offices were approving or denying loans based on the political leaning of the borrower. Members of Jackson's party informed him that the stories of political loans had no basis. Senator Calhoun said the reason the Administration attacked the Bank was because it would not become a controllable element of its agenda. Speeches of John C. Calhoun: Delivered in the Congress of the United States (New York: Harper & Brothers, 1843), 128; Knox, op. cit., 64-66. Govan, op. cit., 112-122.
6. Govan, op. cit., 140-141.
7. U.S. Congress, Committee to Investigate the Bank of the United States, op. cit.
8. Joseph Morgan Rogers, Thomas Hart Benton (Philadelphia: G.W. Jacobs Co., 1905), 139-140.
9. Out of its numerous loans to newspapers, two cases coincided with a change in the recipient's opinion from neutrality to support with respect to the Bank's recharter, those of Duff Green's Telegraph, and a loan made indirectly to Webb and Noah's Courier and Enquirer. A detailed review of these suspicious loans indicated they did not equate to bribery. James L. Crouthamel, "Did the Second Bank of the United States Bribe the Press?," Journalism Quarterly 36, no. 1 (March 1959): 35-44.
10. The majority report put the positive actions of former Bank president Cheves in contrast to Biddle, while the negative actions of the former, such as the charge of excessive interest, were made to be compared with the latter, though they took place ten years before. A witness claiming Bank president Biddle was guilty of embezzlement was found to have perjured himself on the stand. The majority investigation was unable to show that the Bank had any major losses since 1819. U.S. Congress, House, Committee to Investigate the Bank of the United States, Bank of the United States, "Report of Mr. Adams," 22nd Congress, 1st Session, April 30, 1832, No. 460 (Washington: 1832), 389-410.
11. Knox, op. cit., 69.

12. "Mr. Clayton of Georgia," Niles' Weekly Register 46 (June 7, 1834): 251-252.

13. Benton echoed the tenor of the statement days later, stating "You may continue to be for a bank and for Jackson, but you cannot be for this bank and for Jackson… the whole government would fall into the hands of the moneyed power. An oligarchy would be immediately established, and that oligarchy in a few generations would ripen into a monarchy." Carl Schurz, Henry Clay, Vol I (Boston and New York: Houghton, Mifflin and Co., 1899), 379.

14. "Politics of the Day," Niles' Weekly Register 42 (August 4, 1832): 407, 424-426.

15. "James Madison to Charles J. Ingersoll," June 25, 1831, founders.archives.gov

16. Henry Cabot Lodge, Daniel Webster (Boston and New York: Houghton Mifflin Company, 1911), 209.

17. Govan, op. cit., 208-212.

18. Andrew Jackson, "Annual Message of the President," December 4, 1832.

19. Eugene Irving McCormac, James K. Polk: A Political Biography (Berkeley: University of California, 1922), 30.

20. McCormac, op. cit., 34.

21. "Louis McLane to Andrew Jackson," Correspondence of Andrew Jackson, edited by J.S. Bassett, Vol. 5 (Washington: Carnegie institution of Washington, 1926-1935), 75-101; M. Grace Madeleine, "Monetary and Banking Theories of Jacksonian Democracy" (New York: Kennikat Press, 1943).

22. McLane, op. cit.

23. William John Duane, Narrative and Correspondence Concerning the Removal of the Deposits (Philadelphia: 1838), 129-130.

24. Knox, op. cit., 70.

25. U.S. Congress, "An Act to Incorporate the Subscribers to the Bank of the United States," April 10, 1816.

26. Speech of William Ellsworth, March 27, 1834, Register of Debates in Congress, Part III of Vol. X (Washington: Gales and Seaton, 1834), 3261-3262; Govan, op. cit., 244-246.

27. John Quincy Adams, Register of Debates in Congress, Part III of Vol. X (Washington: Gales and Seaton, 1834), 3494-3495.

28. John Quincy Adams, "Documents Relating to the Removal of the Deposits," Hazard's Register of Pennsylvania, Vol. XIII, January-July 1834 (Philadelphia: WM. F. Geddes, 1834), 90.

29. Adams, op. cit. 3492.

30. Govan, op. cit., 245-259.

31. After first underplaying the crisis, the Administration then said the Bank was hoarding gold and silver, though it had been stressing its insolvency for the previous year. Govan, op. cit., 253-255.

32. A resolution passed the Senate on March 28 censuring the President for having "assumed upon himself authority and power not conferred by the Constitution and laws." In April and May 1834, many memorials on the subject were sent to the U.S. Senate from around the country reporting distress and displeasure with Administration. One stated that while its public justification for removal was that the Bank possessed unlimited power and was a threat to liberty, the action which the Administration took was an assumption of unlimited power by the executive, claiming both purse and sword. Another stated that the effects against those doing business on borrowed capital would do more toward creating an aristocracy than its claims against the Bank by limiting enterprise and business to those with large reserves of wealth. As former Treasury Secretary Mclane had told Jackson, some of the resolutions said that if he succeeded in his war against the Bank, without regulation and control, the currency would be ruined by the control of unrestrained state banks. U.S. Congress, Senate, Public Documents Printed By Order of the Senate, 1st Session, 23rd Congress (Washington: 1834).

33. Govan, op. cit., 259.

34. Their own ordinary individual deposits were only $25 million. Knox, op. cit., 80.

35. This growth increase is not comparable with the periods previous. From 1822 to 1829, $1.2 million per year of revenue was raised from

the sale of land on average, with a growth rate per year of about 6%. For comparison, from 1825-1829, the average was $1.3 million per year with an annual growth rate of 9%. From 1829-1833 land sales increased to $3 million per year on average, increasing at an average annual growth rate of 36%. American Almanac and Repository of Useful Knowledge for the Year 1839 (Boston: Charles Bowen, 1838), 101.

36. Knox, op. cit., 82.

37. Andrew Jackson, "Seventh Annual Address," December 1835.

38. U.S. Congress, "An Act to Regulate the Deposits of the Public Money," June 23, 1836, in The Public Statutes at Large of the United States of America, Vol.V (Boston: Charles C. Little and James Brown, 1850), 52-56.

39. Ibid, 36-41.

40. Ibid, 36.

41. Ibid, 36-41.

42. Ibid. Nicholas Biddle suggested that a proper execution of the distribution law and a repeal of the specie circular would restore confidence in twenty four hours, and repose in a month.

43. From 1833-1837, the Bank of England lost 6 million of its 10 million pounds in specie in that time, though its liabilities remained at 32 million. Carey, Answers to Questions, op. cit., 27; Govan, op. cit., 305-308.

44. "Message of the President to Congress," December 5, 1837, The Financial Register, Vol. 1 (July 1837 to July 1838): 394-396.

45. Given his strong advising role and authorship of many of its policies, Van Buren did not inherit the Jackson Administration's financial crisis as much as share the public face for policies he had helped to design. "Speech of Mr. Burges." Niles Weekly Register 40 (April 16, 1831): 119

46. "Message of the President to Congress," September 4, 1837, The Financial Register, Vol. 1 (July 1837 to July 1838): 321-325, 337-342.

47. "I am willing to see the charter expire, without providing any substitute for the present bank. I am willing to see the currency of the Federal Government left to... hard money... Every species of paper

might be left to the State authorities, unrecognized by the Federal Government, and only touched by it for its own convenience when equivalent to gold and silver." Senator Thomas Hart Benton, February 2, 1831, Abridgment of the Debates of Congress, Vol. XI (New York: D. Appelton & Co., 1859), 143-161.

48. "Mr. Biddle's Letter," op. cit.

49. "Henry Clay to Nicholas Biddle," May 30, 1838, in The Correspondence of Nicholas Biddle Dealing with National Affairs, op. cit., 309.

50. President Martin Van Buren, "Third Annual Message to Congress," December 2, 1839. millercenter.org.

51. Knox, op. cit., 82.

52. Ibid., 84.

53. Andrew Jackson, "Annual Address to Congress," December 4, 1832.

54. U.S. Congress, House, Committee to Investigate the Bank of the United States, Bank of the United States, "Report of Mr. Adams," 22nd Congress, 1st Session, April 30, 1832, No. 460, (Washington: 1832), 407-408.

55. In 1837, Robert Hare put forward a proposal for a national loan office system structurally similar to the branches of the Bank of the U.S., based on national credit as their reserve rather than specie alone and without as much power. The proposal was similar to that put forward in "On Banks and Paper Currency," Analectic Magazine, December 1815, op. cit. National regulation of the currency would be accomplished by an institution built up from state associations through the creation of a national trust fund system that state banks would join. The national currency regulation which the second Bank of the United States had accomplished, haphazardly, was to be streamlined by splitting banking into two categories: private banks for deposits and general discounts, and a national loan office system which would make loans on personal account. State banks that wished to resolve themselves into the national system would receive national trust fund notes in proportion to the federal and state stocks which they agreed to deposit in the trust fund. The state banks subscribing would then no longer be able to issue their own currency. Their issues would be founded on the trust fund made up of those stocks, and its operations would be confined to the issue of national loan office bills of credit. In order to account

for the increase of state banking, he proposed its circulation be increased to $255 million, with $55 million in security, rather than the $35 million capital of the Bank in 1817. The trust fund would perform the role of furnishing a sound uniform currency for the nation and making loans, not partaking in the exchange trade and making discounts on commercial paper—that would be left to state banks, or perhaps an exchange office, though he only hinted at the latter. In the same manner, the state banks engaging in discounts of commercial paper would no longer be able to make loans on personal security and personal assets—that would be the function of the national loan office trust. As an example, only the national loan office would make loans to joint stock companies, for making canals, railways, bridges, etc. In addition, the notes would be more secure than the Bank of the U.S. by the manner of redemption, as the offices would be authorized to redeem notes in 5% certificates instead of specie, unless they had ample specie or preferred to redeem their notes in specie. Hare's plan was a very interesting compromise, along with containing some improvements upon the Bank of the United States. Many of its elements were seen later with the establishment of the National Banking System in 1863. Robert Hare M.D, Suggestions Respecting the Reformation of the Banking System," (Philadelphia, John C. Clark & Co., 1837).

Part IV: The Return to Currency Management and the Promise of the National Banking System

Chapter 12. The Independent Treasury and State Banking

1. Banks opposed the subtreasury as it threatened to cause an abnormally large redemption of notes of specie paying banks, as during the period under the Specie Circular. Knox, op. cit., 86-90.
2. Colwell, *The Ways and Means of Payment,* op. cit., 104, 605-623.
3. Ibid., 104.

4. Not having a federal bank system involved in managing domestic payments did not preclude the ability to facilitate the business exchanges of the country. In the 1840s and 1850s the government of France used its revenues to facilitate domestic exchanges, standing in for the role of banks. Colwell, op cit., 605-623.

5. Stephen Colwell, *Remarks and Suggestions Upon the State and National System of Banks* (Philadelphia: Caxton Press of Sherman & Co., 1864), 17.

6. With the crash of 1857, imports declined and banks were relieved of the demand of specie for foreign commerce, and the duties going into the treasury fell by one half. After the crash, a number of proposals were put forward to remedy the systemic errors in the financial system and increase the efficiency of the Subtreasury system. Among them were those of banking expert Stephen Colwell, a former official of the Mint. Since the Bank of the United States had been a politically dead issue since the middle of the 1840s, and the subtreasuries were forbidden from working with the state banks, he proposed the use of treasury notes, payable on demand, with and without interest. They were modeled on relation between the Exchequer and the Bank of England, where government expenditures and revenues were paid in and out without transfer of actual money from the Exchequer, and prior to receiving anticipated taxes. The Exchequer accomplished this in a manner similar to the way the general public made payments with their own bank accounts, using the credit of deposited commercial securities to pay debts by means of bank discounts while the paper was running to maturity. Though the Treasury had issued notes under Gallatin and Dallas, Colwell's plan was of a much larger scope. In addition to interest free treasury notes, Colwell proposed bills with interest but very short maturities of six to twelve months, allowing them to absorb excess circulation. He also proposed a domestic exchange office to regulate and reduce the friction of exchanges, rather than leaving them in the hands of the states, and to distribute public revenues without risk and to the benefit of the public, rather than keeping it idle as it was in the subtreasury. The Lincoln Administration utilized a very similar method in their use of non-interest demand and legal tender notes from 1861-1865. Colwell, *The Ways and Means of Payment,* op. cit., 605-623.

7. Willis, *American Banking,* op. cit., 218-220; Knox, op. cit., 91-92.

Chapter 13. The Departure from the State Banking Era

1. H. C. Carey, "The Currency Question," *Letters to the Hon. Schuyler Colfax*, (Philadelphia: H. C. Baird, 1865), 1-2; Willis, *American Banking*, op. cit., 221.

2. These were part of Congress' authorized loan of $250 million in the Acts of July 17 and August 5, 1861, consisting largely of 20 year loans of 6% interest, and 3 year, 7.3% bonds (7.30's), exchangeable for 20 year 6% bonds. U.S. Treasury, *Annual Report of the Secretary of the Treasury*, by Salmon Chase (Washington: 1861), 7-28; U.S. Treasury, *Annual Report of the Secretary of the Treasury*, by Salmon Chase (Washington: 1863) [These reports were issued on December of each year, and published the following year. To avoid confusion, the dates listed for annual reports of the Secretary of the Treasury and the Comptroller of the Currency are report dates, not publication date.]; Colwell, *Remarks and Suggestions Upon the State and National System of Banks*, op. cit., 3-5.

3. Colwell, 1864, op. cit.; "The Government to Place Itself in the Hands of the Associated Banks, Orange N.J.," *New York Times*, September 30, 1861; Willis, *American Banking*, op. cit., 221. The New York Times article began as follows: "Government, as I understand, are to pay certain creditors with demand notes, bearing no interest, to the extent of $50,000,000, and the coin for these remains partly in the banks and partly in the Sub-Treasury, until needed for the redemption of these demand Treasury notes, or any other demands that comes upon the Sub-Treasurers. If this is carried out, in the true intent and meaning of the present understanding, the SubTreasury will at no time have large balances of coin; but will call, from week to week, for about what they are to disburse. . . . I would suggest that Congress make this loan agency permanent during the war, and also exclusive, leaving it to the banks to seek at home and abroad for takers. . . . Under this arrangement, our Government might agree with some one or more of our principal banks to redeem the demand Treasury notes made payable here; the banks of Philadelphia and Boston to redeem such as were made payable at those places. This would make them current and receivable on deposit at any of the banks in the cities where they are respectively made payable, and they, no doubt, be current in all the loyal States."

4. Knox, op. cit., 1-34; Colwell, 1864, op. cit.

5. Wesley Clair Mitchell, *A History of the Greenbacks, (*University of Chicago Press, 1903), 24-26; Cowell, 1864, op. cit.; Knox, op. cit., 1-35. Mitchell surmises that Chase expected the specie would be able to go back in circulation fast enough to not have exhausted the banks. Other potential reasons for Chase's action include: fear of a popular reaction against working closely with the banks, a personal conviction about specie or the state banks, or very likely, an expectation that the implementation of his planned national banking system would not be possible under such an arrangement.

6. In December 1839, state representative Abraham Lincoln gave a lengthy speech opposing the subtreasury and defending the Bank of the United States. On March 1, 1843, among resolutions he submitted to a Whig meeting in Springfield, Illinois, was the following: "That a National Bank, properly restricted, is highly necessary and proper to the establishment and maintenance of a sound currency, and for the cheap and safe collection, keeping, and disbursing of the public revenue." On July 1, 1848, Lincoln wrote speech notes he thought proper for candidate Zachary Taylor, including: "Should Congress see fit to pass an act to establish [a National Bank] I should not arrest it by the veto, unless I should consider it subject to some constitutional objection from which I believe the two former banks to have been free." Abraham Lincoln, *Complete Works*, edited by John Nicolay and John Hay, Vol. 1 (New York: The Century Co., 1894), 21-37, 72, 134.

7. Gabor S. Boritt, *Lincoln and the Economics of the American Dream* (University of Illinois Press, 1978), 137-233.

8. See Part III, Chapter 8, Note 20; See Part III, Chapter 11, Note 55. "On Banks and Paper Currency," *Analectic Magazine*, op. cit.; Hare, *Suggestions*, op. cit. The New York Banking law of 1838 requiring that collateral security be pledged for the redemption of a bank's circulation was another precedent.

9. Chase, *Annual Report*, 1861, op. cit. Lincoln and Chase's further statements on the subject are reviewed in detail in the next chapter.

10. Borrit, op. cit. Lincoln's lack of involvement in Treasury policy such as the floating of bonds, borrowing from banks, and the legal tender issues apparently caused great frustration to Chase and friction

between the two men. Borrit argues that Lincoln's political requirements did not permit his direct involvement. That Lincoln went out of his way to promote the National Banking plan to Congress further underscores its priority for him.

11. John Hay, December 25, 1863, *Lincoln and the Civil War In the Diaries and Letters of John Hay* (New York: Dodd Mead & Co, 1939), 144-145.

12. Chase, *Annual Report,* 1861, op. cit.

13. U.S. Treasury, *Annual Report of the Secretary of the Treasury,* by Salmon Chase (Washington: 1862).

14. James Blaine, *Twenty Years of Congress: from Lincoln to Garfield,* Vol. I (Norwich: H. Bill Publishing. Co., 1884), Chapter XIX.

15. The Treasury Department had issued treasury notes in anticipation of revenues for payment since the time of Treasury Secretary Oliver Wolcott. It was the action of making these bills a legal tender which was unprecedented under the U.S. Constitution. Congressman E. G. Spaulding of New York, the sponsor of the legal tender bill, explained in his speech on the subject, that through its power to regulate the value of coin, Congress may determine that treasury notes issued on the credit of the government hold equal value to them. He referenced a twenty-five year period in Great Britain where the Bank of England's notes were made a virtual legal tender by the suspension of the statutory clause requiring specie payments. He said that under necessity, the government could issue promissory notes on the basis of its taxation power of a national property then equal to $16 billion, just as banks issue promises to pay which were not backed by sufficient gold, but by economic wealth. Spaulding also reviewed numerous other arguments and cited *McCulloch vs. Maryland.* In his speech in Congress on February 4, 1862, Congressman John Bingham of Ohio addressed those who pointed to a lack of authorization to make notes legal tender in the Constitution. He said the same held true for coin, and that Congress had determined coin to be legal tender through its power to regulate commerce. In response to another legal argument in opposition to the bill, which stated that impairing the obligation of contracts by making treasury notes legal tender for all debts was unconstitutional, Bingham stated that impairing contracts is only prohibited for States, not the Federal Government. E. G. Spaulding,

A History of the Legal Tender Paper Money Issued During the Great Rebellion (Buffalo: Express Printing Co., 1869), 28-40, 48-50.

16. "This note is a legal tender for all debts, public and private, except duties on imports and interest on the public debt, and is exchangeable for U.S. six per cent twenty year bonds, redeemable at the pleasure of the United States after five years."
17. Though not technically redeemable on demand in specie, they remained "redeemable" in the sense of their acceptance for the payment of taxation.
18. Chase, *Annual Report,* 1863, op. cit., 15.
19. Carey, "The Currency Question," op. cit., 2-7; Eleazar Lord, "A Letter on National Currency Addressed to the Secretary of the Treasury" (New York: A. D. F. Randolph, 1861).
20. Chase, *Annual Report,* 1862, op. cit., 1-30.

Chapter 14. Banking & Funding Strategy 1863-1865

1. The account provided in this chapter is of special reference for Part V.
2. The notes issued by the U.S. Treasury to national banks became known as national bank notes. When Chase wrote "United States note circulation, furnished to banking associations," to describe them here, and elsewhere in the report as "similar notes" to "United States notes," he did not mean to equate them with the legal tender notes, legally named "United States notes," but only that they were similarly "notes" of the "United States" This somewhat confusing description of the national banking notes in 1862 by Chase before the bill became law, simply reflects his emphasis that the notes of national banks would be national notes secured by the Treasury, rather than issued by the banks themselves, and equally as uniform as the legal tender notes which had grown in popularity that year.
3. Chase, *Annual Report,* 1862, op. cit., 17.
4. Ibid., 20-21.
5. Ibid., 19-20.

6. Chase, *Annual Report,* 1862, op. cit., 17; William Elder, *Questions of the Day: Economic and Social* (Philadelphia: H.C. Baird & Co., 1871), 153-156.

7. Abraham Lincoln, "Second Annual Message," December 1, 1862. presidency.ucsb.edu

8. Ibid.

9. Knox, op. cit., 97; *Annual Report of the Comptroller of the Currency* (Washington: 1863); Milton Ailes, "The National Banking System and Federal Bond Issues," in *Banking Problems* (Philadelphia: American Academy of Political and Social Science, 1910), 114-128.

10. Chase, *Annual Report,* 1863, op. cit., 1-27, 42-47.

11. Elder, 1871, op. cit., 145. In 1871, its amount was still 82% greater than any time before the war.

12. Knox, op. cit., 137.

13. Spaulding, op. cit., 189-190; Annual Report of the Secretary of the Treasury, "Statement of Indebtedness" tables, 1862-1864. On July 1, 1863, the convertibility of greenbacks to 5-20 bonds was removed, citing the difficulty of selling them while this provision was in force. Despite the success of their sale, Spaulding warned of the consequences of the action for the depreciation of the legal tender notes relative to the price of gold, and wrote that it was one of the worst mistakes of the war. Knox writes that as far as the convertibility was concerned, the bonds were always virtually convertible into legal tenders since they could be used as collateral for loans. Knox, op. cit., 137; Spaulding, op. cit., 190-195. See Appendix I.

14. Chase, *Annual Report,* 1863, op. cit., 1-27.

15. "The Treasury Report and Mr. Secretary Chase," *The Continental Monthly* 5, no. 2 (February 1864).

16. Beginning in August 1861, Chase reincorporated and expanded the use of internal excises taxes which had died out after 1820. In addition, stamp taxes and an income tax of 3% on all incomes of $800 was laid, eventually amounting to $73 million per year. On July 1, 1862 an internal revenue law was passed, providing for a levy of duties on various domestic manufactures, and upon trades and occupations. Congress increased duties on imports on July 14, 1862. These revenues formed a substantial basis on which to rest the

credit of the government for the large issues of its notes, bonds, and other obligations. They provided for the ordinary expense of government, the interest on the war debt, and liquidation of a considerable portion of the principal of the debt.

17. Compare with Colwell, *The Ways and Means of Payment,* op. cit., 605-621

18. Colwell, 1864, op. cit.; Spaulding, op. cit., 190-198.

19. As of June 30, 1865, $180 million of compound interest notes had been issued. U.S. Treasury, *Annual Report of the Secretary of Treasury,* by Hugh McCulloch (Washington: 1865).

20. Many of the banks instead became party to the speculation in gold, costing the government and the public. See Appendix I; Colwell, 1864, op. cit.

21. U.S. Treasury, *Annual Report of the Secretary of the Treasury,* by William Fessenden (Washington: 1864), 1-30.

22. Knox, op. cit., 98; *Annual Report of the Comptroller of the Currency* (Washington: 1863, 1864).

23. Colwell, 1864, op. cit., 19.

Part V: The Challenges and Problems of the National Banking System

Chapter 15. Circulation Limitation and Other Errors of Implementation 1865-1870

1. In 1865 there was enough currency, but it was not evenly distributed. In October of 1865 the national banks in the eastern states held large reserves of legal tender notes of $193 million in addition to $19 million of their own not in circulation, and $16 million of state banks. The whole amount of national banknotes in circulation was then $171 million. The total unemployed circulation in the hands of national banks in the east was therefore $228 million. U.S. Treasury, "Report of the Comptroller," by Freeman Clarke in *Annual Report of the Secretary of the Treasury* (Washington: 1865), 65-67.

2. Knox, op. cit., 100-101; Clarke, op. cit.

3. U.S. Treasury, "Report of the Comptroller," by Hiland Hulburd, in *Annual Report of the Secretary of the Treasury* (Washington: 1866), 72-73; Knox, op. cit. 138; *The Bankers Magazine and Statistical Register* Vol. 40 (July 1885 to June 1886): 177-179; Willis, *American Banking*, op. cit., 225.

4. Hulburd, "Report of the Comptroller," 1866, op. cit., 72-73; Knox, op. cit., 106, 295-304.

5. Henry Parker Willis, *The Theory and Practice of Central Banking:With Special Reference to American Experience 1913-1935* (New York and London: Harper & Brothers, 1936), 69-70.

6. Colwell, 1867, op. cit; Willis, *American Banking*, op. cit., 226.

7. Hulburd, "Report of the Comptroller," 1866, op. cit., 73.

8. Knox, op. cit., 147; U.S. Treasury, "Report of the Comptroller," by Hiland Hulburd, in *Annual Report of the Secretary of the Treasury*, (Washington: 1867), 10-14.

9. Clarke, op. cit., 67.

10. *The Bankers Magazine*, op. cit., 177-179. A Treasury redemption service was belatedly established in 1874.

11. U.S. Treasury, *Annual Report of the Secretary of the Treasury*, by Hugh McCulloch (Washington: 1868), xxx.

12. U.S. Treasury, *Annual Report of the Secretary of the Treasury*, by Hugh McCulloch (Washington: 1867), iv.

13. The amount of 520 bonds outstanding on the Treasury's balance sheet grew from $606 million to $1,267 million between June 1865 and November 1867. In the same period, certificates of indebtedness went from $116 million to zero, 3 year 6% compound interest notes from $194 million to $63 million, 1-2 year 5% interest notes from $42 million to zero, 3 year 7.3% treasury notes from $671 million to $334 million, and temporary loans from $90 million to zero, and legal tenders from $433 million to $357 million. McCulloch, *Annual Report*, 1865, op. cit.; U.S. Treasury, *Annual Report of the Secretary of the Treasury*, by Hugh McCulloch (Washington: 1866); McCulloch, *Annual Report*, 1867, op. cit.

14. To combat the influence of contraction, which had been felt by the economy, prolonged discussion took place in the winter of 1866, an Act was passed on March 2, 1867, to neutralize some of its effects. Since national banks used the Treasury's 6% compound interest notes as part of their reserve, the rapid funding of them required legal tenders to be absorbed in their stead, leading to a contraction of currency in circulation. The bill authorized the Treasury to exchange newly issued certificates of deposit at 3% for the compound interest notes, allowing the 3% notes to be counted as part of the reserve of national banks, reducing the effect. Blaine, op. cit., Vol. II, Chapter XIII.

15. Knox, op. cit., 71; McCulloch, *Annual Report,* 1868, op. cit.

16. Blaine, op. cit., Vol II.

17. U.S. Treasury, "Report of the Comptroller," by Hiland Hulburd, in *Annual Report of the Secretary of the Treasury* (Washington: 1869), 37-38.

18. Knox, op. cit., 147.

19. John Sherman, *Selected Speeches and Reports on Finance and Taxation from 1859 to 1878* (New York: D. Appleton & Co., 1879), 259.

20. Knox, op. cit., 106-109;

Chapter 16. Speculation and the Crisis of 1873

1. Willis, 1935, op. cit., 69; H. Parker Willis, *The Banking Situation* (New York: Columbia University Press, 1934), 894; Knox, op. cit., 103.

2. Another plan for a national institution at that time came from one D. H. London who advocated an Exchequer Bank that would issue circulation against government debt and gold, negotiate and fund government loans, and be its fiscal agent. D. H. London, "The Establishment of the Exchequer of the United States of America," Memorial to the Senate, Referred to the Committee on Finance on December 18, 1871, printed in *Miscellaneous Documents of the Senate,* 1872; Knox, op. cit., 115.

3. U.S. Treasury, *Annual Report of the Comptroller of the Currency,* by John J. Knox (Washington: 1874), 1-9; Knox, *History of Banking,* op. cit., 187.

4. U.S. Treasury, "Report of the Comptroller," by Hiland Hulburd, in *Annual Report of the Secretary of the Treasury* (Washington: 1871), 70-72.
5. Ibid.
6. Elder, *Questions of the Day*, op. cit., 155.
7. Hulburd, "Report of the Comptroller," 1871, op. cit., 72.
8. Ibid.
9. Ibid.
10. Knox, op. cit., 182; Willis, *Investment Banking*, op. cit., 225-226.
11. Knox, op. cit., 182-183.

Chapter 17. Partisan Wrangling and the Decline of National Bank Circulation

1. Knox, op. cit., 138, 149.
2. Ibid., 148-151
3. Ibid.
4. U.S. Treasury, *Annual Report of the Comptroller of the Currency*, by John J. Knox (Washington: 1879), v; Knox, *A History of Banking*, op. cit., 162.
5. James Garfield, 1877, See Knox, op. cit., 211.
6. Knox, op. cit., 154-155.
7. Ibid.
8. Knox, op. cit., 154-155. Specie had begun to shift from Europe back to the U.S., a migration that would continue for the next 60 years. Liaquat Ahamed, *The Lords of Finance* (New York: Penguin Press, 2009).
9. Knox, op. cit., 139-143.
10. William Elder, *Conversations on the Principal Subjects of Political Economy* (Philadelphia: H.C. Baird & Co., 1882), 232; Elder, *Questions of the Day*, op. cit., 153; Colwell, "Financial Suggestions and Remarks," op. cit.

Chapter 18. National Bank Difficulties and Financial Crisis 1879-1907

1. Knox, op. cit., 199; Willis, *American Banking,* op. cit., 30-231.
2. Between 1885 to 1890 national bank circulation declined from, was $267 million to $123 million, a net decrease of $151 million. Knox, op. cit., 295-304.
3. Willis, *American Banking,* op. cit., 220, 272-273; H. Parker Willis and George Edwards, *Banking and Business* (New York: Harper Bros., 1922), 473.
4. Knox, op. cit., 181-183.
5. Ibid., 207.
6. Ibid., 191.
7. Willis, *The Theory and Practice of Central Banking,* op. cit., 66; Willis, *The Banking Situation,* op. cit., 176-179.
8. Willis, *Banking and Business,* op. cit., 415. After 1890, the surplus disappeared as a tariff that year reduced revenues. This lead the government to borrow instead of purchasing its bonds, and new bonds were issued for national bank circulation, bringing the circulation up $214 million by 1896. Willis, *American Banking,* op. cit., 232.
9. Willis, *Banking and Business,* op. cit. 416-419; Willis, *American Banking,* op. cit., 233-234.
10. Willis, *Banking and Business,* op. cit. 415.
11. Willis, *American Banking,* op. cit., 234, 272.
12. Willis, *American Banking,* op. cit, 235-236; Willis, *Banking and Business,* op. cit., 420. For more on the causes and build up of the crash of 1907, see Roger Lowenstein, *America's Bank: The Epic Struggle to Create the Federal Reserve,* (New York: Penguin Press, 2015), 46-76.

Part VI: The Federal Reserve and the Credit Modifications of the 1930s-1940s

Chapter 19. The Federal Reserve System and its Beginnings

1. Multiple forms of Currency legislation were put forward and debated in 1908, some related to plans previously discussed in 1894, leading to the Vreeland-Aldrich act of that year. The Act allowed "national currency associations of banks" to issue currency on their holdings of commercial paper as a joint liability, and individual banks to deposit other securities besides government bonds for circulation, including state, municipal, or county bonds. However, the provisions of the act were not utilized until 1914, and soon became obsolete. H. Parker Willis, "The Federal Reserve System" (Chicago: Blackstone Institute, 1920), 6; Willis, *American Banking,* op. cit., 236-238. See Lowenstein, op. cit, for a full account of the Federal Reserve Act's creation.
2. M.S. Szymczak, "The Federal Reserve System and the Banking Act of 1935," Forum Dinner of the Trenton Chapter of the American Institute of Banking, Trenton New Jersey, November 18, 1936.
3. Willis, *Investment Banking,* op. cit., 328-330.
4. Henry Parker Willis, "The Federal Reserve Act," *The American Economic Review* 4, no. 1 (March, 1914): 18.
5. In 1896, an investigation into the use of checks and credit instruments by banks showed that the deposits of 5,500 banks consisted almost entirely of checks, a portion of 92.5%, whereas the bank currency made up 6% of its deposits, gold .6% and silver .5%. For wholesale trade, 95.3 percent was financed by credit paper. For retail, 67.5% was transacted with credit paper of banks. It concluded that at least 80% of all business of the country was carried on by checks, drafts, and other credit instruments. Knox, op. cit., 211; see also Appendix II.
6. Willis, *American Banking,* op. cit., 285; Willis, "The Federal Reserve Act," op. cit., 20-21; Willis, *Banking and Business,* op. cit., 154;Willis, *The Banking Situation,* op. cit., 23-26.

7. Willis, *The Banking Situation*, op. cit., 445-446.

8. Ibid., 44.

9. Willis, "The Federal Reserve System," op. cit., 53-56; Willis, *Banking and Business*, op. cit., 421.

10. Willis, "The Federal Reserve Act," op. cit., 21-22.

11. Willis, *The Banking Situation*, op. cit. 179.

12. Willis, *The Theory and Practice of Central Banking*, op. cit., 78.

13. Willis, *American Banking*, op. cit., 241-245.

14. Willis, *The Theory and Practice of Central Banking*, op. cit., 78.

15. Willis, "The Federal Reserve System", op. cit., 44-47.

16. Willis, *The Banking Situation*, op. cit., 35.

17. Ibid., 33-34

18. Willis, *Investment Banking*, op. cit., 229-232.

19. Willis, *The Banking Situation*, op. cit.

20. Liaquat Ahamed, *The Lords of Finance* (New York: Penguin Press, 2009).

21. Willis, *The Banking Situation*, op. cit.

22. For more on the Fed's post war actions which contributed to the speculative build up leading to the crash of 1929, see: Willis, *Investment Banking*, op. cit., 333-336; Willis, *The Banking Situation*, op. cit., 53-57; Perry Mehrling, *The New Lombard Street: How the Fed Became the Dealer of Last Resort* (Princeton University Press, 2011), 38-41.

Chapter 20: Fed Discount Limitation Problems and the Amendments of 1929-1933

1. M.S. Szymczak, "The Federal Reserve System and the Banking Act of 1935," Address before the Cleveland Chapter American Institute of Banking, November 7, 1935.

2. Ibid.

3. Mehrling, op. cit., 33-35.

4. Szymczak, “The Federal Reserve System and the Banking Act of 1935,” op. cit.; Hearings on S. 1715 and H. R. 7617 “Bills to Provide for the Sound, Effective, and Uninterrupted Operation of the Banking System, and for other purposes,” April 19 to June 3, 1935, 296-297.

5. Szymczak, “The Federal Reserve System and the Banking Act of 1935,” op. cit.

6. A. D. Gayer, “Proposed Amendment of the Fed: The Administration Banking Bill of 1935,” *Economic Journal* 45, no. 178 (June, 1935): 286-295.

7. Ibid.

8. Howard H. Hackley, *Lending Functions of the Federal Reserve Banks: A History.* Board of Governors of the Federal Reserve System, May 1973, *Chapter 8.*

9. These discounts could only be made against extremely short-term assets, ninety day promissory notes of industry. Such assets were almost solely possessed by banks and it was therefore hardly likely for individual corporations to possess them. By the end of the year only twenty three discounts were made for less than a million dollars. Hackley, op. cit., Chapter 10; James C. Dolley, “The Industrial Advance Program of the Federal Reserve System,” *The Quarterly Journal of Economics* 50, no. 2 (Feb., 1936): 229-274.

10. A predecessor to the Reconstruction Finance Corporation was the War Finance Corporation (WFC). The WFC was created in 1918 to discount slow and long-term paper during WWI when certain economic classes could not obtain credit. In 1921, it was amended to be able to promote the export of agricultural products to foreign countries in particular cases. Willis, *Business and Banking,* op. cit., 477.

11. Hackley, op. cit., Chapter 8.

12. The March 1933 improvement of Section 10b increased the authorization of loans to member banks significantly during 1933 and 1934. As opposed to the total of $30 million having been advanced throughout 1932 under its earlier form, a total of $280 million additional in loans was authorized by March 1935, when it expired. Dolley, op. cit.

13. Hackley, op. cit., Chapter 8.

14. The liberalizations to Section 10b allowing loans to member banks achieved results, but less than needed to make a serious impact. The provision added to Section 13 allowing direct lending to companies was hardly utilized and only a few million dollars went out to 68 individuals and companies. The amendment to Section 13 authorizing loans to non-member banks needed written approval from a proper state banking commission, and the provision was almost never used.

15. Minutes of the Board of Governors of the Federal Reserve System, March 6, 1935. All "Minutes" references available at fraser.stlouisfed.org.

16. David Lawrence, *Pittsburgh Post Gazette,* February 8, 1934

17. David Lawrence, *The Desert News* (Salt Lake City), November 24, 1933.

18. Black, Eugene, Statement to the House, *Extension of Credits to Industry and Broadening of the Powers of the Federal Reserve,* Hearing on H.R. 8717, May 2, 1934, 73rd Cong., 2nd Session, 1-78; Douglas Raymond Fuller, *Government Financing of Private Enterprise* (Stanford University Press, 1949), 81.

19. In 1932-1933, banking expert and historian H. Parker Willis served on the Senate Subcommittee on Banking. In 1934, he subsequently wrote an excellent treatment on the significance, context, and workings of the committee with respect to the Banking Act of 1933, available in Part I of his book *The Banking Situation.* On the development of investment banking sector and its importance for the consolidation and growth of industry from 1880-1920 see Willis, *Investment Banking,* op. cit., 228-232.

Chapter 21. Credit Supply Initiatives of 1934-1935

1. Minutes, February 7, 1934, op. cit.

2. David Lawrence, *Pittsburgh Post Gazette,* February 8, 1934.

3. Minutes, Feb. 8, 1934, op. cit.

4. Minutes, Feb. 26, 1934. op. cit.

5. A January 30th act of Congress related to credit measures (the "Thomas Amendment") was used by the Roosevelt Administration to lower the weight of a dollar of gold, creating an available fund on which to draw. $140 million of this fund was to be used to pay Federal Reserve banks for the FDIC stock they held, such that the reserve banks could then subscribe to the capital of the proposed industrial credit banks of 1934. In addition, the banks would leverage their capital up to five times by borrowing. Their capital was to be continually loaned and repaid as a revolving fund. The original Feb. 8 draft of Black had a general subscription by the U.S., without specifying the method, for a capital twice that of the final bill of February 26.
6. Minutes, op. cit., March 5, 1934.
7. Ibid., April 12, 1934.
8. Ibid., March 2, 3, 8, 1934.
9. Ernest M. Klemme, "Industrial Loan Operations of the Reconstruction Finance Corporation and the Federal Reserve Banks", *The Journal of Business of the University of Chicago* 12, no. 4 (Oct., 1939): 365-385; U.S. Bureau of the Census, *Survey of Reports of Credit and Capital Difficulties* (Washington: Government Printing Office, 1935); Charles O. Hardy and Jacob Viner, *Report on the Availability of Bank Credit in the Seventh Federal Reserve District* (Washington: 1935).
10. David Lawrence, "Intermediate Credit System for business," *New York Sun*, March 15, 1934.
11. Minutes, op. cit., April 23, 1934.
12. George Durno, *The Citizen Advertiser* (NY), March 12, 1934.
13. U.S. Congress, Senate, S. 3487, "An Act Relating to direct loans for industrial purposes by Federal Reserve banks, and for other purposes," fraser.stlouisfed.org. Bills preceding the act included S.2946, S. 2867, H. R. 8864.
14. M.S. Szymczak, "Recent Relations of the Federal Reserve System with Business and Industry," speech delivered before the Illinois Bankers Association Decatur, Illinois, May 20, 1935.
15. Ibid.

16. The authorization for lending "on a reasonable and sound basis," was a less restrictive provision than that given to the RFC, which was on the basis of "adequate security." By the end of 1935, nearly 2000 applications totaling 125 million had been approved, roughly equal to those made by the RFC in those two years, due to a more liberal provision given to the Federal Reserve. By 1936 this tapered off and the RFC took over most industrial loaning.
17. U.S. Congress. House. "To Extend the Functions of the Reconstruction Finance Corporation." Hearings before the Committee on Banking and Currency on H.R. 4240 (S. 1175) "A Bill to Extend the Functions of the Reconstruction Finance Corporation, etc., and for other purposes," January 21, 22, 23, 24, and 25, 1935.
18. Jesse Jones, *50 Billion Dollars: My thirteen years with the RFC* (New York: 1951); U.S. Treasury, *Final Report of the Reconstruction Finance Corporation*, by Robert Anderson (Washington: 1959).
19. The 1935 Banking Act amended the Federal Reserve Act giving discretion to a centralized board over the powers of setting the discount rate, open market operations, and reserve requirements; the Board was moved from New York to Washington. Many of its provisions were an abandonment of the theory of automatic adjustment of currency and credit. Gayer, op. cit. For a more critical view of the 1935 Banking Act, see Willis, *The Theory and Practice of Central Banking*, op. cit.
20. M. S. Szymczak, "The Banking Act of 1935," New York Banker's Convention, Lake George, New York, June 8, 1935.
21. Henry Steagall, April 19, 1935, Report to Accompany H.R. 7617, 74th Congress, 1st Session, House of Representatives, Report No. 742, fraser.stlouisfed.org.

Chapter 22. Fed Lending Powers and Proposals 1939-1950

1. Klemme, op. cit.
2. Hearings before the Committee on Banking and Currency, House of Representatives, April 18, 1938, 8.
3. Loans had averaged $17 million a month in 1935, and $10 million a month in 1936, and declined to $4 million a month in 1937.

4. David Lawrence, *Appleton Post Crescent,* February 18, 1939; also published in *The Nebraska State Journal* (Lincoln, Nebraska), February 20, 1939.
5. David Lawrence, *San Bernardino Sun,* Vol. 45, May, 23, 1939.
6. David Lawrence, June 14, 1939, *Pittsburgh Post-Gazette.*
7. Senator James Mead, S. 2998, October, 1939.
8. Hackley, op. cit., Chapter 11, 12.
9. Hearing on S. 408, "To repeal section 13b of the Federal Reserve Act, to amend section 13 of the said Act, and for other purposes." April 17, 1947, 18, fraser.stlouisfed.org.
10. May, 1944: S. 1918 (Senator Wagner, 78th Cong., 2d Sess); Feb. 1945: S. 511 (Senator Wagner) Jan. 27, 1947: S. 408, (Senator Tobey), Jan. 27, 1947; February and May 1950: S. 2975 (Senator Mahoney), S. 3625 (Senator Lucas), H.R. 8565 (Mr. Spence), and H-R. 8566 (Mr. Patman);1951: S. 1647; Ibid. Chapter 11.
11. Hearing on S. 408, op. cit.
12. Board of Governors of the Federal Reserve System, "Statement of the FRB in connection with S. 408," by S. R. Carpenter, December 19, 1946. fraser.stlouisfed.org.

Appendices

Appendix I: The Causes of Inflation and Increases in the Price of Gold 1862-1865

1. While there was not an excess of U.S. notes, Chase said that if there was any excess in prices from currency it came from state banks, which were using legal tenders in place of a gold reserve to expand their own issues: "U.S. notes, having been made a legal tender were diverted from their legitimate use as currency and made the basis of bank circulation, that the great increase of the latter began," he wrote. State banks had increased their circulation by $37 million, their deposits had increased from $264 to $344 million, and their increased deposits stimulated loans, which grew from $607 to $677 million. Chase, *Annual Report,* 1862, op. cit., 14-15.

2. Chase, *Annual Report,* 1862, op. cit., 18.

3. Colwell, "Financial Suggestions and Remarks," op. cit., 1-14.

4. Colwell, 1864, op. cit., 49.

5. The high demand for gold forced a continuation of suspension long past the point where banks had accumulated sufficient gold reserves to resume specie payments under normal demand for gold.

6. U.S. Treasury, "Report of the Comptroller," by Hugh McCulloch, in *Annual Report of the Secretary of the Treasury* (Washington: 1864), 52-53.

7. Ibid.

8. Fessenden, *Annual Report,* op. cit., 5.

9. Chase, *Annual Report,* 1862, op. cit.

10. Colwell, 1864, op. cit.

11. Chase, *Annual Report,* 1863, op. cit., 12-14; Chase, *Annual Report,* 1862, op. cit.

12. Chase, *Annual Report,* 1862, op. cit.; Fessenden, *Annual Report,* op. cit., 22-23; McCulloch, "Report of the Comptroller," 1864, op. cit.; Carey, *Letters to Colfax,* op. cit.; H. C. Carey, *Letters to the Hon. B. H. Bristow,* (Philadelphia: Collins Printer & Co., 1874), 5-6.

13. McCulloch, "Report of the Comptroller," 1864, op. cit., 53.

14. Ibid.

15. Colwell, 1867, op. cit., 1-19.

Appendix II: Oversights of the National Banking Acts of 1863 and 1864

1. Colwell, *Remarks and Suggestions Upon the State and National System of Banks,* op. cit., 12. The simple inadequacy of specie to conduct the required services of payments was also illustrated later in an example in 1882 by William Elder. That year the amount of domestic gold and silver was $480 million, deposits in the national banks were $713 million, in state and private banks $397 million, in savings banks $783 million, and their total banknotes $694 million.

There was therefore a total for circulation and deposits convertible into coin of $2.58 billion, in relation to $480 million worth of gold and silver coin, a ratio of 5.3 to 1. Elder, *Conversations on the Principal Subjects of Political Economy,* op. cit., 157-158; Colwell, 1864, op. cit., 12-21; Colwell, *The Ways and Means of Payment,* op. cit., 188-250.

2. Colwell, 1864, op. cit, 11-22.

3. As a simple illustration, a bread maker may have issued a promissory note of 30 day maturity to a miller for the purchase of flour, and the latter would have brought the promissory note to a bank for discount. In this case, the bank would buy the promissory note from the miller with banknotes, paying him an amount less than the full value for maturity. Later, upon maturity of the note in the bank, the bank would receive a payment to the full value of the note from the breadmaker, enough to balance the transaction with a small profit. As with checks between banks transferring deposit credits, this transaction with banknotes did not involve any use of the bank's specie reserves. The banknotes were themselves a credit issued for a credit, and represented commodities in trade. They could be redeemed into coin but they were not a representation of coin, not because there was not enough gold on reserve, but because they came into existence for commodities in production.

4. On the insecurity created by convertibility on demand, and the issue of solvency against convertibility, economist Ralph Robey used a useful metaphor in 1938 to address the assumption that banknotes could not be as good as gold without being convertible instantly into gold. "To defend this view one must be prepared to contend that beef and mutton purchased with banknotes are not as good as if purchased with gold and silver, and that debts paid with banknotes are not as fully extinguished as if discharged in gold or silver. As long as this policy is continued, the banks will resist being forced to stop payment in specie with all the powers of attack and defense that they can wield, and they will claim to be sound frequently because in the attempt to save themselves they will have hurt the public more than the public has damaged them." Like Colwell, Robey saw the convertibility of credits into legal money as an inefficient form of regulation and a poor form of security. Ralph W. Robey, *Purchasing Power: An Introduction to Qualitative Credit*

Control Based on the Theories of Stephen A. Colwell (New York: Prentice Hall, 1938), 45-54.

5. Stephen Colwell, "Financial Suggestions and Remarks," 1867, available at the Princeton Theological Seminary Libraries Special Collections, 1-19.

6. Colwell also proposed the authorization and capitalization of special non-issue deposit and transfer banks. These banks would be capitalized by buying bonds and depositing them in the Treasury like other national banks, but instead of receiving notes for their capital they would only be credited the amount at the Treasury and authorized to transfer the credit of their stock of bonds to other banks for payment. There capital would therefore not be put at the risk of those withdrawing specie, maintaining the distinction between bank credits and legal money. Ibid., 9.

7. Colwell, 1864, op. cit., 27-30.

8. As reviewed in Appendix I, the congressional legislation of 1862 that made import duties paid in coin also made specie reserves much less controllable by the government and fueled speculation in gold. The U.S. had no institution with the power of the Bank of England to raise the discount rate to discourage such speculation. By the summer of 1864, speculation had cost the Treasury $500 million. Ibid.

9. See Chapter 10.

10. Colwell, 1864, op. cit., 26-36.

Bibliography

Adams, John Quincy. *Memoirs of John Quincy Adams.* Vol. IV. Philadelphia: J.B. Lippincott & Co, 1874.

"Documents Relating to the Removal of the Deposits." *Hazard's Register of Pennsylvania.* Vol. XIII, January-July 1834. Philadelphia: WM. F. Geddes, 1834.

The Jubilee of the Constitution: A Discourse. New York: Samuel Colman, 1839.

Register of Debates in Congress. Part III of Vol. X. Washington: Gales and Seaton, 1834.

"*An Act for Reprinting, Exchanging and Remitting all the Bills of Credit of this Province.*" In C. W. MacFarlane. "Pennsylvania Paper Currency." *Annals of the American Academy of Political and Social Science* 8 (Jul., 1896): 51-120.

Ahamed, Liaquat. *The Lords of Finance.* New York: Penguin Press, 2009.

Ailes, Milton. "The National Banking System and Federal Bond Issues." In *Banking Problems.* Philadelphia: American Academy of Political and Social Science, 1910.

American Almanac and Repository of Useful Knowledge for the Year 1839. Boston: Charles Bowen, 1838.

The Bank of the United States. "Report of the triennial meeting of the stockholders." *Niles Weekly Register* Vol. XXXV (September 27, 1828): 73-74.

The Bankers Magazine and Statistical Register Vol. 40 (July 1885 to June 1886): 177-179

Bartlett, John Russell. *Records of the Colony of Rhode Island and Providence Plantations. in New England.* Vol. 5. Providence: A. C. Green, 1860.

Bartram, Ferdinand. *Retrographs: Comprising a History of New York City Prior to the Revolution, Biographies of George Washington, Alexander Hamilton, Nathan Hale, etc.* New York: Yale Publishing Co., 1868.

Benton, Thomas Hart. February 2, 1831. *Abridgment of the Debates of Congress from 1789-1856.* Vol. XI. New York: D. Appelton & Co., 1859.

Biddle, Nicholas. *The Correspondence of Nicholas Biddle Dealing with National Affairs,* 1807-1844. Boston and New York: Houghton Mifflin Company, 1919.
National Gazette of Philadelphia, April 10, 1828. Extracts printed in *Gouge,* Cobbett edition.
"Nicholas Biddle to John Quincy Adams." *The Financial Register* I (July 1837 to July 1838): 342-346.
Pennsylvania House of Representatives. *Debates of the Legislature of Pennsylvania in the Session of 1810-1811.* Reported by William Hamilton. Lancaster: 1811.

Black, Eugene. Statement to the House. *Extension of Credits to Industry and Broadening of the Powers of the Federal Reserve.* Hearing on H.R. 8717, May 2, 1934, 73rd Cong., 2nd Session.

Blackwell, John. "A Discourse in Explanation of the Bank of Credit." In *Colonial Currency Reprints with an Introduction and Notes,* 1682-1751, edited by Andrew McFarland Davis, Vol. I. Boston: John Wilson & Son, 1910.
"Some Additional Considerations on the Bills of Credit." In *Colonial Currency Reprints with an Introduction and Notes,* 1682-1751, edited by Andrew McFarland Davis, Vol. I. Boston: John Wilson & Son, 1910.

Blaine, James. *Twenty Years of Congress: from Lincoln to Garfield.* Vol. I & II. Norwich, Connecticut: Henry Bill Publishing Co., 1886.

Board of Governors of the Federal Reserve System, "Statement of the FRB in connection with S. 408," by S. R. Carpenter, December 19, 1946. fraser.stlouisfed.org.

Boritt, Gabor S. *Lincoln and the Economics of the American Dream.* University of Illinois Press, 1978.

Brown, Roger H. *Redeeming the Republic.* Baltimore and London: Johns Hopkins Univ. Press, 1993.

Bullock, Charles J. *The Finances of the United States From 1775 to 1789.* Madison: University of Wisconsin Press, 1895.

Burges, Tristam. *Memoir of Tristam Burges.* Providence: Marshall Brown, 1835.

Calhoun, John. *Speeches of John C. Calhoun: Delivered in the Congress of the United States.* New York: Harper & Brothers, 1843.

Carey, H. C. *Answers to the Questions: What Constitutes Currency?.* Philadelphia: Lea & Blanchard, 1840.
Letters to the Hon. B. H. Bristow. Philadelphia: Collins Printer & Co., 1874.
"The Currency Question." *Letters to the Hon. Schuyler Colfax.* Philadelphia: H. C. Baird, 1865.

Carey, Mathew. "The New Olive Branch." *Essays on Political Economy.* Philadelphia: H.C. Carey & I. Lea, 1822.
Miscellaneous Essays. Vol. I. New York: Carey & Hart, 1830.

Carlson, Robert. "The Pennsylvania Improvement Society and Its Promotion of Canals and Railroads, 1824-1826." *Pennsylvania History* 31, no. 3 (July 1964).

Chernow, Ron. *Washington: A Life.* New York: The Penguin Press, 2010.

Chevalier, Michael. *Society, Manners, and Politics, in the United States.* Boston: Weeks, Jordan and Co., 1839.

Colwell, Stephen. "Financial Suggestions and Remarks." 1867. Available at the Princeton Theological Seminary Libraries Special Collections.
The Ways and Means of Payment: A full Analysis of the Credit System, with its Various Modes of Adjustment." 2nd edition. Philadelphia; T.B. Lippincott & Co., 1860.
Remarks and Suggestions Upon the State and National System of Banks. Philadelphia: Caxton Press of Sherman & Co., 1864.

"The Comparative Value of Money between Britain and the Colonies." *Coin and Currency Collections.* Department of Special Collections University of Notre Dame Libraries. www.coins.nd.edu

"Continental Congress Motion on Payment of Interest on the Domestic Debt and on Sending a Deputation to Rhode Island," December 6, 1782. founders.archives.gov.

Cowen, David J., Richard Sylla, and Robert E. Wright. "The U.S. Panic of 1792: Financial Crisis Management and the Lender of Last Resort." Working Paper, Stern School of Business, New York University, October 2006.

Crouthamel, James L. "Did the Second Bank of the United States Bribe the Press?" *Journalism Quarterly* 36, no. 1 (March 1959): 35-44.

Dallas, George Mifflin. *Life and Writings of Alexander James Dallas.* Philadelphia: J. B. Lippincott & Co., 1871.

Davis, Andrew McFarland. Introduction to *Colonial Currency Reprints* 1682-1751. Vol. I. Boston: John Wilson & Son, 1910.
"Was It Andros?" *Proceedings of the American Antiquarian Society.* New Series, Vol. XVIII (Oct. 24, 1906-Oct. 16, 1907): 346-361.

Dawson, Henry B. "The Motley Letter." N.Y. July 5, 1861. *The Historical Magazine* 9, no. 3 (March 1871): 177-178.

Dictionary of Political Economy. Edited by Robert Harry Inglis Palgrave. Vol. III. London: Macmillan and Co., 1910.

"The Distressed State of the Town of Boston Considered." In *Colonial Currency Reprints with an Introduction and Notes,* 1682-1751, edited by Andrew McFarland Davis, Vol. I. Boston: John Wilson & Son, 1910.

Dolley, James C. "The Industrial Advance Program of the Federal Reserve System," *The Quarterly Journal of Economics* 50, no. 2 (Feb., 1936): 229-274.

Douglas, Charles H. J. *The Financial History of Massachusetts.* New York: Columbia University, 1892.

Duane, William John. *Narrative and Correspondence Concerning the Removal of the Deposits.* Philadelphia: 1838.

Durno, George. *The Citizen Advertiser* (NY), March 12, 1934.

Edling, Max M. *A Revolution in Favor of Government.* London: Oxford University Press, 2003.

Elder, William. *Conversations on the Principal Subjects of Political Economy.* Philadelphia: H.C. Baird & Co., 1882.
Questions of the Day: Economic and Social. Philadelphia: H.C. Baird & Co., 1871.

Eliason, Adolph Oscar. *The Rise of Commercial Banking Institutions in the United States.* Minneapolis: University of Minnesota Press, 1901.

Elliot, Jonathan. *The Debates in the Several State Conventions on the Adoption of the Federal Constitution.* Vol. I. Washington: 1901.

Ellsworth, William. March 27, 1834. *Register of Debates in Congress.* Part III of Vol. X. Washington: Gales and Seaton, 1834.

"Essays on Colonial Currency." University of Notre Dame. www.coins.nd.edu.

Felt, Joseph. *An Historical Account of Massachusetts Currency.* Boston: Perkins & Marvin, 1839.

Franklin, Benjamin. "Franklin to Robert Morris," December 23, 1782. franklinpapers.org.
Franklin to Robert Morris, December 25, 1783. franklinpapers.org.
"The Legal Tender of Paper Money in America." February 13, 1767. franklinpapers.org.
"A Modest Inquiry Into the Nature and Necessity of a Paper Currency." In *Colonial Currency Reprints with an Introduction and Notes,* 1682-1751, edited by Andrew McFarland Davis, Vol. II. Boston: John Wilson & Son, 1910.
"Remarks and Facts Relative to the American Paper Money." March, 11, 1767. *The Pennsylvania Chronicle.* May 25–June 1, 1767. *The Pennsylvania Gazette.* June 4, 1767. founders.archives.gov.

Fuller, Douglas Raymond. *Government Financing of Private Enterprise.* Stanford University Press, 1949.

Gayer, A. D. "Proposed Amendment of the Fed: The Administration Banking Bill of 1935." *Economic Journal* 45, no. 178 (June, 1935): 286-295.

Goldberg, Dror. "The Massachusetts Paper Money of 1690." *The Journal of Economic History* 69, no. 4 (December 2009).

Govan, T. P. *Nicholas Biddle.* 1959. *Nicholas Biddle: Nationalist and Public Banker.* The University of Chicago Press, 1959.

"The Government to Place Itself in the Hands of the Associated Banks, Orange N.J." *New York Times,* September 30, 1861.

Grubb, Farley. "Benjamin Franklin And the Birth of a Paper Money Economy." www.philadelphiafed.org.

Hamilton, Alexander. "H to Vicomte De Noailles," April-June 1782. *Papers of Alexander Hamilton.* Vol. III. New York: University of Columbia Press, 1961
"Hamilton to George Clinton." May 14, 1783. founders.archives.gov.
"Hamilton to James Duane." September 3, 1780. *Papers of Alexander Hamilton.* Vol. II. New York: University of Columbia Press, 1961

"Hamilton to Robert Morris." April 30, 1781. *Papers of Alexander Hamilton.* Vol. II. New York: University of Columbia Press, 1961

"Hamilton to Oliver Wolcott," August 3, 1796, founders.archives.gov.

"Hamilton to Oliver Wolcott," August 22, 1798, in Henry Cabot Lodge, *The Works of Alexander Hamilton,* Vol. 10. New York and London: G.P. Putnam's Sons, 1904.

"Hamilton to Oliver Wolcott," April 10, 1795, in Henry Cabot Lodge, *The Works of Alexander Hamilton,* Vol. 10. New York and London: G.P. Putnam's Sons, 1904.

"Hamilton to Oliver Wolcott," June 16, 1796, in Henry Cabot Lodge, *The Works of Alexander Hamilton,* Vol. 10. New York and London: G.P. Putnam's Sons, 1904.

"Hamilton to Senator Jonathan Dayton," 1799. founders.archives.gov.

"Letter to ____ December-March 1779-1780," *Papers of Alexander Hamilton.* Vol. II. New York: University of Columbia Press, 1961.

Hamilton, John C. "Introduction." The Federalist: A Commentary on the Constitution of the United States, a collection of essays by Alexander Hamilton, Jay, and Madison, and also The Continentalist and other papers by Alexander Hamilton. Philadelphia: J.B. Lippincott & Co, 1864.

The Life of Hamilton. Vol. I. New York: D. Appleton, 1840.

Hammond, Bray. *Banks and Politics in America from the Revolution to the Civil War.* Princeton University Press, 1957.

Hare, Robert. *A Brief Review of the Policy and Resources of the United States.* Philadelphia: Bradford & Inskeep, 1810.

Suggestions Respecting the Reformation of the Banking System. Philadelphia: John C. Clark & Co., 1837.

Hackley, Howard H. *Lending Functions of the Federal Reserve Banks: A History.* Board of Governors of the Federal Reserve System, May 1973.

Hardy, Charles O., and Viner, Jacob. *Report on the Availability of Bank Credit in the Seventh Federal Reserve District.* Washington: 1935.

Hay, John. December 25, 1863. *Lincoln and the Civil War In the Diaries and Letters of John Hay.* New York: Dodd Mead & Co, 1939.

Holton, Woody. *Unruly Americans and the Origins of the Constitution.* New York: Hill and Wang: 2007.

Jackson, Andrew. "Annual message of the President." December 4, 1832. "Seventh Annual Address." December 7, 1835.

Jones, Jesse. *50 Billion Dollars: My thirteen years with the RFC, 1932-1945.* New York: 1951.

Journals of the American Congress from 1774 to 1788, Vol. I (Washington: Way and Gideon, 1823).

Kent, James. *Commentaries on American Law.* Vol. 1. New York: E. B. Clayton, 1840.

Klemme, Ernest M. "Industrial Loan Operations of the Reconstruction Finance Corporation and the Federal Reserve Banks." *The Journal of Business of the University of Chicago* 12, no. 4 (Oct., 1939): 365-385.

Knox, John J. *A History of Banking in the United States.* New York: Bradford Rhodes & Company, 1900.

Lawrence, David. *Appleton Post Crescent,* February 18, 1939.
The Desert News (Salt Lake City), November 24, 1933.
"Intermediate Credit System for business." *New York Sun,* March 15, 1934.
The Nebraska State Journal (Lincoln, Nebraska), February 20, 1939.
Pittsburgh Post Gazette, February 8, 1934.
San Bernardino Sun, Volume 45, May 23, 1939.
Pittsburgh Post Gazette, June 14, 1939.

Lincoln, Abraham. *Complete Works.* Edited by John Nicolay and John Hay. Vol. 1. New York: The Century Co., 1894.
"Second Annual Message," December 1, 1862. presidency.ucsb.edu

Lodge, Henry Cabot. *Daniel Webster.* Boston and New York: Houghton Mifflin Company, 1911.

Lord, Eleazar. "A Letter on National Currency Addressed to the Secretary of the Treasury." New York: A. D. F. Randolph, 1861.
Principles of Currency and Banking. New York: G. & C. & H. Carvill, 1829.

London, D. H. "The Establishment of the Exchequer of the United States of America," Memorial to the Senate, Referred to the Committee on

Finance on December 18, 1871. *Miscellaneous Documents of the Senate.* 1872.

Lowenstein, Roger. *America's Bank: The Epic Struggle to Create the Federal Reserve.* New York: Penguin Press, 2015.

Lloyd, Gordon. "The Constitutional Convention." teachingamericanhistory.org.

MacFarlane, C. W. "Pennsylvania Paper Currency." *Annals of the American Academy of Political and Social Science* 8 (Jul., 1896): 51

Madeleine, M. Grace. "Monetary and Banking Theories of Jacksonian Democracy." New York: Kennikat Press, 1943.

Madison, James. "James Madison to Alexander Dallas," July 4, 1816. In George Mifflin, Dallas. *Life and Writings of Alexander James Dallas.* Philadelphia: J. B. Lippincott & Co., 1871.

"James Madison to Alexander Dallas," June 16, 1816. In George Mifflin, Dallas. *Life and Writings of Alexander James Dallas.* Philadelphia: J. B. Lippincott & Co., 1871.

"James Madison to Charles J. Ingersoll." June 25, 1831. founders.archives.gov

"Madison on the Tariff," Letter II, Montpelier, October 30, 1828. In *The Debates in the Several State Conventions,* edited by Jonathan Elliot. Vol. IV. (Philadelphia: J. B. Lippincott Co., 1836), 605-608.

"Seventh Annual Message." December 5, 1815. millercenter.org

Mather, Cotton. "Some Considerations On the Bills of Credit." In *Colonial Currency Reprints with an Introduction and Notes,* 1682-1751, edited by Andrew McFarland Davis, Vol. I. Boston: John Wilson & Son, 1910.

McCormac, Eugene Irving. *James K. Polk: A Political Biography.* Berkeley: University of California, 1922.

McDonald, Forrest. *Hamilton.* New York & London: W. W. Norton & Co., 1982.

McLane, Louis. "Louis McLane to Andrew Jackson." *Correspondence of Andrew Jackson.* Edited by J.S. Bassett. Vol. 5. Washington: Carnegie institution of Washington, 1926-1935.

Mead, James. Senator. S. 2998. October 1939.

Mehrling, Perry. *The New Lombard Street.* New Jersey: Princeton University Press, 2011.

"Million Dollar Club." *Neversink Valley Museum.* neversinkmuseum.org.

Minutes of the Board of Governors of the Federal Reserve System, February 7, 1934, February 8, 1934, February 26, 1934, March 2, 1934, March 3, 1934, March 5, 1934, March 8, 1934, April 12, 1934, March 6, 1935, April 23, 1934. fraser.stlouisfed.org.

Mitchell, Wesley Clair. *A History of the Greenbacks.* Chicago: University of Chicago Press, 1903.

Morris, Robert. "Morris to Franklin," November 27, 1781. franklinpapers.org.
"Morris to Franklin," January 7, 1782. franklinpapers.org.
"Morris to Franklin," September 30, 1784. franklinpapers.org.
The Papers of Robert Morris, 1781-1784. Edited by E. James Ferguson. "February 7 - July 31, 1781." (University of Pittsburgh Press, 1973).
A Statement of the Accounts of the United States of America During the Administration of the Superintendent of Finance. Commencing with His Appointment on the 20th Day of February 1781, and Ending with His Resignation on the 1st Day of November 1784 (Philadelphia: 1785).

"Mr. Biddle's Letter." *Niles National Register* 54 (April 14, 1838): 98-100.

"Mr. Clayton of Georgia." *Niles' Weekly Register* 46 (June 7, 1834): 251-252.

"New York and the Federal Constitution." *Magazine of American History.* Vol. II, no. 7 (July, 1878):391-392.

Niles, Hezekiah. *Niles' Weekly Register* 43 (September 22, 1832): 50.

Oberholtzer, Ellis Paxon. *Robert Morris, Patriot and Financier.* New York: MacMillan Co., 1903.

"Politics of the Day." *Niles' Weekly Register* 42 (August 4, 1832): 407, 424-426.

Potter, William. *The Key of Wealth.* London: R.A., 1650.

Pownall, Thomas. *The Administration of the British Colonies.* 4th Edition. London: 1768.

"A plan proposed for a general paper currency for America, to be established by the British government." *The Administration of the British Colonies.* 5th Edition. Vol. I. London: 1774.

Rakove, Jack N. *The Beginnings of National Politics.* New York: Alfred A. Knopf, 1979.

"Report on the Currency." *American Quarterly Review* Vol. XI (March & June 1832): pp. 245-248

The Resolutions of Congress of the 18th of April 1783. New York: Carroll & Patterson, 1787.

Robey, Ralph W. *Purchasing Power: An Introduction to Qualitative Credit Control Based on the Theories of Stephen A. Colwell.* New York: Prentice Hall, 1938.

Rogers, Joseph Morgan. *Thomas Hart Benton.* Philadelphia: G.W. Jacobs Co., 1905.

Rossiter, Clinton. *1787: The Grand Convention.* New York: W.W. Norton, 1987.

Schurz, Carl. *Henry Clay.* Vol I. Boston and New York: Houghton, Mifflin and Co., 1899.

Sherman, John. *Selected Speeches and Reports on Finance and Taxation from 1859 to 1878.* New York: D. Appleton & Co., 1879.

"Some Considerations Upon the Several Sorts of Banks." In *Colonial Currency Reprints with an Introduction and Notes,* 1682-1751, edited by Andrew McFarland Davis, Vol. I. Boston: John Wilson & Son, 1910.

"Some Proposals to Benefit the Province." In *Colonial Currency Reprints with an Introduction and Notes,* 1682-1751, edited by Andrew McFarland Davis, Vol. II. Boston: John Wilson & Son, 1910.

Sparks, Jared. *The Life of Gouverneur Morris.* Vol. I. Boston: Gray & Bowen, 1832.

Spaulding, E. G. *A History of the Legal Tender Paper Money Issued During the Great Rebellion.* Buffalo: Express Printing Co., 1869.

"Speech of Mr. Burges." *Niles Weekly Register* 40 (April 16, 1831): 119.

Steagall, Henry. April 19, 1935. Report to Accompany H.R. 7617. 74th Congress, 1st Session, House of Representatives, Report No. 742. fraser.stlouisfed.org.

Sumner, William Graham. *Robert Morris: The Financier and the Finances of the American Revolution.* Vol. II. New York: Dodd, Mead, & Co., 1892.

Szymczak, M. S. "The Banking Act of 1935." New York Bankers' Convention. Lake George, New York, June 8, 1935.
"The Federal Reserve System and the Banking Act of 1935." Forum Dinner of the Trenton Chapter of the American Institute of Banking, November 18, 1936, Trenton New Jersey.
"The Federal Reserve System and the Banking Act of 1935." Address before the Cleveland Chapter American Institute of Banking. November 7, 1935.
"Recent Relations of the Federal Reserve System with Business and Industry." Speech delivered before the Illinois Bankers Association, Decatur, Illinois, May 20, 1935.

"The Treasury Report and Mr. Secretary Chase," *The Continental Monthly* 5, no. 2 (Februrary 1864).

Trumbull, James Hammond. *First Essays at Banking and First Paper-money in New-England.* Worcester: American Antiquarian Society, 1884.

U.S. Bureau of the Census. *Survey of Reports of Credit and Capital Difficulties.* Washington: Government Printing Office, 1935.

U.S. Congress. "An Act to Incorporate the Subscribers to the Bank of the United States," April 10, 1816.
"An Act to provide more effectually for the collection of the duties imposed by law on goods, wares and merchandise imported into the United States, and on the tonnage of ships or vessels," August 4, 1790.
"An Act to Regulate the Deposits of the Public Money," June 23, 1836. In *The Public Statutes at Large of the United States of America.* Vol.V. Boston: Charles C. Little and James Brown, 1850.
Committee on Ways and Means. Senate Committee on Finance. *Official documents, &c. in relation to the Bank of the United States.* 21st, 1st session, April 13th, 1830, March 29, 1830. Steubenville: J. Wilson, 1830.

House. Committee to Investigate the Bank of the United States. *Bank of the United States.* 22nd Congress, 1st Session, April 30, 1832, No. 460. Washington: 1832.

House. Hearings Before the Committee on Banking and Currency. April 18, 1938.

House. Hearings on S. 1715 and H. R. 7617, "Bills to Provide for the Sound, Effective, and Uninterrupted Operation of the Banking System, and for other purposes." April 19 to June 3, 1935.

Senate. "An Act Relating to direct loans for industrial purposes by Federal Reserve banks, and for other purposes." S. 3487. 73rd Congress, 2nd Session, May 10, 1934. fraser.stlouisfed.org.

Senate. Committee on Banking and Currency. "A Bill to Extend the Functions of the Reconstruction Finance Corporation, etc., and for other purposes." H.R. 4240 (S. 1175). January 21, 22, 23, 24, and 25, 1935.

Senate. Committee on Banking and Currency. "To repeal section 13b of the Federal Reserve Act, to amend section 13 of the said Act, and for other purposes." S. 408. April 17, 1947. fraser.stlouisfed.org.

Senate. *Public Documents Printed By Order of the Senate.* 1st Session, 23rd Congress. Washington: 1834.

U.S. Treasury. *Additional Supplies for 1792,* by Alexander Hamilton. In *The Works of Alexander Hamilton,* Vol. III, edited by John C. Hamilton. New York: John F. Trow, 1850.

Annual Report of the Comptroller of the Currency. Washington: 1863.

Annual Report of the Comptroller of the Currency. Washington: 1864.

Annual Report of the Comptroller of the Currency, by John J. Knox. Washington: 1874.

Annual Report of the Comptroller of the Currency, by John J. Knox. Washington: 1879.

"Annual Report of the Treasury," by Richard Rush, December 6, 1828. In The Register of Debates in Congress, Vol. V, Appendix. Washington: Gales & Seaton, 1830.

Annual Report of the Secretary of the Treasury, by Hugh McCulloch. Washington: 1865.

Annual Report of the Secretary of the Treasury, by Hugh McCulloch. Washington: 1866.

Annual Report of the Secretary of the Treasury, by Hugh McCulloch. Washington: 1867.

Annual Report of the Secretary of the Treasury, by Hugh McCulloch. Washington: 1868.

Annual Report of the Secretary of the Treasury, by Salmon Chase. Washington: 1861.

Annual Report of the Secretary of the Treasury, by Salmon Chase. Washington: 1862.

Annual Report of the Secretary of the Treasury, by Salmon Chase. Washington: 1863.

Annual Report of the Secretary of the Treasury, by William Fessenden. Washington: 1864.

Final Report of the Reconstruction Finance Corporation, by Robert Anderson. Washington: 1959.

Financial Operations of the Late War—Money Matters of 1815—Support of Public Credit—National Circulating Medium, by Alexander J. Dallas, December 6, 1815. In The Funding System of the United States and Great Britain, edited by Jonathan Elliot. No. 86. Congressional Series of United States Public Documents. Washington: Blair & Rives, 1845.

"Letter from Treasury Department to House of Representatives," November 27, 1814, by Alexander J. Dallas. In George Mifflin Dallas. Life and Writings of Alexander James Dallas. Philadelphia: J. B. Lippincott & Co., 1871.

"Mr. Dallas's Plan of a National Bank," by Alexander J. Dallas, December 24, 1815. In The Funding System of the United States and Great Britain, edited by Jonathan Elliot. Congressional Series of United States Public Documents. No. 87. Washington: Blair & Rives, 1845.

"Origin of the National Banking System." The Historical Magazine 9 (August 1865): 252-256

"Report of the Comptroller," by Freeman Clarke. In Annual Report of the Secretary of the Treasury. Washington: 1865.

"Report of the Comptroller," by Hiland Hulburd. In Annual Report of the Secretary of the Treasury. Washington: 1866.

"Report of the Comptroller," by Hiland Hulburd. In Annual Report of the Secretary of the Treasury. Washington: 1867.

"Report of the Comptroller," by Hiland Hulburd. In Annual Report of the Secretary of the Treasury. Washington: 1869.

"Report of the Comptroller," by Hiland Hulburd. In Annual Report of the Secretary of the Treasury. Washington: 1871.

"Report of the Comptroller," by Hugh McCulloch. In Annual Report of the Secretary of the Treasury. Washington: 1864.

"Report on a Plan for the Further Support of Public Credit," by Alexander Hamilton, January 16, 1795. In Papers of Alexander Hamilton. Vol. XVIII. New York: University of Columbia Press, 1961.

"Second Report on the Further Provision Necessary for Establishing Public Credit (Report on a National Bank)," by Alexander Hamilton, December 13, 1790. In Papers of Alexander Hamilton. Vol. VII. New York: University of Columbia Press, 1961. 236-342.

"Report on Public Credit," by Alexander Hamilton, January 9, 1790. In Papers of Alexander Hamilton. Vol. VI. New York: University of Columbia Press, 1961.

"Report on the Subject of Manufactures," by Alexander Hamilton, December 5, 1791. In Reports of the Secretary of the Treasury, Vol. I. Washington: Duff Green, 1828.

"State of the Finances," by Alexander J. Dallas. Communicated to the Senate, December 8, 1815. In American State Papers: Documents, Legislative and Executive. Part III, Volume III, No. 454. Washington: Gales & Seaton, 1834.

"Support of Public Credit by a System of Taxation—National Bank—Debenture Certificates," by Alexander J. Dallas, October 17, 1814. In The Funding System of the United States and Great Britain, edited by Jonathan Elliot. Congressional Series of United States Public Documents. Vol. 440. Washington: Blair & Rives, 1845.

Van Buren, Martin. "Message of the President to Congress," September 4, 1837. *The Financial Register* I (July 1837 to July 1838): 321-325, 337-342.

"Message of the President to Congress," December 5, 1837. *The Financial Register* I (July 1837 to July 1838): 394-396.

"Third Annual Message to Congress," December 2, 1839. millercenter.org.

W. "On Banks and Paper Currency." *Analectic Magazine* Vol. VI (December 1815): 489-518.

Willis, H. Parker. *American Banking.* LaSalle Extension University: 1916.

Banking and Business. New York: Harper Brothers., 1922.

The Banking Situation. New York: Columbia University Press, 1934.

"The Federal Reserve Act." *The American Economic Review* 4, no. 1 (March, 1914): 18

"The Federal Reserve System." Chicago: Blackstone Institute, 1920.

Investment Banking. New York and London: Harper Brothers, 1936.

The Theory and Practice of Central Banking. New York and London: Harper & Brothers, 1936.

Wilson, James. "Considerations on the Bank of North America, 1785." *The Works of the Honourable James Wilson L. L. D.* Vol. III. Philadelphia: Lorenzo Press, 1804.

Woodbridge, John. "Severals Relating to the Fund." In *Colonial Currency Reprints with an Introduction and Notes,* 1682-1751, edited by Andrew McFarland Davis, Vol. I. Boston: John Wilson & Son, 1910.

Wright, Robert. "Origins of Commercial Banking in the United States, 1781-1830". EH.Net Encyclopedia, edited by Robert Whaples. March 26, 2008.

"York County (PA.) Memorial," May 19, 1834. *Register of Debates in Congress.* Part IV of Vol. X. Washington: Gales and Seaton, 1834. 4188.

Index

D

E

F

G

H

I

J

K

L

M

N

P

www.ingramcontent.com/pod-product-compliance
Lightning Source LLC
LaVergne TN
LVHW050302210926
848481LV00014BA/438
9781622730766